BUDDY HOLLY

Icons of Pop Music

Series Editors: Jill Halstead, Goldsmiths, University of London, and
Dave Laing, University of Liverpool

Books in this series, designed for undergraduates and the general reader,
offer a critical profile of a key figure or group in twentieth-century pop
music. These short paperback volumes focus on the work rather than on
biography, and emphasize critical interpretation.

Published:

The Velvet Underground
Richard Witts

Bob Dylan
Keith Negus

Elvis Costello
Dai Griffiths

Björk
Nicola Dibben

Forthcoming:

Elton John
Dave Laing

Joni Mitchell
Jill Halstead

Brian Wilson
Kirk Curnutt

James Brown
John Scannell

BUDDY HOLLY

DAVE LAING

INDIANA
University Press
Bloomington & Indianapolis

This book is a publication of

Indiana University Press
601 North Morton Street
Bloomington, Indiana 47404-3797 USA

www.iupress.indiana.edu

Telephone orders   800-842-6796
Fax orders   812-855-7931
Orders by e-mail   iuporder@indiana.edu

First published in the United Kingdom by Equinox Publishing Ltd.

Manufactured in Great Britain

Cataloging information is available from the Library of Congress.

ISBN 978-0-253-22168-1 (paperback)

1 2 3 4 5 15 14 13 12 11 10

Contents

Contents

Introduction

This book appears more than 50 years after the accidental death of its subject at the age of 22. Despite (and in part because of) that foreshortened life and career. Buddy Holly's music has continued to fascinate successive generations of musicians and listeners since 1959. To document and try to explain the reasons for that fascination is one of the aims of this book. The others are to re-create Holly's musical world and career in the emergence of rock 'n roll as a genre and an industry in late 1950s America, and to examine Holly's corpus of recordings.

The opening chapter aims to reconstruct the musical networks in Lubbock, Texas, of which Holly was a part, as they operated in the formative period from about 1950 to 1956. Various dimensions of his career form the basis of subsequent chapters, apart from Chapter 4, which considers the archive of recordings as musical texts. The later evolution can be said to have two main phases: the brief years of national prominence and stardom (1957–1959), considered in Chapters 2 and 3, and the posthumous or post-mortem career since 1959, the subject of Chapters 5 and 6.

While the chapter structure broadly follows a chronological sequence, there are some overlaps: for example, Chapter 2 discusses some early recordings made in 1954–5, during the "apprenticeship" phase of Holly's career which is mainly considered in Chapter 1. To aid the reader's understanding of the chronological sequence, a "Timeline" can be found as an appendix to this book. The Timeline includes a chronology of the posthumous career to 2009.

A few readers may be aware that in 1971 I wrote a brief monograph on Buddy Holly. Mainly because of the large amount of Holly scholarship that has been published in the intervening period, the current volume is almost entirely different from that earlier one, except perhaps in the author's continuing enthusiasm for Buddy Holly's music.

1 The West Texas Musicscape and Buddy Holly's Musical Idiolect, 1950–1955

More than 50 years after his death at the core of what we now know as "Buddy Holly" is his archive of recordings and a set of iconic images involving his guitar and heavy-rimmed spectacles. The recordings have often been presented as evidence that Holly was an unusual individual, a genius. But it is important to realize that "Buddy Holly" was equally the precipitate of a network of practices involving numerous other individuals (e.g. musicians, disc jockeys, promoters, producers), technologies (e.g. radio, jukebox, phonography, electric guitar), and artefacts, most notably sound recordings.

The Holly network

This approach to understanding the making of the Holly *œuvre* is influenced by the actor-network theory (ANT) developed by Bruno Latour and others (Latour 1987) to study the interdependent social practices that constitute work in science and technology. Some of the main features of ANT are the recognition that a network is heterogeneous, and will have both human and non-human (e.g. technological) participants; that participants are 'actants' that may at different stages (or simultaneously) be either active or passive, acting or acted upon; that the network has both a local (e.g. Lubbock-based) and non-local topology, where the non-local may include long-distance broadcasts from Dallas or Shreveport or recordings made in Nashville, New York or New Orleans; and that the network has diachronic as well as synchronic dimensions – events and artefacts from the past may be equally or more determining than present-time events.

Methodologically, ANT has two main approaches. One is to follow the actor, through interviews and ethnographic research. The other is to examine what ANT calls "inscriptions" which include written and recorded texts, images and other documentation. Inscriptions make action at a distance possible by stabilizing work so that it can travel across space and time to be combined with other work. A prime example of the productivity of such inscriptions in Buddy Holly is the existence of recordings by other artists that provided material for his cover version performances and inspiration for the "original" songs he played and recording.

While a "paper trail" of inscribed items is a central feature of actor-networks in scientific enquiry, the opposite is the case in the study of much popular music. Here, limited amounts of written material must be supplemented by interview material with participants and eyewitnesses. Therefore, apart from the semiotic analysis of recordings in Chapter 4, the primary methodological orientation of this book is necessarily that of oral history: "necessarily" because the contemporary documentary inscription of Buddy Holly's life and career is extremely meagre. There is one autobiographical document from his high-school years, a few letters and contracts, recording session logs, tour itineraries and occasional set lists, but little else. Also, the popular music press of the 1950s was parsimonious in its approach to interviews and documentation of artists' careers, influences, etc. Holly died before the era of *Rolling Stone*.

Nevertheless, in the years since 1959, but mainly in the 1970s and later, a number of researchers have diligently interviewed Holly's associates (members of the network in my terminology) and created a body of published work that amounts to a distinctive archive of niche knowledge, which I will call the product of Hollyology, in tribute to its practitioners. Hollyology has been (and continues to be) an important component of the posthumous actor-network and it is discussed directly in Chapter 5. But, as key Hollyologists will be quoted throughout this book, I will introduce the main published sources in this field here.

Although shorter books by myself (Laing 1971) and Elizabeth Peer and Ralph Peer II (1972) were published in the early 1970s, the first substantial product of Hollyology was John Goldrosen's biography of 1975. Goldrosen's book was later slightly amended and two decades later was republished with additional material as a collaboration with John Beecher (who supplied discographical and touring information) titled *Remembering Buddy* (Goldrosen and Beecher 1996). The later version of Goldrosen's book appeared almost simultaneously with two new large-scale biographies by Ellis Amburn (1995) and Philip Norman (1996). The fourth major contribution is the series of interviews by Dick Stewart published in an online journal of South-West popular music, the *Lance Monthly*, between 2002 and 2006 (Stewart interviews).[1] Aspects of Holly's career are the subject of books by Alan Mann (2009) and Larry Lehmer (1997), while the 50th anniversary of Holly's death was commemorated in books by John Gribben and Spencer Leigh. To these should be added the work of the dean of Hollyologists, Bill Griggs. As well as editing the magazine *Reminiscing* for the International Buddy Holly Memorial Society, he has compiled a day-by-day listing of Holly's life (Griggs 1997).

Almost all these works rely heavily on interview material. This is a necessary methodology but one that has a major limitation, namely the absence of direct testimony from Buddy himself. Because of this, Buddy Holly the individual exists only through the ventriloquism of others. This has been a key problem for many of the Hollyologists since their primary generic orientation is biography.[2] The focus is on the unique individual, even though to a greater or lesser degree these authors acknowledge the contributions of others to Holly's work. This limitation is less relevant to the approach taken by the present work, although that will be for the reader to judge!

After a brief section on the city of Lubbock, the remainder of this chapter describes five sites or musicscapes in which Buddy Holly and his informal network of friends and collaborators were immersed in the mid-1950s. The term "musicscape" is derived from the concept of soundscape elaborated by Canadian musicologist Murray Schafer, who defined it as the acoustic landscape (Schafer 1977). A musicscape is the musical dimension or portion of a general soundscape. The five musicscapes that mattered to Buddy Holly's Lubbock network were those of Family, Church, School, Live Shows and Mediated Music.

Lubbock and West Texas

> We often walked away from town in the late afternoon sunset. There were no paved roads and no fences – no trees – it was like the ocean but it was wide, wide land . . . The evening star would be high in the sunset sky when it was still broad daylight. That evening star fascinated me . . . I had nothing but to walk into nowhere, and the wide sunset space with the star. (O'Keeffe 1976/1917)

Almost 20 years after the painter Georgia O'Keeffe wrote this lyrical description of the Texas Panhandle, Buddy Holly was born in Lubbock, the *de facto* capital of West Texas. He was formed by the cultural and musical ethos of the region, which had its obverse side to that evoked by O'Keeffe. In his biography of Jimmie Rodgers, Nolan Porterfield evoked the West Texas landscape in the 1970s:

> The High Plains region is dotted with dozens of crumbling little burgs . . . half-deserted villages with little future and even less past. Most of them hardly existed before World War I; they flourished briefly in the Twenties with an influx of settlers from the farmed-out, boll weeviled bottoms of East Texas and beyond, and then gradually rotted away, victims of future shock, fast living and freeways, of cultural homogenization and changing economic patterns that doomed the quarter-section cotton farm and replaced it with "agribusiness" conglomerates. (Porterfield 1992: 198)

The novelist Larry McMurtry chronicled West Texas in fiction. One of his novellas was filmed by Peter Bogdanovich as *The Last Picture Show* (1971). McMurtry once said that the 1950s in Texas were "a dying twinge of depression: gray, dust-blown, intolerant" (Friedman 1990: 104) and his story portrays a small West Texas town in 1951, said to be Odessa, some 60 miles south-west of Lubbock and the nearest town to Roy Orbison's birthplace of Wink. Carl Bunch, Holly's drummer on the fatal final tour, grew up in Odessa: "all there was back then were mesquite bushes, horny toads, diamond-back rattlesnakes and tired jackrabbits" (Stewart interviews).

Gary Tollett, a backing vocalist on Buddy Holly's first big hit with the Crickets, 'That'll Be The Day', grew up in the 1940s on a family cotton farm near Littlefield, 30 miles north-west of Lubbock: "We thought more about work than we did about playing. Even as a youngster, I had to milk cows, feed and water chickens and hogs and do other farm chores We lived 14 miles from school . . . We all enjoyed listening to our little battery-operated radio at night (we didn't have electricity yet)" (Stewart interviews).

Small towns such as Littlefield and Odessa were part of the hinterland of Lubbock, the largest settlement in West Texas. The city is described by Holly's biographers as "the hub city of the South Plains" (Goldrosen and Beecher

1996: 8) and "the buckle on the Bible belt" (Amburn 1995: 7).

Lubbock had been founded in the 1880s as part of the movement west-ward of ranchers and farmers. The city's later prominence was a product of the 20th-century growth of cotton farming on the Texas plains. In 1919, Lub-bock County produced fewer than 14,000 bales of cotton. By 1932 this had risen to 100,000 and similar growth took place in surrounding counties.

As well as acting as the commercial and financial centre of a large rural area, Lubbock's principal impetus for growth in the mid-century was the foundation in 1923 of the Texas Technological College, known colloquially as Texas Tech. The population of Lubbock grew from 20,000 in 1930 to 72,000 in 1950 and increased again during the 1950s to reach 129,000 in 1960. The spirit of the town was described in the 1960s by a Texas historian as that of "small town individualism, together with a rather strait-laced moral attitude charac-teristic of much smaller communities. A certain suspicion of such attributes of a modern industrial nation as government bureaucracy, labor unions and commitment to foreign nations is to be noted" (Meinig 1969: 186).

Music historians present mixed views of the city. Holly biographer Ellis Amburn can scarcely conceal his animus for Lubbock and its citizens and even the mild-mannered historians of West Texas country music waspishly note that for professional musicians it was "the place to be from, if not the place to be" (Carr and Munde 1995: 162). In a 1974 interview, Waylon Jennings, himself a West Texan, was more blunt. Asked why so much music came from the region, he said that "it's a way to get up and away from something bad . . . you'll do anything to get out of West Texas" (Denisoff 1974: 118).

The city has also featured in songs by later generations of local musicians. Lubbock-born Mac Davis, whose best-known composition is the 1969 Elvis Presley hit 'In The Ghetto', was inspired in 1980 to write an autobiographical song called 'Texas In My Rear View Mirror'. It describes how the youthful Davis "thought happiness / was Lubbock, Texas / in my rear view mirror" and how "I ran off chasing a distant star / If Buddy Holly could make it that far / I figured I could too". However, by the end of the song the mature Davis knows that "happiness is Lubbock Texas / Growing nearer and dearer . . . and when I die you can bury me / in Lubbock, Texas, in my jeans".

Much later, Natalie Maines of the Dixie Chicks, and the daughter of a leading local musician of the 1960s,[3] composed the less amenable 'Lubbock Or Leave It', a track that appeared on the 2006 album *Taking The Long Way*. The song was written in response to the overwhelmingly hostile attitude of

Maines's fellow citizens to her public criticism of president George Bush's decision to go to war in Iraq.

The individuals belonging to the Lubbock-centred Holly network included musicians with whom he would perform locally, tour nationally and internationally and also record. Among these were:

- Jack Neal, guitarist and songwriter, who performed with Buddy as Buddy & Jack in 1953–4
- Bob Montgomery, guitarist and songwriter, who performed with Buddy as Buddy & Bob in 1954–5
- Larry Welborn, bass player with Buddy & Bob in 1954–5 and the Crickets in 1957
- Jerry Allison, drummer and songwriter, recording and touring member with Holly and the Crickets (1956–8)
- Don Guess, bass player with Holly in 1955–6
- Sonny Curtis, fiddler, guitarist and songwriter, played with Holly in 1954–7
- Joe B. Mauldin, bass player, recording and touring member of the Crickets in 1957–8
- Niki Sullivan, guitarist, recording and touring member of the Crickets in 1957
- Waylon Jennings, DJ, singer and bass player who was recorded by Holly and accompanied Buddy on his final tour, 1958–9
- Bob and John Pickering with Bob Lapham, a.k.a. the Picks, harmony singers who performed uncredited on numerous Holly and Crickets tracks in 1957–8
- Gary and Ramona Tollett, backing singers on 'That'll Be The Day' (1957)
- Bob Linville, Ray Rush and David Bigham, a.k.a. the Roses, another vocal trio who performed on Crickets tracks and toured with the group in 1958

Others involved were Peggy Sue Gerron (after whom one of Holly's biggest hits was named – a close friend of Holly and later wife of Jerry Allison), Sue Parrish (co-writer of two songs with Holly), Tinker Carlen (high-school contemporary of Holly and local musician) and some older figures such as Clyde Hankins (guitar salesman and teacher), Dave Stone (radio station manager) HiPockets Duncan (radio DJ and club owner) and Ben Hall (radio DJ and bandleader).

The family musicscape

Many members of the Lubbock network had their first taste of music-making at home in the late 1940s or early 1950s. Some were made to take formal lessons on piano, violin or other instruments, while several came from musical families where parents, siblings or other close relatives were active singers or instrumentalists, either professionally or as a pastime or hobby.

Both Sonny Curtis and the Pickering brothers came from families of professional musicians. The uncles of Sonny Curtis were the Mayfield Brothers, Lubbock's leading bluegrass band of the late 1940s and 1950s. Bill and John Pickering of the Picks came from a leading family of professional Southern gospel singers headed by their father John Murchison Pickering. He was a member of an early professional white travelling gospel quartet and taught music for leading Christian music publishers, leading a quartet that demonstrated songs to church members. His son John (born 1933) told Dick Stewart: "They entertained at churches, school auditoriums and singing conventions, in and outdoors. There were no microphones in those days. So they became experts in voice projection" (Stewart interviews). John Pickering and his brother joined the family singing group as small children.

Apart from families of professional musicians, many of the network members came from homes that made their own entertainment. The Holleys[4] sang and played at "get-togethers". Peggy Sue Gerron's relatives played guitar, fiddle and drums. Ben Hall was 12 years older than Buddy and a local bandleader with whom the young Holly played and one of whose songs was recorded by Buddy. Hall's aunts and uncles would "sit around at night and sing and play . . . old songs like the Carter Family sang . . . and I wanted a guitar real bad from the earliest times" (Carr and Munde 1995: 149). And Gary Tollett's father was "an excellent singer and guitar player" who "often played for Saturday night dances in the community and picked up a few dollars to support the community" (Stewart interviews).

The Holley family was one in which children were encouraged to learn one or more musical instruments. Buddy was given a toy fiddle at five, playing it at a local talent contest with his brothers (who played fiddle and accordion) in 1941. Buddy was given a small prize. This seems to have been his only musical activity until he took a course of piano lessons in 1947, at the age of 11. This was his only formal music training and his teacher reported that he learned quickly by ear. After being given a steel guitar the following year, on which

Buddy Holly aged four

Hulton Archive. Reproduced by permission of Getty Images.

he took 20 lessons, he asked to exchange it for an acoustic guitar. His brother Larry taught him the basics of the instrument on this new Epiphone.

Joe Mauldin, bass player with the Crickets, was also made to learn classical piano as a small child. At 13 he switched to learning steel guitar and then trumpet. But he didn't find his own place in music until a member of his peer group, Terry Church (who as Terry Nolan would later perform on the same New York bill as Holly), showed him how to play the "bass fiddle" (double bass) and invited him to join his band, the Four Teens (Goldrosen and Beecher 1996: 53–4).

Almost all families, rural or urban, had radio sets, which were an important source of music for tyro performers. Buddy Holly was reported to have the ability to "hear a song on the radio and then sing it and play the guitar part" (Carr and Munde 1995: 122). Some households in the city had phonographs or record players. The Holley home had a phonograph – one source says there were old 78s of "such early stars as Jimmie Rodgers and the Carter Family" (Stambler and Landon 2000: 204). The Holleys also had access to domestic recording equipment. One source says that Holly recorded a Jimmie Rodgers song and a mandolin solo at home (Mann 2009: 19). In 1949 the 13-year-old Buddy made a home recording of 'My Two-Timin' Woman' by country and western star Hank Snow. Three more home recordings made in 1952 with Bob Montgomery survive. The songs were by Rose Maddox ('Take These Shackles From My Heart'), Bill Monroe ('I'll Just Pretend') and the traditional 'Footprints In The Snow'. These early tracks were probably captured on a magnetic wire recorder, a domestic recording machine that used similar technology to the Dictaphone and telephone answering machines. The wire recorder was "a flashy technology with a great deal of 'high tech' appeal, and its sales seemed to be taking off in 1946 and 1947, when Americans purchased tens of thousands of them" (Morton 2000: 137–8).

The church musicscape

Lubbock earned the soubriquet "buckle on the Bible belt" because of the large number of Christian congregations in the city. Almost all were of Protestant denominations and the intensely conservative Baptist, Church of Christ and Methodist religious ethos of the city enforced both racial segregation and prohibition during Holly's lifetime.

As a centre of Christian Protestant fundamentalism, where even the state high school attended by Buddy held early-morning religious meetings,

Lubbock generated strong sectarian differences both with other Christian churches and between the Protestant sects. Peggy Sue Gerron was one of the small number of (non-Hispanic) Roman Catholics and felt isolated. Buddy Holly's teenage relationship with a classmate, Echo McGuire, foundered in part on their families' differing religious allegiances. Echo belonged to the Church of Christ which excluded musical instruments from their acts of worship and believed that only its members were "saved". Holly's family belonged to the congregation of the Tabernacle Baptist Church, which included hymns in its services, although the minister had highly conservative and reactionary views on secular music.

Much singing in church was unharmonized. Country music historian Bill C. Malone has written that "to the extent to which harmony did exist, in the church or elsewhere, it was probably a product of the southern gospel quartets and of the four-part emphasis of the shape-note singing schools" (Malone 2002a: 21). The shape-note system was a form of notation in which "the pitch of musical notes was indicated by their shape independent of the lines and spaces of the staff" (2002a: 22). The shape-note movement was fuelled by hymnal publishers such as Stamps-Baxter of Dallas who employed itinerant quartets like that led by John Pickering Senior to popularize

> their style of harmony (usually first tenor, second tenor, baritone, and bass) in country churches, at singing schools at schoolhouse concerts, and at the famous all-day-singings with dinner on the grounds . . . described as "singing conventions". People thronged to the conventions as much to gorge themselves on the sumptuous feasts laid out on the ground or on picnic tables as they did to sing gospel songs with their neighbors. (2002a: 21–2)

According to John Pickering of the Picks, the Holley family would attend such events in Lubbock where the Pickering Family Quartet was among the performers.

Religious music could also be heard on radio. Gary Tollett recalled listening to the Chuck Wagon Gang on WBAP from Fort Worth in the 1940s. This popular mixed (male and female) gospel group had begun their career as the Carter Quartet at KFYO Lubbock in 1935 and made the first recording of Albert E. Brumley's white gospel classic 'I'll Fly Away' in 1948.

The Pickering Family Quartet had a regular weekday 15-minute pro-gramme in the early morning on KTRH Lubbock until the sudden death of John Pickering Senior in 1953. In the mid-1950s, John Pickering sang on dif-ferent Lubbock radio stations with the gospel groups Central Baptist Church Quartet (on KFYO) and Happy Rhythm Boys (on KSEL). And, as leader of the Picks, he arranged and led the backing vocals on recordings by the Crickets, notably 'Oh Boy!'

Buddy Holly had heard and liked black gospel singing. His biographers state that he had a particular love of Mahalia Jackson's singing and that a favourite recording was 'I'll Be All Right' by the Angelic Gospel Singers, a female group founded in South Carolina by singer and pianist Margaret Allison in the 1940s and still performing in the 1990s. 'I'll Be All Right' was one of many record-ings made by the group for the Nashville-based Nashboro label. It inspired the melody of Buddy Holly's song 'True Love Ways' and it was played at his funeral in 1959.

One of the Holly biographers, Ellis Amburn, has argued that there was a fundamental conflict between rock 'n roll and religion in his life, akin to that which wracked Little Richard at the same time. Amburn claimed that, as late as the 1990s, "in Lubbock I heard people say that God killed Buddy Holly to prevent the spread of rock 'n' roll" and that Buddy's internal conflict explains "the suffering that underlies his darker-hued ballads such as 'Learning the Game', written only days before his death" (Amburn 1995: 7).[5]

The evidence for this view, however, is inconclusive. Peggy Sue Gerron recalled a conversation with Buddy after his split with Echo McGuire: "Buddy told me that he did not believe God intended him to give up his music and that he could not live without his music or without God. He did not believe music was a sin. She did" (Stewart interviews).

And, despite the antagonism of church ministers to rock 'n roll, they accepted donations from Holly. Amburn claims that Holly told a friend in December 1958 that "I want to get in a business more acceptable to being able to work for the Lord." Earlier in the year, though, Buddy told his elder brother he would record albums of religious songs; the later comment may be related to this (Amburn 1995: 215–6, 139). There was also an unconfirmed report by a local studio owner that he had privately recorded some gos-pel songs towards the end of his life (Mann 2009: 230). Holly's only known recordings of religious songs were 'I Saw The Moon Cry Last Night' and 'I Hear The Lord Callin' For Me' made in 1953 with Jack Neal, the song's author, and unreleased until 1986, many years after Holly's death.

The school musicscape

There were no integrated schools in Lubbock until 1955 (the year Holly graduated from high school) and in the 1970s prolonged opposition to the bussing of children to integrated schools prevented the construction of any new school buildings. From 1949 to 1955, Buddy Holly's daily routine revolved around his studies and extra-curricular activities at J. T. Hutchinson Junior High and Lubbock High schools. Here he met and made music with some of his later collaborators. There were official school musical activities as well as opportunities for Holly's early groups to perform for classmates and parents.

With school friend Bob Montgomery (the son of the owner of the Gin Café), the 14-year-old Buddy performed at a junior high Parents' Night function in 1950. They chose to play 'Too Old To Cut The Mustard' – a risqué comic song associated with 'Jumping' Bill Carlisle, whose comic alter ego was 'Hot Shot Elmer' and whose other novelty songs included 'No Help Wanted' and 'Is Zat You Myrtle?' (Shelton 1966: 115–6). The sexual nature of the comedy embraced by 14-year-olds caused a minor scandal.

At Lubbock High, which he attended from 1952 to 1955, Buddy was a member of the 40-strong Senior A Capella Choir, the school orchestra and the "music society". The saxophone-playing Peggy Sue Gerron came to Lubbock High shortly after Buddy had left: "I was in the band, which made me a nerd. I was in marching band and symphony [orchestra]" (Stewart interviews).

An annual event at the high school was Round-Up, described in the *Lubbock High Yearbook 1954–5* as "a time of western costumes and western festivities, a day when everyone relives the history of the 'Old West' . . . On the night of Round-Up, an assembly is held at which Wranglers are presented and a Western 'shindig' follows in the gym" (Peer and Peer 1972: 16). There were contests for best slogan, poem, poster and song. 'Flower Of My Heart' (by Bob Montgomery and Don Guess) was chosen as the best song of 1955 and Holly and Montgomery and Larry Welborn (bass) played at the school's "Westerner Day" in February 1954. In the same year, Buddy Holly wrote letters to other schools, looking for performance opportunities. The letters offered the services of his band to help raise funds, describing the group as "one of the leading hillbilly and western bands in Lubbock".

At school, too, Buddy wrote an essay in 1953 in which he expressed his intention to take up music as a career. In it he wrote that "I have thought about making a career in Western music if I am good enough."

Performance venue musicscapes

Despite the conservatism of Lubbock's religious leaders, there were numerous opportunities to play and hear live music within as well as outside the
city limits. Buddy Holly's earliest public performances took place late in 1953,
with Jack Neal as Buddy & Jack, on shows linked mostly with the radio station KDAV (see below). Over the next two years he performed with a range
of musicians, but mostly as Buddy & Bob, a group whose nucleus was Buddy
and Bob Montgomery on guitars and vocals. The duo were augmented variously by Larry Wellborn on double bass, Sonny Curtis on guitar or fiddle and
Jerry Allison on drums. Additionally, Buddy occasionally sat in with bands led
by older Lubbock-based country musicians.

For entry-level musicians such as Buddy & Bob and Sonny Curtis, the
places to play were "car lots, grocery store parking lots, teen parties, Bob's
garage (no audience), fair booster tours and anywhere else people wanted
to hear some music, and some places they didn't" (Sonny Curtis; Stewart
interviews). Among the "anywhere else" venues mentioned in the Hollyology literature were roller rinks, drive-ins, "community shows", sock hops and
other high-school dances.[6]

In the early 1950s, the principal styles of music provided for the white
population were mainstream (white) American popular music epitomized
by singers such as Bing Crosby and Doris Day, white gospel music and various
types of what would later be called country music. These included bluegrass
and western swing, two styles that would be ever-present to Buddy Holly in
his early teens. There was enough work in the city itself and its surrounding
region to support a number of semi-pro and full-time musicians, notably in
bluegrass, western swing and other country styles.

Commenting on the choice of Buddy & Bob to play bluegrass-inspired
music, John Goldrosen states that "while most bluegrass musicians hailed
from the eastern South, the style was not alien to areas like Texas where
fiddle music was popular" (Goldrosen and Beecher 1996: 15). He might have
added that the Lubbock area was in fact home to the Mayfield Brothers, a
talented bluegrass band that included Edd Mayfield, a guitarist who was a
member of bluegrass founder Bill Monroe's own group for periods during
the 1950s. According to bluegrass historian Rod Moag, the Mayfield Brothers
"were the first full band to specialize in Bill Monroe style music in the Lone
Star State" and from the late 1940s they were featured on the Saturday-night

Western Jamboree show on Lubbock radio station KSEL (Moag and Campbell 2004).

The Mayfields' guitar-playing nephew Sonny Curtis made his first public appearances here, at the age of 11 or 12 in the late 1940s. The band made some recordings at Norman Petty's studio in Clovis, NM, around 1955, a year before Buddy met Petty. These tracks were not issued at the time and only became available in 2006 on a CD from the heritage label Patuxent. West Texas music historians Joe Carr and Alan Munde state that "Sonny Curtis, Waylon Jennings and Buddy Holly all heard and were inspired by the music of the Mayfield Brothers" (Carr and Munde 1995: 96). In the late 1940s, the Mayfield band was the support act for such leading country acts as the Maddox Brothers and Rose, Tennessee Ernie Ford and Hank Snow when they visited Lubbock. Bill Myrick, a former member of Monroe's band, led the Mayfield group for a period and later led his own band at clubs in Lubbock.

The Lubbock musicscape was enlivened by visiting artists, usually performing at clubs outside the city limit such as the Cotton Club, Glasserama and the 16th and J. Holly, Montgomery and Welborn would sometimes be the opening act for visiting artists, notably Bill Haley (in October 1955), Marty Robbins (later that year) and above all for Elvis Presley. Nevertheless, at this time, John Pickering says, "Buddy's fans in Lubbock were mostly teenagers and fans of Elvis Presley. Buddy was considered an amateur country singer and only a few people went to see him at the skating rink or the Cotton Club" (Stewart interviews).

If bluegrass was centred on the south-east of the country, western swing was quintessentially Texan, with that genre's dominant figure, Bob Wills, hailing from Turkey, Texas, a small settlement about 70 miles north-east of Lubbock. Wills and others created dance music out of rural tunes, polka rhythms, swing orchestra material and even jazz and blues elements.

A key figure in Lubbock's western swing scene was fiddler Tommy Hancock, who led his seven-piece Roadside Playboys band, which in the late 1950s included two local Hispanic musicians – Louis Martinez (guitar) and Alex Martinez (steel guitar). A sometime owner of the Glasserama club, in the 1940s and 1950s, Hancock was a member of the house band at the Cotton Club. Here, he backed visiting country and western artists as well as Little Richard and Elvis Presley.

Hancock's website quotes Sonny Curtis as citing Hancock and his singer wife Charlene Condray as "a strong influence on Buddy and us all" and Philip

Norman states that Hancock was "the idol and role model of most teenage musicians in the Lubbock area" (Norman 1996: 49). Certainly, the choice of Rhythm Playboys as the name of a short-lived Holly, Montgomery and Don Guess trio around 1954–5 was more than a nod to western swing bands like Hancock's and Bob Wills's Texas Playboys, as well a recognition of the importance of the beat (and, possibly, even of R&B) for the 17-year-old Holly.

One of the most active country bands in Lubbock was led by radio announcer Ben Hall. According to Carr and Munde, "at various times Ben Hall's band included Sonny Curtis, Buddy Holly, Weldon Myrick and Hall's wife Dena on bass" (Carr and Munde 1995: 143). Weldon Myrick (no relation to Bill Myrick) was a young steel guitarist who co-wrote with Hall 'It's Not My Fault', a song Holly took to Nashville and recorded there. Myrick himself went on become one of country music's most prolific session musicians and a regular on the *Grand Ole Opry* for over 30 years until his retirement in 1998.

Although the Federal ban on alcohol had been lifted in 1933, the sale and consumption of alcohol in public places remained prohibited in Lubbock until 1972, at which time it was the largest "dry" city in the United States. This prohibition extended only to the city limits, however, and in the 1950s, there was "a string of clubs, honky-tonks and liquor stores lying just beyond the town line along the highways leading out of the city" (Goldrosen and Beecher 1996: 9). Many of the venues and stores were in the sections inhabited by non-whites. Lubbock's population was over 90 per cent white with small enclaves of African-Americans and Hispanics outside the city limits. According to singer John Pickering, whose group the Picks provided the backing vocals on many Crickets records:

> In the 1950s and earlier, there were few permanent Mexican families in Lubbock. Most of the Mexicans were migrant workers who spoke little or no English and had little money, or they wouldn't have been there. Many of the permanent Hispanic families lived north of town and the black families lived on the east side of Lubbock. Many of the teenagers only came into contact with them when they would drive by for "bootleg" liquor. (Stewart interviews)[7]

Whites and blacks were permitted to attend the same concerts at larger venues, but at shows by black artists "whites usually sat together in the orchestra, while blacks watched shows from the balcony" (Goldrosen and Beecher 1996: 28). Margaret Lewis, a white rock 'n roll and country singer who grew up in Levelland near Lubbock, however, claimed that the audiences for black R&B acts at the Cotton Club on the Lubbock outskirts was wholly or mainly white (Tapp 2009: 16).

One of the very few African Americans to impinge on the lives of Holly's network was "Stubbs" (C. B. Stubblefield), the chef at the Hi-D-Ho drive-in diner, "who did a lot for Lubbock and a lot for us kids", according to Peggy Sue Gerron. "Whether you were hungry or not, Stubbs didn't let you leave hungry . . . [he] continued to do a lot for the musicians who came though town" (Stewart interviews).[8]

Goldrosen and Beecher make the point that the teenage Holly "had only limited contact with local blacks and their music" (Goldrosen and Beecher 1996: 9), while Carr and Munde conclude that "Sonny [Curtis], Buddy and other musical friends took advantage of the few entertainment venues for local blacks and touring acts that did exist" (Carr and Munde 1995: 125). Buddy Knox, from Dumas, 200 miles south of Lubbock, could not recall hearing a record by a black artist until he went to New York after his record 'Party Doll' had become a national hit early in 1957 (Gillett 1970).

Whatever the accuracy of that anecdote, West Texas was not a major source of black music, although local country bandleader Ben Hall recalled the singing of African-American workers in the cotton fields of the 1930s: "they would start singing and get in time with it, and each one of them would have perfect rhythm across that field" (Carr and Munde 1995: 150). The few better-known blues musicians to have lived in the region included Blind Arvella Gray and Texas Alexander, who were, according to Paul Oliver, "following the migrant cotton-workers who were now being driven out in trucks to the labourers' camps that served the newly opened-up fields" in the 1920s and 1930s (Oliver 1969: 137). A minor figure in blues history, John Hogg, recorded a version of Alexander's 'West Texas Blues' for the Octive label in the early 1950s.

In the late 1950s, the only nationally known black act from the area was the doo-wop group the Velvets. Their lead singer Virgil Johnson was a year older than Buddy Holly and attended Dunbar High, the Lubbock black school in the segregation era. He qualified as a teacher and did not form the Velvets (with four of his school students) until 1959. With Roy Orbison's help, they gained a record deal with Nashville label Monument, scoring a minor hit with 'Tonight (Could Be The Night)' in 1961.

Despite the relatively small proportion of African-Americans in West Texas, Lubbock's status as the only large town of the region meant that it was a regular calling point for tours by leading R&B acts and black dance bands. There was at least one venue for black audiences in the late 1940s: the Hi-Hat club, which featured "Tony Ford Jr and his Jive Jump All-Colored Orchestra". In the mid 1950s, Fats Domino, Ivory Joe Hunter and Little Richard were all booked to play at the Cotton Club, "drawing a racially mixed audience" (Carr and Munde 1995: 125). Sonny Curtis was invited to attend Charles Brown's R&B show by Brown's guitarist and found himself to be the only white person in the club but "I don't remember being made to feel uncomfortable once that evening" (1995: 219).

While Holly attended some of the Cotton Club shows (notably that of Little Richard), there are only two references to his hearing locally based black musicians in all the interview-based literature on his formative years. Firstly, Philip Norman quotes Jack Neal on Buddy's visits to black "cafes and joints" in Lubbock's African-American suburbs where "there'd be one guy with a guitar and another with a horn, and usually barbeque cookin' in a pit" (Norman 1996: 55). The second account of Buddy Holly and Lubbock's African-American music scene was given to interviewers as recently as the early 21st century by Tinker Carlen, a controversial figure for Hollyologists. Carlen was a school contemporary of Buddy who had made his first appearance in the Holly literature as an informant on Buddy's early sex life (Amburn 1995: 15–16) but he later claimed to have played with young African-American musicians from Lubbock's black high school to audiences that included Holly; and that Buddy had also sat in with these musicians (Stewart interviews).

Other parts of Carlen's claims about his role in Buddy's musical development have been shown to be untrustworthy[9] but his account at least provides a sketch of the racial divide in music in Lubbock and a claim that it had been transcended, at least temporarily. Such direct interaction (in person rather than on records or radio) was not unknown in the early rock 'n roll years especially in states such as Tennessee and Louisiana where blacks and whites were not so geographically separated, particularly in rural areas. In Tennessee, Elvis Presley, Jerry Lee Lewis and Carl Perkins found direct inspiration from local black musicians. Carl Perkins said that:

> I was raised on a plantation in the flatlands of Lake County
> Tennessee, and we were about the only white people on

it . . . working in the cotton fields in the sun, music was the
only escape. The colored people would sing, and I'd join in,
just a little kid, and that was colored rhythm & blues, got
named rock and roll, got named that in 1956, but the same
music was there years before, and it was my music. (Lydon
1968: 32)

Carlen's claims about Holly's interest in an integrated band would be consistent with the evidence provided by the literature of his, sometimes naïve,
enthusiasm for black music and musicians. Buddy's elder brother recalled
how, in a "colored beer joint" near San Angelo in Texas, when working for the
family building contractor business, Buddy sat in with a three-piece band,
singing 'Sexy Ways', a 1954 hit for the Midnighters, whose 'Work With Me
Annie' he was later to record (Goldrosen and Beecher 1996: 28).

On another occasion, following a Cotton Club show by Little Richard,
Buddy invited the singer to visit his parents' house for dinner, much to their
consternation (Norman 1996: 74). In summer 1958, he gave his wristwatch
to a black "shoeshine attendant" in Lubbock who had admired it (Amburn
1995: 167). Ellis Amburn also saw proof of a lack of racial prejudice in Buddy's
decision to call his cat "Booker": Booker T. Washington was a leading figure in
the fight for equal rights at the start of the 20th century (1995: 14). More pertinent, perhaps, was Holly's comment to his mother after touring with black
artists in late 1957 (see Chapter 3). When she asked him how he felt about it,
he is reported to have "replied that he was a negro too; he felt black, he said"
(1995: 115–6).

Mediated music soundscapes

Beyond the soundscape of live music was the mediascape of jukebox, records
and radio that brought rhythm & blues as well as mainstream pop into
Lubbock. The mediascape was the domain of what Murray Schafer called
"schizophonia", the technologically induced separation of sound from its
source and image from sound (Schafer 1986: 139). As Jody Berland states,
"listening practices are continuously transformed by technical innovation in
music reproduction . . . enabling us to carry music 'belonging' to one loca-
tion or spatial scale into other places" (Berland 1998: 133). "Belonging" is a
key term here: clear channel radio, jukeboxes and shellac and vinyl discs enabled music "belonging" to the African-American community to be re-sited in

white Lubbock and to transform both the listening and performing practices of the Holly network. The rare opposite process – the transportation of white youth to the place where black music belongs – was exemplified by Sonny Curtis's seat on stage next to Charles Brown's guitarist.

Two types of radio station were available to Lubbock youth in the 1950s. The city had several local music stations that actively promoted events and provided outlets for local musicians in addition to their DJ shows of recorded music. There were also the "clear channel" stations from elsewhere in the South that were permitted by the broadcast licensing authorities to operate with the much greater power of 50,000 watts and with non-directional antennae, enabling them to reach listeners hundreds of miles away in all directions. Between sunset and sunrise, local stations were not allowed to transmit programmes on the same wavelengths as the clear channel broadcasters.

Music radio in general went through two major changes in the 1950s. Firstly, record shows hosted by disc jockeys replaced live performances introduced by announcers, and later in the decade programming choices were made on the basis of sales charts rather than the preferences of the disc jockeys themselves (Jensen 1998). It is arguable whether these processes affected stations specializing in country music and/or based in more rural regions more slowly than the generalist popular music stations in the big cities. Philip Ennis estimates that in the 1950s there were some 650 stations in the Southern and Western states broadcasting live shows by country performers (Ennis 1992: 170) and Diane Pecknold says that KDAV in Lubbock did not change from DJ choice to tight playlisting until the early 1960s (Pecknold 2007: 146). Throughout the 1950s, Lubbock stations continued to programme some live music shows in the early morning and at weekends.

Lubbock's first radio station had been launched in 1932 and, by the 1950s, the city had three significant music-based stations: KLLL, KDAV and KSEL. The typical rural local station was described by Waylon Jennings to journalist John Grissim. Jennings made his broadcast debut with a 15-minute country music show at the age of 12 or 13 on KVOW in Littlefield, near Lubbock, a station owned by the local newspaper publisher: "It had the old-style block programming: fifteen minutes of this and fifteen minutes of that, the Hillbilly Hit Parade, pop standards, Mantovani – real backwoods programming. Finally I got the owner to let me play two hours of country music [records] in the afternoons" (Grissim 1970: 72).

All three Lubbock stations were more country-oriented than KVOW by the mid-1950s. They programmed "a mixture of rockabilly and older country styles, including western swing and honky-tonk" (Goldrosen and Beecher 1996: 107), and KSEL even introduced in about 1954 a half-hour of black popular music at 4 pm on weekdays, called *Sepia Parade*.

KDAV was the newest of these stations. It was launched in October 1953 by Dave "Pappy" Stone, the former general manager of KSEL. At that station, Stone had introduced a limited amount of country music, including the *Saturday Night Jamboree*, into the station's conventional schedule of mainstream popular song and talk shows. Among the on-air personalities was Ben Hall, whose promotional literature proclaimed him to be "the Country Drifter" and host of the *Western Roundup* and *Western Hit Parade*.

KDAV, in contrast, was a wholly vernacular music station, with country and gospel shows named *Sunset Trading Post*, *Corral Club*, *Bethel Chapel*, *Old Camp Meeting*, etc. In this respect, is it noteworthy that a religious item composed by Jack Neal, 'I Hear The Lord Callin' For Me', was one of four songs performed by Buddy & Jack on their first Sunday afternoon broadcast in November 1953, the others being Hank Williams's 'Your Cheatin' Heart', Marty Robbins's 'I Couldn't Keep From Cryin'' and another country number, 'I Got You On My Mind'. Soon after this, the *Buddy & Jack Show* was replaced on KDAV by the *Buddy & Bob Show*, as Holly's partnership with Neal was replaced by one with Bob Montgomery.

These broadcasts led to Holly's first efforts at songwriting. Sue Parrish, a KDAV listener, sent two lyrics she had written to Buddy and he set them to music. The songs, 'Don't Come Back Knockin'' and 'Love Me', were recorded in Nashville in January 1956. Parrish moved to the West Coast soon afterwards and sent more lyrics to Holly, but none was turned into a song.

Another of the Lubbock stations, KLLL, was bought in early 1958 by the Corbin family of Lubbock who introduced a format that "might be described as a Hillbilly Top 40 or a McLendon type, something we feel is just a little bit different", according to an interview with its new owners in *Cashbox* (Goldrosen and Beecher 1996: 128).[10] KLLL was now "an all country station" (1996: 107), or a "hillbilly rock" station (Norman 1996: 268) but one that was fast-paced and played a lot of jingles.

One biographer says that, when Buddy was in Lubbock in the summer of 1958, KLLL "became the new focus of his professional life" (Amburn 1995: 181). On a visit to the station, Holly composed the song 'You're The One' with KLLL disc jockey and musician Waylon Jennings and Slim Corbin, one of three brothers who had recently bought the station. Holly also sang background vocals to the commercials read out by Jennings and made promotional jingles for the station using the tunes of his hits 'Everyday' and 'Peggy Sue'. The latter's doggerel was: "if you knew what I do / You'd tune our way the whole day through / to music K Triple L – uh L uh huh / well it's country style on K L Double L".

Radio stations such as KDAV and KLLL broadcast three types of show based on live music rather than records: the sponsored 15- or 30-minute show by a specific artist or group; the weekend evening "barn dance"-type show, exemplified by the *Grand Ole Opry* broadcast across the South and West from WSM Nashville and the *Louisiana Hayride* from KWKH in Shreveport, LA; and a looser type of talent show open to beginners in music as well as established performers. A fourth type, featuring performances of current hit songs (e.g. the nationally syndicated *The Lucky Strike Hit Parade*) had all but disappeared, to be replaced by disc-based hits shows.

The artist-based live shows survived in Lubbock until the mid-1950s. Vicky Billington Pickering recalled listening at home to early-morning gospel shows featuring her future husband John Pickering (Stewart interviews). There were also remote broadcasts from various venues in the city (Amburn 1995: 30). Buddy Holly and Jack Neal had their 30-minute *Buddy & Jack's Sunday Party* show from November 1953 (Norman 1996: 46–7) and Holly and Montgomery had their own *Buddy & Bob Show* on KDAV in late 1954 and early 1955, although this seems to have been a segment of the station's *Sunday Party* talent show (Amburn 1996: 25). In this half-hour appearance Buddy & Bob played requests and featured an eclectic mixture of bluegrass, R&B (for example, Hank Ballard and the Midnighters' 'Work With Me Annie') and songs recorded by Elvis Presley.

The premier barn dance show on Lubbock radio was *Western Jamboree* on KSEL, which for a while featured the Mayfield Brothers band. It could not compete in prestige and reach with the *Opry* (founded 1925) or the *Hayride*, which had made its mark as "the *Opry*'s brash younger cousin" (Guralnick 1994: 136). Elvis Presley had joined the *Louisiana Hayride* in October 1954 and early the next year told Buddy in Lubbock that he could get Buddy & Bob a slot on the show. Because of this, Holly, Welborn and Montgomery drove over 500 miles to Shreveport but were turned away from the show because Elvis was not there on that occasion (Norman 1996: 64).

During the early 1950s, generalist music radio stations throughout the USA began to introduce rhythm & blues music to white youth audiences. In a study of this process of musical desegregation, Kloosterman and Quispel wrote that "After 1950, due to the advancement of radio in American society, it became increasingly possible for white youths to get acquainted with a black culture as propagated by blacks to blacks. Here, the prejudice-upholding shackles of 'labelled interaction' did not exist" (Kloosterman and Quispel 1990: 161).

The rate at which this mediated desegregation occurred varied considerably according to local taste, the attitudes of station owners and the speed with which the nomenclature "rock 'n roll" spread throughout the music and radio industries. Although the argument about which was the first rock 'n roll record is fundamentally undecidable, it is documented that a Cleveland, OH, disc jockey, Alan Freed, adopted the term in 1952 (Ennis 1992: 18). In the same year, a former Cleveland DJ reported the situation in a "large, central Texas city":

> There is no teenage activity in this town. There are only two or three dances a year because of the Baptists here. The kids like either pop or hillbilly. They're real fanatic and here the kids, white, lean to R&B. They call it cat music, so I play some rhythm & blues. I started it in Cleveland and was surprised it went down so well. I continued it here, but not the real "low down" stuff. (Ennis 1992: 170)[11]

It took two more years, however, for rock 'n roll radio to reach West Texas. By 1954 Lubbock stations were beginning to cater to the youth audience with relatively brief shows devoted to putative rock 'n roll music. KSEL was offering a one-hour show each weekday after high school had ended, and the following year (1955) KDAV started a competing show called *Rock 'n Roll Hit Parade* (Goldrosen and Beecher 1996: 28). KSEL also broadcast a late evening *Hi-D-Ho Hit Parade* between 9 pm and 11 pm, sponsored by the drive-in café of that name. According to Norman's informant, DJ Jerry Coleman, Buddy would sometimes sit in with him to comment on the R&B records by such acts as New York vocal group the Drifters and New Orleans blues shouter Smiley Lewis. Norman adds that KSEL "had moved from easy-listening pop to all-out rock 'n roll", a statement belied by the existence of KSEL's long-running *Western Jamboree* show (Norman 1996: 72).

Rock 'n roll established a generational divide in musical taste. According to John Pickering, "Many of the students at Tech were listening to rhythm & blues groups as well as pop songs by the Diamonds, the Four Aces and the like. Perry Como and Pat Boone were popular with most adults" (Stewart interviews). Carl Bunch, from Odessa, told an interviewer:

> Chuck Berry, Little Richard, Fats and the rest got good air-play on some stations in West Texas, and might as well as have been banned on others. We weren't deep enough in the South to hear all the hateful slurs they faced in Alabama, Louisiana and Mississippi, but parents in general from our neck of the woods faced it like most parents now have to deal with rap. They wouldn't allow it in the house, but couldn't keep us from listening when we were out of the house. After a while they got weary of the fight and let us play our 45s at home. (Stewart interviews)

All of these programmes on local stations offered a limited number of rhythm & blues records, but to hear such sounds on a large scale (including the "low down" stuff) it was necessary to tune in to one of the long-distance clear channel stations licensed to broadcast with a 50,000 watt transmitter such as XERF from Del Rio and KWKH from Shreveport, LA, the station from which *Louisiana Hayride* originated: "not only did KWKH blanket the Ark-La-Tex area, but the station's AM frequency also bounced and skipped its way west across much of North Central and West Texas" (Specht 2003: 2). By tuning into his parents' car radio, Holly and his circle were able to listen to R&B from KWKH on a late-night show sponsored by Stan's Record Shop.

The KWKH R&B disc jockey was Frank Gatemouth Page, a white man who sounded black to his teenage listeners. The show's title was *Stan's Record Review* (Goldrosen and Beecher 1996: 54) but was recalled by Sonny Curtis as *Stan's Record Rack*. Joe B. Mauldin recalled that "it came on at 10.30 at night and we could barely tune it in on our car radios" (Goldrosen and Beecher 1996: 54). Curtis said he and Buddy would "go out to the car at midnight and listen to *Stan's Record Rack* out of Shreveport. He would play everything: Lonnie Johnson, Ray Charles, Bill Haley, Little Richard etc. It was mightily enlightening" (Stewart interviews). "Stan" was Stan Lewis, a white Shreveport record shop owner, jukebox operator, one-stop distributor[12] and record producer. Lewis was involved with both country and R&B music – his store and jukeboxes were in the African-American section of Shreveport (Leadbitter 1973–4).

In one interview, Bob Montgomery stated that his and Buddy's blues favourites were such artists as Muddy Waters, Little Walter and Lightnin' Hopkins rather than younger vocal groups (Goldrosen and Beecher 1996: 16), though there is no report of Buddy & Bob performing songs associated with these artists. The music of such artists was also broadcast on another 50,000 watt station, WLAC Nashville. According to "Hoss" Allen, a (white) DJ at WLAC in the 1950s:

> White guys growing up in Tennessee, Louisiana, Mississippi, Arkansas, Texas, Alabama, if they were musically inclined they played country music but they listened to WLAC, as well as the *Grand Ole Opry* on WSM, and it influenced them all. They started trying to hold those guitar chords like the blues guys, play in minor keys and stuff, but it didn't come out like Muddy Waters or Howling Wolf, it came out rockabilly, and from rockabilly came white rock 'n roll. (Palmer 1996: 20)

Another prime source of schizophonic experience was the jukebox, to be found in most cafés and drug stores. The repeal of prohibition by the Federal government in 1933 had led to the opening of thousands of new venues where jukeboxes could be installed; and the relocation of millions of young members of the armed forces during World War II to camps with service clubs containing these machines had greatly enhanced the role of jukeboxes in disseminating music. Until 1948, the machines had contained only 24 single-sided discs, but the launch of the Select-O-Matic 100 by Seeburg in that year increased the selections to 50 singles, both of whose sides could be chosen. This enabled a much wider range of musical styles to be represented on a single box. Jukeboxes in the Lubbock and West Texas region were operated by the Jordan Music Company, whose owner Bob Jordan was reported in 1958 as saying that "Elvis Presley is probably the most popular recording artist on the juke boxes here, but the Crickets and Sonny Curtis are also well liked" (*Lubbock Avalanche-Journal* 1958).

Niki Sullivan recalled how black music had been available in 1954 from jukeboxes in Lubbock as well as long-distance stations: "I started listening to rhythm and blues in high school . . . in my junior year, the Midnighters were very popular – where I ate lunch they had those records like 'Work With Me Annie' on the jukebox" (Goldrosen and Beecher 1996: 47–8). Peggy Sue Gerron had direct access to jukebox records. She explained that she, Buddy and Jerry Allison would "talk about the records that I was getting from Dallas . . . I believe one of the artists we talked about was Hank Ballard . . . My brother-in-law had a friend that changed the juke-boxes for all the cafes. I had all the early rhythm and blues records" (Stewart interviews).

As the Gerron quote indicates, If Buddy and his circle could not find music on radio or Lubbock's jukeboxes, there were also records themselves. One anecdote tells of his introduction to African-American music through a disc by Fats Domino played to him by Jerry Allison around 1953. Buddy was already 16, but local stations did not yet programme black music, and Niki Sullivan's comments suggest that R&B records may have been scarce or absent from jukeboxes in the city until 1954 when hits by the Midnighters arrived.

A local newspaper article reporting the popularity of rockabilly in Lubbock provides a sort of inventory of the city's recorded music business in 1958. Among those quoted are record shop proprietor U. V. Blake and "local record store chain owner" Wayne Allen, whose Wayne's Record Rack near the high school sold new 45 rpm releases to local teenagers. Blake commented that Broadway show albums were among his bestsellers and that the advent of stereo meant "we are converting a lot of standard record players over to stereophonic by adding the stereo cartridge". The article added that "grocery and drug stores are adding record racks to their stocks to meet the demand for the waxie maxie carriers" (*Lubbock Avalanche-Journal* 1958).

In the early 1990s, Buddy Holly's record collection was donated to the memorabilia collection in Lubbock. It included singles by a range of African-American artists including six by Ray Charles, and others by Little Walter, Bo Diddley and Jimmy Reed. There were also records by white female singers the McGuire Sisters, Valerie Carr and Peggy Lee (Mann 2009: 245).

Musical instrument shops were another nexus for information about new music. Sonny Curtis worked in the Adair musical instrument shop in Lubbock in 1956–7, with his guitar teacher Clyde Hankins: "It was under his tutelage that my music reading skills developed. He introduced me to jazz and classical guitar. He made me understand that if I learned to play jazz, I wouldn't forget how to play bluegrass" (Stewart interviews). Buddy Holly also had lessons from Clyde Hankins, who was a master of all musical genres, having been an arranger for Stan Kenton's band and an accompanist for the Andrews Sisters. He also recorded an album at Norman Petty's studio and appeared on the *Dude Ranch* show of Lubbock's first television station, KDUB (which opened in 1952) (Carr and Munde 1995: 122).[13]

Finale: the Presley effect

John Goldrosen has provided an instructive list of music genres that constituted Holly's "musical background". These were country & western, western swing, bluegrass, blues, rhythm & blues and black and white gospel music. To these we can add folk revival song, although his introduction to this genre may not have occurred until 1957 when he played on a recording session for Texas folk singer Carolyn Hester.[14]

The picture so far in this chapter is of Buddy Holly and the teenage members of his network absorbing and/or recreating this range of musics during the first half of the 1950s. To a great extent, the "range" remained just that: the songs in Buddy's developing repertoire that were added or discarded derived from one or other genre or music style, but there was no synthesis of these styles, as the occasional use of a description for Buddy's music showed; in 1953, for example, it was "western" and, a year later, "western and bop" on the business cards of Buddy & Bob.

"Bop" or even "Be-bop" was an epithet also applied to Elvis Presley at the time. Joe Specht has explained the use of this term for the music of young white Southerners:

> "Bop" in this case was, obviously, being used as a code word. It meant more than just a "Negro" beat. Bop was also something new and cool, and it involved an element of dance, too. The sexuality oozing from Presley could not be ignored either. In a 1960 interview, Elvis coyly confided, "I can't dance to rock and roll. I can slow dance but I never learned to bop". But his fans knew better and so did the media and the public at large. Presley's stage moves were described in Tulsa, Oklahoma, as the "dirty bop". The Alabama White Citizens Council was even more explicit when it railed against "this animalistic nigger bop". (Specht 2003: 6)

It took the arrival of Elvis Presley to demonstrate to Buddy Holly and other young musicians how a new music could be constructed from a combinatory of the various genres. When Buddy saw Elvis he witnessed a condensation of these musics through an unprecedented Dionysiac bopping stage act.[15]

Presley's popularity in West Texas was reported to *Billboard* magazine in June 1955 by Cecil Hollifield, the owner of record shops in Midland and Odessa (both over 100 miles from Lubbock) and an occasional concert promoter:

> West Texas is his hottest territory to date, and he is the teen-agers' favourite wherever he appears. His original appear-ance in the area was in January with Billy Walker to more than 1600 paid admissions. In February, with Hank Snow in Odessa, paid attendance hit over 400. On April 1 we booked only Elvis and his boys, Bill and Scotty, plus Floyd Cramer on piano and a local boy on drums for a rockin' and rollin' dance for teenagers and pulled 850 paid admissions . . . Incidentally, Presley's four records have beat any individual artist in our eight years in the record business. (Guralnick 1994: 183)

While there is conflicting evidence in the Hollyology literature, the defini-tive *Elvis Day by Day* shows that, during 1955, Elvis Presley performed five times in Lubbock (Guralnick and Jorgenson 1999). Buddy Holly was present for all five, four of them playing as co-leader with Bob Montgomery of a sup-port band. It is probable that, apart from acts who toured with Elvis (who were generally established country singers), few other bands played so often on the same bill as Elvis in this early phase of his career.

Presley's impact, it seems, was immediate. Elvis first played the Fair Park Coliseum in Lubbock on either January 2 or January 6 in a show with country singer Bill Walker and Jimmy & Johnny, regulars on the *Louisiana Hayride* and proto-rockabilly singers. It is also reported that Elvis played a late-night set at the Cotton Club on the same visit, as he was said to have done in June and in October (Frame 1998: 9). Holly and Curtis were in the audience and "the day after Elvis left town, we turned into Elvis clones", according to Curtis, who can be pardoned a certain exaggeration ". . . and we was bookin' out as an Elvis band" (Norman 1996: 61).

On February 13, an advertisement in the *Lubbock Avalanche-Journal* announced the return "By Popular Demand" of "Elvis Presley the Be-Bop

Western Star of the Louisiana Hayride". The event was a 4 pm matinee at the Fair Park Coliseum. Also on the bill were the *Grand Ole Opry* comedian Duke of Paducah (catchphrase: "I'm going to the waggon, boys. These shoes are killing me"), Charline Arthur ("Miss Dynamite of the *Big D Jamboree*"), whose singing was "bold, brassy and slightly blues-flavoured" (Allen 1998: 3), Jimmy Rodgers Snow (son of country star Hank Snow) and West Texas country singer Ace Ball. The Buddy & Bob group, bottom of the bill, were followed onstage by another Lubbock band, Bill Myrick and the Rainbow Riders.

Elvis returned to play the Cotton Club on April 29. Although Philip Norman (1996: 63) says Buddy was in the audience, Bill Myrick claims to have enabled Holly's group to open the show. The biography on his MySpace Music page states:

> After letting Buddy Holly and his group sit in with him on stage at the Cotton Club in Lubbock, Bill Myrick would actually be the reason Buddy Holly took the stage that fateful night at the Elvis Presley concert in Lubbock on which Bill Myrick was Elvis's opening act. But a rowdy crowd who arrived two hours early prompted Myrick to intervene and send out Buddy Holly and his band playing with Bill's band's instruments. They subsequently brought the house down and began Holly's meteoric rise in rockabilly music.[16] This may also have been when Buddy Holly is said to have taught Elvis the words of 'Money Honey' by the Drifters (Mann 2002) and Elvis offered to get Buddy and Bob a spot on the *Louisiana Hayride*.

On June 3, Elvis played the Fair Park Coliseum as part of a package show that included Ferlin Husky, gospel singer Martha Carson and Bill Carlisle, author of 'Too Old To Cut The Mustard' (Guralnick 1994: 163). Buddy Holly and Bob Montgomery led the band that opened the show. This visit also included separate sets by Buddy and Elvis on the back of a flatbed truck at the opening of a Pontiac automobile showroom (Norman 1996: 63; Goldrosen and Beecher 1996: 29). All the musicians later went together to the Lindsay theatre to see *Gentleman Prefer Blondes*, starring Marilyn Monroe and Jane Russell.

Elvis made his fifth visit to Lubbock on October 15. His growing celebrity had made him the star of the show. The Elvis Presley Jamboree was also weighted towards the rockabilly wing of country music with Johnny Cash, Wanda Jackson and Carl Perkins on the bill alongside country acts Porter Wagoner and Floyd Cramer. This was the first time Presley had come to the city as the leader of a four-piece group with a drummer, D. J. Fontana, joining guitarist Scotty Moore and bass player Bill Black. Philip Norman says this was the catalyst for Jerry Allison to join the Holly group (Norman 1996: 65). On this show, Buddy, Bob and double bass player Larry Welborn were joined by Sonny Curtis on lead guitar.

For much of 1955, Holly seems to have simply reproduced Elvis's stylistic motifs. Sid King, a country bandleader of the Five Strings, who played often in Lubbock and met Buddy & Bob there, said that, when he found the duo a slot on the *Big D Jamboree* show on Dallas radio station KRLD, "he was on an Elvis Presley kick – he just idolised the guy. He sounded exactly like Elvis" (Goldrosen and Beecher 1996: 30–1).

Presley's final show in Lubbock took place in April 1956. By that time, Buddy Holly had begun to go beyond emulation of Elvis to embark on a journey towards his own musical style, although this would not crystallize until 1957.

2 A Studio Career: Nashville–Clovis– New York, 1956–1959

This chapter and the following one trace the brief professional career of Buddy Holly as a recording artist (Chapter 2) and performer (Chapter 3) between 1956 and 1959.

Buddy Holly's professional recording career lasted from 1956 to 1958 and consisted of three phases differentiated by studio sites and organizational practices. Between January and November 1956, Holly recorded in Nashville for the Decca label. When Decca failed to renew his contract, he recorded between January 1957 and December 1958 in Clovis, New Mexico, with producer Norman Petty. Through Petty he had gained recording contracts with the New York-based labels Brunswick (for the Crickets) and Coral (for his solo recordings). During the latter part of 1958, Holly made a small number of recordings in New York with musicians and producers chosen by Coral.[1]

Before discussing his recording career, this chapter begins with a section on earlier tracks made by Holly with Bob Montgomery and others during the period covered in Chapter 1.

Apart from the occasional tracks recorded at home between 1949 and 1953 for his family to hear or at local radio station KDAV in 1953 with Jack Neal, the first substantial tranche of Holly recordings were made in 1954–1955 with Montgomery and several other Lubbock musicians at Nesman Studios in Wichita Falls, about 200 miles east of Lubbock and at KDAV in 1955. These were mainly cut as demos to be used to try to get a recording contract. Some were given to a local representative of Columbia Records but no contract ensued (Goldrosen and Beecher 1996: 30).

The Wichita Falls tracks are a representative sample of the repertoire of Buddy & Bob in their early bluegrass and country phase. Five tracks resulted from the first of these sessions, on which Holly and Montgomery singing harmony vocals and playing acoustic guitars were accompanied by Sonny Curtis (on fiddle rather than guitar) and either Don Guess or Larry Welborn on double bass. In keeping with the conventions of the bluegrass genre, the group was without a drummer. Among the tracks was 'I Gambled My Heart', a Holly–Montgomery collaboration and Buddy's first known composition. The other tracks – 'Door To My Heart', 'Soft Place In My Heart', 'Flower Of My Heart' and 'Gotta Get You Near Me Blues' – were written by Montgomery alone.[2]

Nearly all the singing is in close harmony, of the plaintive kind typical of country music, including bluegrass. The Everly Brothers also began from this harmonic tradition and forged an individual style out of it. Buddy & Bob, however, never managed to surpass the convention to reach a more personal style. One exception is 'Soft Place In The Heart', where Holly's solo singing shows that the unusual melismatic quality of his voice (sometimes called the "hiccupping" effect) was already developed.[3] It also indicates how much his style owed to the country and western examples of Hank Williams and others.

The songwriting is undistinguished and somewhat repetitive with four of the five songs including "heart" as the last word of their title! Most lyrics repeat the melancholic feelings found in much country music. Curtis's old-timey fiddle playing reinforces the depressive message of 'I Gambled My Heart', where the only consolation for the singer is that the girl who turned him down might get the same treatment herself one day. While the songs written by Felice and Boudleaux Bryant for the Everly Brothers a few years later were love songs about high-school situations intended to correspond to the experience of their teenage audiences, Montgomery's lyrics are hand-me-downs from Hank Williams or Hank Snow.

On these country and western ballads, the guitar playing tends to be of the rich chorded style containing echoes of Mexican and Hawaiian music. It is a smoother sound than that of Hank Williams, made popular in the 1950s by such younger country stars as Marty Robbins, whom Buddy & Bob were to support in concert in Lubbock in October 1956.

The up-tempo 'Got To Get You Near Me Blues' is the least typical of these recordings. Holly's guitar break has some similarities with the rockabilly playing of Carl Perkins, but the remaining instrumental work is taken straight from the dance music of western swing bands. The fiddle again predominates. The singing crams as many words as possible into each line. This style originated from the technique of auctioneers at auctions for crops such as tobacco and cotton. The auctioneers' speedy delivery inspired both square dance callers and singers of country novelty songs, notably Leroy Van Dyke who was to have a 1957 hit called 'The Auctioneer' and Hank Snow with 'I've Been Everywhere' (1962).

There is no precise date for those recordings, which may have been made in 1954 when Holly was 18 years old. However, John Beecher's discography dates the next Wichita Falls sessions at June 1955 by which time Holly and his colleagues had fallen under the Presley spell. For these three tracks, the duo added the drumming of Jerry Allison and one of the recordings was a version of 'Baby Let's Play House' (sometimes listed as 'I Wanna Play House With You'), an R&B song originally recorded by Arthur Gunter and covered by Elvis Presley. The Elvis version had been recorded in February 1955 and was released on May 1, a few weeks before the Buddy & Bob session.

Also recorded at this time was another Montgomery ballad, 'You And I Are Through' and 'Down The Line' – the only song of these recordings that Holly had a hand in writing. 'Down The Line' is a fast boogie with a jangling electric guitar introduction. The guitar solo is very similar to some of the breaks played by Scotty Moore on early Presley records and to the solo by Danny Cedrone on Bill Haley and the Comets' 'Rock Around The Clock'. The vocal excitement is generated by the way the chorus line "I gotta roll" is sung. The word "roll" is repeated several times, sung alternately by each voice. On both 'Baby Let's Play House' and Down The Line', the drumming has an accented off-beat instead of reinforcing the guitar rhythm as country music drummers often did.

The guitar playing on this track is again in the amplified style characteristic of many Sun Records recordings produced by Sam Phillips in Memphis. The opening bars of 'Baby Let's Play House' sound much like the playing of black artist Dr Ross on such Sun titles as 'The Boogie Disease'; and this track is perhaps the closest Buddy Holly came to performing in the rockabilly style pioneered by Sun's white acts.

The KDAV tracks, recorded in August 1955, exhibit a harder sound derived from R&B and from the influence of Elvis Presley. Five songs were recorded at the radio station including new versions of 'Soft Place In My Heart' and 'You And I Are Through'. The new songs were 'Memories' by Montgomery, 'Queen Of The Ballroom' by Don Guess, and 'Baby It's Love', credited to Bob Montgomery and Buddy's mother, Ella Holley. On these songs the guitars of Holly and Montgomery are again supplemented by Larry Welborn on double bass and Sonny Curtis on fiddle (and guitar on one track).

The Nashville sessions with Owen Bradley

Buddy Holly's first commercial recording sessions came about through the efforts of Eddie Crandall, a talent scout, booking agent and manager of Marty Robbins, and Lubbock radio station owner Dave Stone. Crandall saw Holly perform in Lubbock at the end of 1955 and subsequently cabled Stone from his Nashville office, asking him to make demo recordings of Holly, adding "don't change his style at all".[4]

In December 1955, Holly returned to the Wichita Falls studio to record four tracks. Two – 'Don't Come Back Knockin'' and 'Love Me' – had been co-written with Sue Parrish. The others were Holly's 'I Guess I Was Just A Fool' and 'Baby Won't You Come Out Tonight?' by Don Guess. These demos were sent to Crandall and given by him to music publisher and Nashville veteran Jim Denny who in turn persuaded Paul Cohen of Decca Records to record Holly as a solo singer. This relay of agent/manager to publisher to record company was extended by Cohen to the record producer Owen Bradley. Three sessions were held at the Bradley's Barn studio on 16th Avenue South in Nashville during 1956.

Owen Bradley (1915–1998) was a former radio station staff producer who had recently built his own studio in a Quonset hut, a prefabricated building made of corrugated iron and lined with wood for use by the armed services during World War II. After 1945, these were sold off for $1,000 each for business use.[5]

Bradley was later to work on recordings by Patsy Cline, Loretta Lynn, Conway Twitty and Brenda Lee, and had a penchant for pop-country. He was not known for sympathy with rockabilly and treated the Buddy Holly sessions as a routine assignment. Holly's biographers report that the first Nashville session pitted Holly as solo singer against a gaggle of unenthusiastic session musicians. Later, he was permitted to use more of his own accompanists, which was more supportive, but the results were equally uninspired as a rookie musician met an uncomprehending producer.

In an interview conducted in the 1970s, Bradley reacted somewhat defensively to the suggestion that the recordings were unsuccessful, stating that he had no clear instructions from Paul Cohen as to which style Holly should be recorded in:

> When Paul Cohen sent Buddy over, Paul said he wanted it
> country – at least that was my understanding . . . We had

> been very successful with a country formula; we were all
> into country and it's hard to change patterns . . . I remember
> Buddy wanted the drummer to do something, and the drum-
> mer just couldn't do it. Buddy was trying to make sort of a
> rock 'n roll record and he should have had guys with a black
> feel – our guys had a country feel. (Goldrosen and Beecher
> 1996: 36)[6]

Whether or not Cohen "wanted it country", Bradley's understanding that this was the case is understandable. The standard history of country music states that "much of Nashville's evolution towards musical pre-eminence is attrib-utable to Paul Cohen", who had "inaugurated the modern era of recording in Nashville in the spring of 1945" (Malone 2002a: 209).

The mid-1950s was a critical phase in the evolution of what was becoming known as "country" music. Those involved in the Nashville scene and in radio stations across the South were scrambling to fix an identity and bounda-ries, even down to the name of their favoured music. In the period before World War II it was often referred to as "hillbilly", and Buddy Holly had used another widely used term when he referred to "western" music in his 1953 high-school essay. By 1955, however, the Nashville establishment had settled on "country", dispelling connotations of rural hicks and singing cowboys. A Country Music Association was set up to regulate and promote this industry, with Owen Bradley among its board of directors.

In 1956, neither of the twin processes was quite complete by which "coun-try music" established a distinctive and strongly policed identity for itself and by which Nashville was to become the unchallenged metropolis of the coun-try music recording and music publishing industry. Consequently, the arrival of Elvis Presley and "rockabilly" provoked a minor crisis of identity for the Nashville-based idea of what country should aspire to be. The uncertainty is evident in the variety of generic descriptions attached to Elvis in 1954–55 before "rockabilly" became the default definition of his music. Most of them expressed a paradox in the mind of the publicist, journalist or promoter coining the phrase. Sometimes he was the "Folk Fireball" – linking him to rural music but possibly posing an arsonist threat to it; at other times he was a "Hillbilly Cat" or a purveyor of "Western bop". Even "rockabilly" was not entirely satisfactory to the new country music establishment, since their branding of their industry as "country" was in part an attempt to repress the term "hillbilly" and its connotations of rural idiocy.

In her study of the rise of the country music industry, Diane Pecknold asserts that "rockabilly was perceived as country music" and that country record executives and publishers "embraced rock and roll even before the immensity of its commercial potential was entirely clear" (2007: 86). However, the treatment of Buddy Holly indicates that such a sweeping statement must be qualified. Bradley's reference to "guys with a black feel" shows there was a racial undertow to his musicians' incomprehension of Holly's music, and Pecknold herself comments that "there is no doubt that racism underlay much of the country industry's response to the growing influence of R&B" (2007: 86). Paul Ackerman, editor of *Billboard*, was more direct. In a 1958 article he stated that the reaction of some Nashville executives to Presley was "he sings nigger music" (Ackerman 1958: 37).

And, even when the Nashville establishment appeared less antipathetic to rockabilly, the new music could still come up against the conservatism of the old. When Jimmy Bowen and Buddy Knox, West Texas singers with rockabilly hits, were booked to appear on the *Grand Ole Opry*, Bowen recalled that he "was introduced to the difference between the worlds of country and rock. When we arrived at the artists' entrance, a guard saw our drummer with all his gear and said 'Whoa, we don't have drums in the *Grand Ole Opry*'. They refused to let him in the door" (Bowen with Jerome 1997: 51).

In this still fluid situation, members of the country music business were split in their response to the challenge of the new music of young white southerners, epitomized by Elvis Presley. As Pecknold points out, Elvis was at first regarded by most as part of country – one of his early promotional descriptions was "the Hillbilly Cat", the adjective linking him to the past but the noun suggesting his connection to something else. But Elvis certainly divided the country audience. The music historian Bill Malone was an undergraduate student at the University of Texas, Austin, in 1955. When he saw Elvis perform, he felt "the barbarians had entered the gates of country music" (Malone 2002b: 10). A country musician's perspective was given to Neil Rosenberg by Vic Mullen, a Canadian country act of the 1950s, who told him that some of the audience would:

> yell for 'Blue Suede Shoes' and these other big rock songs, and
> if you happened to do one of those on the show, this group,
> wherever they were in the building, would, of course, get all
> carried away . . . and the guy on stage would say, "hey, this is

what we should be doing". Forgetting that the quiet country
music crowd were sitting down there hoping that he'd get
back to a country song . . . what it did was discourage the
country fans from going to any country show that was adver-
tised because they found out after they got there, most of the
show was going to be rock. (Rosenberg 2005: 118)

Another of Rosenberg's informants had a less apocalyptic view of the relationship between country and rock 'n roll. The bluegrass banjo player Rusty
York was a year older than Buddy Holly. He formed a banjo and guitar duo,
"then Elvis came along . . . and even country boys started liking Elvis you
know. And we had to switch over to electric guitar . . . and switch over to
electric bass, and we finally had to have drums and turn into modern country" (Rosenberg 2005: 124). York went on to record one of several cover versions of Holly's hit record 'Peggy Sue', for King Records of Cincinnati. Unlike
Holly, however, he did not commit himself wholeheartedly to rock 'n roll,
continuing to play bluegrass as well as occasionally making rock recordings.

While many in Nashville and mainstream country music were at first
indifferent to, or suspicious of, rockabilly, it was said to be different in West
Texas. Interviewed by John Goldrosen, Dave Stone of Lubbock station KDAV
asserted that "we thought of rockabilly as just being another kind of country music, so we always played it. And I know I did well in the 1950s . . . our
decline came in the early 1960s when there weren't so many country musicians involved in rock 'n roll" (Goldrosen and Beecher 1996: 108). However,
Stone's view should be balanced against that of leading Hollyologist Bill
Griggs who has stated that Lubbock was "primarily a country music town
and rock 'n roll here was a tiny island surrounded by boot-skipping country
fans" (Stewart interviews).

The Decca Records contract and the Nashville sessions represented the
first watershed in Holly's career, something underlined by his decision to buy
a new guitar to take to Nashville. He borrowed a thousand dollars from his
brother Larry and acquired a Fender Stratocaster, the state-of-the-art solid-
bodied guitar that had been launched in 1954 for the Californian western
swing band market, with its revolutionary cutaway design to enable the
body of the guitar to fit comfortably at the hip of the player (Minhinnett and
Young 1995). Holly was among the first of the younger generation of putative
rockabilly and rock 'n roll musicians to adopt the Stratocaster.

For the journey to the first Nashville session in January 1956, he also took Sonny Curtis and Don Guess, from the band that had played on the demos that secured the Decca contract. Jerry Allison could not join them because of high-school commitments. When they arrived, they first had to join the American Federation of Musicians (since Nashville sessions were a closed shop, excluding non-union members). Then, Bradley decreed that Buddy could not both play rhythm guitar and sing. Instead, Bradley brought in his regular session players, Grady Martin on guitar and drummer Doug Kirkham, to work with Holly, Curtis and Guess.

It was presumably Kirkham to whom Bradley was referring in his comment quoted above that "the drummer just couldn't do it" – "it" being to play in a rock 'n roll style. For the later sessions, Bradley at first relented, allowing the full Lubbock band (including Allison) to play on five tracks recorded in a three-hour session in July but then reversed this policy so that, in December 1956, only bass player Guess was permitted to accompany his colleague, alongside several more of Nashville players including noted pianist Floyd Cramer and Bradley's brother Harold on guitar!

A total of 11 tracks were produced by Bradley. Of these only one – 'Midnight Shift' – was a recording of a song supplied by a Nashville source (publisher Jim Denny) rather than by Buddy and his supporting musicians. To add to the general uncertainty about how Holly should be recorded, this and several other songs were firmly in an R&B or rockabilly mode, contrasting with the country flavour of several other songs. The country-styled tracks were 'Girl On My Mind' and 'You Are My One Desire', both by Don Guess, Ben Hall's 'Blue Days, Black Nights', 'Modern Don Juan' by Guess and Jack Neal, and the Holly–Parrish composition 'Love Me'.

'Midnight Shift' was composed by Alabaman musician Luke McDaniel, although credited by him to two aliases, Earl Lee and Jimmy Ainsworth. This was because McDaniel was under contract to the top country and western publisher Acuff-Rose who "didn't handle that type of material", according to McDaniel. The type of material was what McDaniel described as "old-type Saturday night blues" (Goldrosen and Beecher 1996: 38).

Country music lyrics, especially in their honky-tonk variant, had plenty of "cheating" or "slippin' around" (the title of a 1949 song by Floyd Tillman), but the less moralistic treatment of the theme of infidelity marks 'Midnight Shift' as owing most to R&B, as does the name of its "heroine", Annie. The Midnighters with lead singer Hank Ballard had made a series of records in

1954 recounting the exploits of a character called Annie. They included 'Work With Me Annie' and 'Annie Had A Baby'. They were sometimes banned by radio stations and had inspired answer records such as the Etta James hit 'Roll With Me Henry', a reply to 'Work With Me Annie'. Although Luke McDaniel told John Goldrosen that he hadn't been influenced by the Annie saga, the lyrics read like an extension of the Midnighters' sequence of songs where "Annie's been working on the midnight shift".

A decade after his death, Holly's exuberant, deadpan delivery of 'Midnight Shift' caught the attention of rock critic Greil Marcus. He described Buddy's phrasing as "simply what we know as pure Dylan" (Marcus 1969) quoting as an example:

> If she tells you she wants to use the cahhh
> Never explains what she wants it fahhh

The track is also outstanding instrumentally. It drives along from a sprightly introduction played on the bass strings of the guitar to a neatly picked rockabilly solo by Curtis, reminiscent of Carl Perkins's work. But it is the lyric that lifts 'Midnight Shift' above most of the other Nashville tracks:

> Early in the morning when the sun comes up
> You look at old Annie and she looks kinda rough
> You tell her "honey, get outa that bed"
> She says "leave me alone, I'm just about dead"

Joining 'Midnight Shift' as clearly non-country or post-country (proto-rockabilly) songs were 'Ting-A-Ling', 'Rock Around With Ollie Vee', 'Changing All Those Changes', 'Don't Come Back Knockin'' and 'That'll Be The Day', the first recorded version of one of Holly's best-known songs. 'Ting-A-Ling' was the only cover version among the Nashville recordings. It had been recorded by black vocal group the Clovers and composed by Atlantic Records' Ahmet Ertegun under his palindromic pseudonym Nugetre.

The lyric of 'Rock Around With Ollie Vee' (composed by Sonny Curtis) declares "we're gonna rock to the rhythm and blues", and Ollie Vee herself is said to be from Memphis, Tennessee, home of Elvis Presley and Sun Records. Here, Holly uses a range of vocal effects. The swiftness of his delivery of the lyric, the lengthening of syllables and the primitive echo added by Bradley combine to make the words slither together. There is a notable vocal touch on the line "I'm gonna shake it just a bit *in the middle of the night*", where the voice suddenly drops an octave for the italicized words. But, while Elvis Presley managed to get a menacing sexual growl by a similar effect, Buddy Holly comes across as playful rather than deeply sensual: it is a wink, not a snarl.

The otherwise banal ballad 'Girl On My Mind' is also notable for Holly's experimentation with melismatic vocal motifs, whereby a single syllable or phoneme expands to cover several beats or even bars of the music. Whereas on 'You Are My One Desire' he holds notes by singing them straight and going slightly out of tune, on this song the country quiver in the voice becomes the first full appearance of the "hiccup" technique that was become a crucial feature of Holly's mature singing style. Here the single syllable "girl" becomes the polysyllabic "gir-hir-hir-hirl-hirl" and "mind" is transformed into "mi-hi-hi-hiya-hind". At least one monosyllabic word in most phrases of the lyric receives this treatment, and, together with the heavy echo and high-pitched voice, made this track into something strange and original. Although Presley had used this way of bending notes on slow ballads, here it dominates the song and conveys an obsessional feeling about the "girl on my mind".

'Changing All Those Changes', 'Don't Come Back Knockin'' and 'That'll Be The Day' are among the four songs composed or part-written by Buddy Holly and recorded in Nashville in 1956 (three of the others were by Don Guess). Of these, only 'That'll Be The Day' is outstanding: the others come across as conventional rockabilly or rock 'n roll dance tracks, in which lyrics and tune cede the foreground of the sound to the rhythm and instrumental playing.

'Don't Come Back Knockin'' has two contrasting guitar solos by Sonny Curtis. The first consists of a battery of chords, the second of sequences of single notes. During the vocal sections a melody line is played faintly on guitar in addition to the customary rhythm guitar. One line stands out from the conventional lyric: "like a talent scout you want some love that's new". It recalls Holly's meeting with Eddie Crandall at the Lubbock concert.

During 1956, Decca had issued two singles from the 11 Nashville tracks. 'Blue Days, Black Nights' / 'Love Me' was released in April, receiving a review in the leading music industry weekly *Billboard* that stated "if the public will take more than one Presley or Perkins, as it well may, Holly stands a strong chance" (Goldrosen and Beecher 1996: 38). 'Blue Days, Black Nights' is an up-tempo country song with a rhythm section led by the bass, similar to some early Johnny Cash rockabilly pieces such as 'I Walk The Line'.

Holly later told a Lubbock newspaper reporter that by June the record had sold 19,000 copies. This was not enough to make it either a regional or national hit. In December Decca released 'Modern Don Juan' / 'You Are My One Desire'. 'Modern Don Juan' edges towards an urban pop sound with a buzzing saxophone (said by some to be played by famous Nashville virtuoso Boots Randolph, although John Beecher's sessionography names the player as E. R. "Dutch" McMillin). This single was equally unsuccessful and Paul Cohen informed Buddy that he would not be taking up the option on his recording contract. Holly's first attempt at a recording career had been a failure.

In late 1956, Buddy made many more recordings of song associated with various rock 'n roll acts in the garage of the Holley home with drummer Jerry Allison and a local recording engineer. Jerry Allison later stated that these were songs that the duo "always played . . . at dances" around Lubbock and they put them down on tape "just to see what [they] sounded like" (Allison 1993). Like the 1954–55 tracks, these were issued posthumously, at first with overdubs and later in their original form. They are discussed further in Chapter 6.

The Norman Petty recordings

In the early 1960s, Norman Petty was interviewed by the British music magazine *New Record Mirror*. In answer to the question, "When did you begin to think that Buddy Holly would be a big star?", he said:

> Right back in 1956, when I first met him, when he wandered into my studio in Clovis, New Mexico, to make a demonstration tape. I said then he was a diamond in the rough and I was right. Although I discovered him, I let him go his own way. He knew what he wanted and I knew how to record him. He respected my ability and I respected his personality and talent. I was no magician where Buddy was concerned. You don't create talent – it's there. (Quoted in Laing 1971: 30)

The next phase of the recording career was the most important – Buddy's collaboration with Norman Petty at the latter's studio in Clovis. Petty was the main difference between the 1956 Holly records and those made in 1957 and 1958. As well as operating an independent recording studio, Petty was a professional musician with a recording career stretching back to the late 1940s. His preferences were for easy listening music, a factor that gave him an advantage over Owen Bradley in his work with Buddy Holly. While Bradley could recognize the country element in Buddy's music and work to repress the non-country part, the wholly dissimilar nature of Petty's musical tastes made him – like George Martin, the Beatles' producer – more willing to take risks and go further afield in the search for new sounds necessary to achieve popular success. Sometimes his mainstream light music taste hindered rather than enhanced Holly's music. But, more often, his musical inventiveness matched his sensitivity to Holly's potential.

Petty was an unusual combination of a talented musician and a creative recording engineer and producer. His interest in recording technology was evident from a young age. Born in 1927 into a musical family in Clovis, Norman learned the piano at a very young age. Philip Norman says that "As well as being able to play anything instantaneously by ear, he had such abnormal sensitivity to tone and pitch that he was soon getting lucrative work as a part-time piano-tuner" (Norman 1996: 100).

At eight or nine he wired a microphone into a radio set, so he could broadcast his own shows. At 15, he was recording the singing of a schoolmate, the future country singer Billy Walker (Carr and Munde 1995: 146) and his own amateur group, the Torchy Swingsters, on a wire-operated recorder. Petty bought a disc-cutter and recorded such items as greetings from service personnel to their families. He also worked as a disc jockey at the local radio station KICA while still at high school (Norman 1996: 100–1).

Petty had an eclectic musical background, absorbing country music, pop and classical styles. In 1949, he formed an instrumental trio with his wife Violet Anne (Vi) on piano and vocals and guitarist Jack Vaughn to play what would now be classified as easy listening instrumental music. With Norman Petty on organ, the trio had a hit in 1954 on the Columbia label with a harmony vocal version of Duke Ellington's 'Mood Indigo' and in 1957 pianist Roger Williams reached the top 30 with a recording of Petty's composition 'Almost Paradise'. Most sources state that with the proceeds from these hits Petty equipped and opened a recording studio, but Philip Norman refers to a letter written by Don Guess to Holly in March 1954, telling him about the new studio in Clovis, which suggests that the project was planned and carried out before the royalties from 'Mood Indigo' had reached Petty.

The studio was built in a small single-storey building which had previously been a grocery store run by Norman Petty's aunt. It consisted of a small lobby, a control room housing Petty's Altec single-channel recording desk, an Ampex reel-to-reel tape recorder (he later acquired additional tape recorders) and a lathe for cutting demo discs, two small adjoining recording rooms and a kitchen and "guest room" where Holly and the Crickets would sometimes sleep after a late-night session. The main studio space was "no bigger than an average-size living-room" (Norman 1996: 95) and housed a stand-microphone, guitar amplifier, grand piano and celesta. It had polycylindrical walls designed to reflect sound and eliminate dead spots and distortion. A smaller room was large enough to isolate one performer. Buddy Holly would often be recorded in here singing and playing rhythm guitar, although Jerry Allison was placed in the small room for the recording of 'Peggy Sue' (Goldrosen and Beecher 1996: 61).

Next door to the studio was the gas station and two-storey house owned by Petty's parents, where the Pettys and Norman's parents lived. In 1957 he enlisted the help of the musicians and Buddy's elder brothers to convert a room above an adjoining garage into a "live" echo chamber. John Goldrosen explains that "the sound produced in the studio was fed through a speaker in [this room] . . . picked up by a microphone in the same room and channelled back to the control room" (Goldrosen and Beecher 1996: 61). Before the construction of the echo chamber, Petty would also use the Lyceum Theatre in Clovis for some recordings that needed a "live" feeling and live echo – for example, the first Clovis tracks made by Sonny West, co-author of 'Oh Boy!'.

Petty's was one of the very few professional recording studios on the High Plains and soon drew musicians from a wide radius. Lubbock's bluegrass band, the Mayfield brothers, recorded there, as did country singer Jimmy Self and, in 1956, the Teen Kings, featuring Roy Orbison. That group recorded several demos including 'Ooby Dooby', which would be Orbison's first hit after he re-recorded it for Sam Phillips's Sun label in Memphis. In late 1956, Petty produced his first rockabilly hits with Buddy Knox, Jimmy Bowen and their group the Rhythm Orchids.

Buddy Holly and his cohort of musicians contacted Petty on the rebound from the unhappy Nashville experience. Holly, with Curtis, Guess and Allison, had previously used the Clovis studio between February and April 1956 to make song demo recordings of seven songs. Of these, only one ('I'm Changin'

All Those Changes' composed by Holly) would later be re-recorded and pro-duced in Nashville by Owen Bradley.

The other songs from these initial Clovis sessions were four composed by Buddy ('I Guess I Was Just A Fool', 'I'm Gonna Set My Foot Down', 'Because I Love You' and 'Rock-A-Bye Rock'), one by bass player Don Guess ('Baby Won't You Come Out Tonight?') and 'It's Not My Fault', written by Ben Hall and Weldon Myrick, two musicians from the Lubbock network. None of these demos, or other versions of these songs, were released in Buddy's lifetime.

The first recording session of 1957 at Clovis found Holly, Welborn and Allison recording two songs by current R&B artists who were also rock 'n roll stars. These were 'Brown Eyed Handsome Man' by Chuck Berry and Bo Diddley's eponymous signature song. It's not immediately clear why the trio should have chosen to do cover versions in a professional studio, but a month or so earlier the cover versions Holly and Allison had taped had included those two songs. At Clovis, the duo created a fuller sound, being augmented by Larry Welborn on bass and an unknown second guitarist.

That was the prelude to the creation of Holly's greatest sequence of record-ings. Between February 1957 and September 1958, Buddy Holly and his musi-cians went to Clovis for 15 separate recording sessions, producing between one and four tracks at each one. There was another session to cut four tracks at an air force base in Oklahoma City in September 1957. Petty booked these facilities because the Crickets were on tour and unable to return to Clovis. In total, versions of 36 songs were recorded under Petty's guidance, almost all of which were released as by Holly or the Crickets prior to the February 1959 plane crash.

On another ten days in 1957–58, Buddy Holly and others travelled to Clovis to play as session musicians on tracks by local singers such as Jim Robinson, Gary Tollett and folk singer Carolyn Hester, who would include a Crickets number ('Fool's Paradise') in her performances in Greenwich Village folk clubs a few years later. In July 1957, Holly played lead guitar on 'Sugartime' by local singer Charlie Phillips. Published by Petty, the song would become a major hit in versions by the McGuire Sisters, Guy Mitchell and British singer Jim Dale.

The first session produced the crucial breakthrough for Holly. He and Allison brought two songs to Petty: 'I'm Looking For Someone To Love' and 'That'll Be The Day', the song already recorded for Decca but which was unre-leased at this time.

The process of recording those two tracks was typical of the numerous later sessions and a total contrast to the Nashville recording system. All recordings in Nashville were made in conformity with a national agreement between the large record companies and the American Federation of Musicians (AFM). Nashville sessions, like those of New York, Los Angeles and other major recording centres, were timed in three-hour blocks for which musicians received a minimum fee from producers. Hence, all of Holly's Nashville sessions lasted for exactly three hours – in the evening or the morning.

At Clovis, recording sessions could not begin until the next-door gas station had closed for the day, because of the danger of picking up external sounds from the station and passing traffic. For their first session, Holly, Allison and Welborn with three backing singers (Niki Sullivan, Gary Tollett and Ramona Tollett) arrived in the late evening and spent three or four hours rehearsing the two songs before Petty began to record. 'I'm Looking For Someone To Love' was the first song to go down, in a large number of takes. The recording was done "live", because of the single-track machine. The three backing vocalists had to share one microphone. It was 3 am when they turned to 'That'll Be The Day', by which time "there was a party atmosphere", according to Gary Tollett. "We were having fun, not concentrating real hard . . . At about the fourth take, Norman said, 'Right, that's it'" (Norman 1996: 116).

The extended length of this session and the technical perfectionism of Norman Petty (which some authors state was matched by Buddy Holly's own) seem to have been typical of the Clovis recording dates. But there were also a number of specific effects, techniques and instrumental arrangements that enhanced particular tracks.

The specifics of the process of bricolage necessary to convert spaces intended for other uses into a recording studio contributed to the special sound qualities of recordings by Holly and others at Clovis. In this respect, Albin Zak mentions the "acoustic characteristics of the room above Petty's father gas station, which served as the studio's ambient chamber" and the improvised drum kit used on 'Not Fade Away'. Summarizing an account based on an interview with Petty's assistant (Jackson 1996), Zak states that the small size of the studio made it impossible to record a full drum kit without drowning out other musicians. After unsuccessfully moving Jerry Allison into a foyer, Petty decided to substitute a cardboard box for the kit: "the box's light popping sound seems odd for a driving Bo Diddley-style beat, but . . . it makes a good counterpart to the backing vocals . . . In this case, a distinctive aspect of the musical work resulted not from compositional design but from logistical consistency" (Zak 2001: 101–2). When 'Peggy Sue' was recorded, the drum kit was set up and separately miked in the hallway of the studio building.

Norman Petty had already used this technique with the Rhythm Orchids. In his memoirs, Jimmy Bowen describes Petty's studio sound improvisations:

> Petty decided to rig up a large cardboard box to sound like drums. He buried one of the mikes inside a towel, then stuffed the towel inside the box . . . it was amazing, but once [Rhythm Orchids' drummer Dave] Alldred got into an R&B-style double backbeat on that box with one half-shut drum brush and a stick, the sound just worked. That muffled percussive sound of Petty's became a true fifties rockabilly signature (Bowen with Jerome 1997: 40).

On another occasion, Allison used his own body sounds in place of a drum kit. He accompanied the lighter, keyboard-led sound of 'Everyday' by slapping his knees in time. That track illustrated one of Norman Petty's key innovations in recording Holly and the Crickets. On several occasions, Petty augmented the guitar, bass and drums sound with a keyboard instrument. On 'Everyday' it was the celesta or celeste, a type of xylophone keyboard invented in 1886 by Auguste Mustel in Paris. The keys of the celesta operate hammers that strike steel bars, underneath which is a series of wooden resonators. Elsewhere, piano or Baldwin electronic organ was added. Vi Petty played piano on several tracks including 'Fool's Paradise', 'Look At Me' and 'Think It Over', while Norman played organ on 'Take Your Time'. Both keyboards were included on the cover version of Fats Domino's hit 'Valley Of Tears'.

Petty also brought his skills as a recording engineer to the task of production. As well as installing the live echo system, he was an expert in microphone positioning (even placing a small microphone on the body of Joe Mauldin's acoustic bass) and in overdubbing. This last technique was particularly difficult to apply to a one-track recording system. However, Petty frequently added backing vocals to tracks scheduled for release by the Crickets and on several occasions he double-tracked Holly's singing or guitar playing. Without multi-track recording machines, the overdub method was adopted whereby an initial recording was played back on a single-track machine with the second vocal and/or guitar part played and recorded live over it.

Backing vocals by local singers the Picks (and, later, the Roses), were added to finished tracks at separate sessions that could occur within a few days or many weeks of the original recording being made. For example, while 'Fool's Paradise' and 'Think It Over' were overdubbed by the Roses within a few days of the Crickets recording the track in February 1958, backing vocals to 'Send Me Some Lovin'' and 'It's Too Late' were not added by the Picks until October 1957, almost three months after the original recording session.

As will be discussed in Chapter 4, these backing vocals were one of the less successful of Petty's aesthetic contributions. In contrast, the effectiveness of several of Holly's solo recordings was due in large part to the use of double-tracking to enhance the sounds of Holly's voice and guitar. John Goldrosen points out that, though the technique had been pioneered by Les Paul and Mary Ford almost a decade earlier, it "had been used sporadically since then, but Holly was probably the first rock 'n roll artist to use vocal and instrumental overdubbing" (Goldrosen and Beecher 1996: 65–6).

The first of five tracks created by this type of overdub was 'Words Of Love', recorded at Clovis in April 1957. On this song, Holly's voice and guitar were both double-tracked, with the vocal appearing as a close-harmony duet and the instrumental playing as a lead line dubbed over a rhythm guitar part. In his *America on Record*, Andre Millard writes that double-tracking involved "superimposing the second [vocal] on the first with a slight delay, giving the vocal more density and depth", noting that 'Words Of Love' "gives the impression of several voices in harmony" (Millard 1995: 293–4).

As with 'I'm Looking For Someone To Love', it took as much as six hours of studio time for Holly and Petty to perfect the sound of 'Words Of Love'. The technique of double-tracking was repeated on the recordings of 'Listen To Me', 'I'm Gonna Love You Too', 'Love's Made A Fool Of You' and 'Wishing'.

During all these recording sessions, the respective roles of the participants were clear. Holly and his colleagues were there to perform: all production decisions and many on arrangements were made by Petty. In September 1958, however, Holly made his debut as a producer at the Clovis studio. He organized and oversaw a session by Waylon Jennings. One of the songs was 'Jole Blon', a standard of Cajun music, a genre that originated in the French-speaking communities of Louisiana. This choice of song did not necessarily indicate an involvement with Cajun on Holly's part, however. 'Jole Blon' was also part of the standard repertoire of western swing bands, such as the Texas Wanderers, with whom Moon Mullican had played: Mullican had toured with Buddy as part of Tommy Allsup's band earlier in 1958.

At the same session, Holly introduced the first African-American musician to set foot in the Clovis studio. The saxophonist King Curtis, who earlier in the year had played the solo on the Coasters' hit 'Yakety Yak', was flown in from New York to contribute to the Jennings tracks and two recordings by Buddy Holly: 'Come Back Baby' (credited to Petty and Fred Neil, the folk revival singer whose best known song was 'Everybody's Talkin'', the title theme of the 1969 film *Midnight Cowboy*) and Curtis's composition 'Reminiscing'.[7]

In addition to producing the Clovis tracks, Norman Petty played a crucial role in Holly's successful career as a recording artist. Given the relative isolation of West Texas from the main centres of the popular music business in the mid-1950s, Petty was an important industry intermediary. Through his own recordings for the Columbia label and its influential A&R director Mitch Miller, he had become plugged into industry networks. Now he was "the conduit for a large number of West Texas performers to the record companies and bookers located in the North and Northeast" (Carr and Munde 1995: 220).

Research in the files and tape library of the Petty studios by John Ingman and others has shown that, in the late 1950s, Petty's work with Holly and the Crickets was only a small proportion of the recordings made at Clovis and subsequently issued to the public. While some of these were distributed only within New Mexico and West Texas – for instance on Petty's own Petsey label[8] – many Clovis masters were placed by Petty with such record companies as Imperial on the West Coast, Dot in Tennessee, Starday in Texas, and Epic and Kapp in New York. Additionally, the Norman Petty Trio continued to perform and record, creating two minor hits in 1957: 'Almost Paradise' and 'The First Kiss'.

The means by which he acted as such a conduit was by offering master recordings produced at his studio to New York-based record companies with national distribution and the publishing rights to the songs on those tracks to New York music publishers. In order to do so, however, Petty required musicians to publish their songs with his Nor Va Jak company and to cede to him ownership of the copyright in their recordings. In his memoir, Jimmy Bowen is complimentary about Petty's "extraordinary patience as engineer and producer", but adds that the Rhythm Orchids walked out of the studio "with our master tapes – probably the last group ever to leave Clovis with their masters. After us Norman got smart: he signed people to publishing and recording contracts. When Buddy Holly and the Crickets later recorded there, Petty

Publicity shot of Buddy

Redferns/Charlie Gillett Collection. Reproduced by permission of Getty Images.

owned the records and their publishing rights" (Bowen with Jerome 1997: 41).

In many cases, too, Petty claimed part authorship of the original songs recorded at the Clovis studio. Carl Bunch, the Crickets' drummer on the final tour, had recorded at Petty's studio with Odessa group the Poor Boys. His somewhat exaggerated view was that: "Norman was a businessman. He put his name on every song that came out of his studio and that was just a given – part of the price you paid to get his influence in obtaining a recording deal" (Stewart interviews).

Nor Va Jak Music was linked to Southern Music of New York, which organized the publication of sheet music and licensed the songs for foreign recordings on behalf of Petty. Southern had been founded in the 1920s by Ralph Peer, the talent scout and record producer who had "discovered" Jimmie Rodgers, the Carter Family and many other rural artists. Southern had become one of the most powerful music publishers in New York and its general manager Murray Deutch was Norman Petty's first point of contact in seeking to place Clovis recordings with labels.

Soon after they had been recorded, Petty sent the masters of 'That'll Be The Day' and 'I'm Looking For Someone To Love' to Deutch, who took them to a number of record company executives.[9] Among those who refused to issue the tracks was Jerry Wexler of Atlantic. The tracks were eventually accepted by Bob Thiele, head of the Coral label, who agreed to "buy" them from Petty. Strictly speaking, Thiele licensed them from Petty for the life of copyright, agreeing to pay a 5% royalty on 90% of the price for each copy sold. In his somewhat self-serving autobiography, Thiele claimed to have overcome strong opposition from his bosses at the Decca corporation (of which Coral was a part). Thiele stated that he clinched the argument by suggesting that the single be issued on Brunswick, a Decca-owned label known mainly for its roster of African-American pop and R&B acts (Thiele with Golden 1995: 52).

The acquisition of the two tracks by a Decca-owned label brought complications for Buddy Holly. His contract with Decca's Nashville subsidiary had included a standard clause by which the artist agreed not to re-record any songs cut under the Decca contract for at least five years. These songs included 'That'll Be The Day'. When Holly explained this difficulty to Petty, it was agreed that Buddy's name could not be on the Brunswick version of the song and that a group name should be chosen. Hence, Holly, Allison, Sullivan and Mauldin became the Crickets.[10] Subsequently, Petty, Holly and Bob Thiele agreed that some of the Clovis recordings should be issued as by Buddy Holly the solo singer (Thiele with Golden 1995: 53).

Recording in New York, 1958

'That'll Be The Day' by the Crickets was released by Brunswick in May 1957. It entered the American charts in August and stayed there for five months, peaking at number 3.[11] The next Crickets single to be issued was 'Oh Boy!' backed with 'Not Fade Away', in October 1957. It was a Top 10 hit at the end of the year.

The success of 'That'll Be The Day' and the obvious fact that Buddy Holly was the star of the group had led Bob Thiele to agree to issue a separate contract for Buddy as a solo singer, with the records issued on the Coral label. The first single was 'Words Of Love' coupled with 'Mailman Bring Me No More Blues' (a song co-written by Thiele himself under a pseudonym).[12] The first solo hit, however, was 'Peggy Sue' / 'Everyday' which entered the charts alongside 'Oh Boy!', eventually reaching number 3.

The gathering momentum of these record releases meant that, as 1957 progressed, commercial considerations played an ever-greater role in the scheduling of recording sessions and the choice of songs. In particular, the decision of Bob Thiele to issue an album by the Crickets (*The Chirping Crickets*) in late 1957 and the eponymous album by Buddy Holly early the next year necessitated the swift creation of several new tracks for each release. As Buddy Holly and Jerry Allison did not have enough unrecorded compositions, Petty drew on material by other writers, often including himself. Thus, three of the four Crickets tracks recorded at the Oklahoma officers' club at the end of September were by non-Crickets writers, and two were co-authored by Petty.

The need to get tracks made quickly also led to Holly's first New York City recordings. 'Rave On' (composed by 'Oh Boy!' writers West and Tilghman with Petty) was cut at Bell Sound Studios in January 1958 so it could appear on the *Buddy Holly* album two months later. According to Thiele, Bell Sound "featured a revolutionary 'dead sound' – sound that wasn't travelling all over the room – which allowed producers to isolate the individual musicians and achieve a literally unheard of depth of sonic separation, vibrancy and excitement" (Thiele with Golden 1995: 55). The musicians were a mixture of Clovis people – Allison, Mauldin and Petty on piano – and NYC session players led by lead guitarist Al Caiola. Crucially, however, Petty was not invited to produce these tracks. He had to cede control to a Coral staff producer, Milton De Lugg, who, like his Nashville contemporaries, worked to corporate standards.

The next New York City recordings were made in June 1958 under circumstances that had more to do with Big Apple music industry politics than aesthetic decisions made by Holly or Petty. Buddy and Norman were already in New York when Coral's new A&R head Dick Jacobs approached them to record two songs by Bobby Darin: 'Early In The Morning' and 'Now We're One'. A few months earlier, Darin's contract with the Atlantic company had been close to its conclusion. Jacobs organized a clandestine session for Darin to record these songs to be issued by Coral as soon as his obligations to Atlantic were over. However, in the meantime, Atlantic issued a novelty record by Darin, 'Splish Splash'. It became a surprise number 1 hit and the company promptly gave Darin a new contract.

Unable to issue Darin's own version of the songs, Jacobs persuaded Petty and Holly that Buddy should "re-record" them using the same arrangements and backing musicians. The six-piece band and four female backing singers included some of the leading New York session players, the New Orleans-born drummer Panama Francis and saxophonist Sam "The Man" Taylor, bandleader for Alan Freed tours. The two tracks were recorded in two hours.

Although he was an established recording artist with his own hits, the machinations of rival record companies meant that Buddy had, in effect, been persuaded to make a cover version. His single of 'Early In The Morning' was issued in July 1958 as was a version by Darin himself, rush-released by Atlantic under the name of the Rinky Dinks. While Holly's version reached number 32 in the charts, the highest place of the Rinky Dinks' record was number 24.

In what was to be his final studio session, Holly recorded four more tracks in three hours in October 1958 with Dick Jacobs and a large orchestra including a 12-piece string section (eight violins, two violas and two cellos). 'Early In The Morning' had retained some links with vernacular music through its gospel feel, but these tracks found Holly almost wholly detached from his habitual rock 'n roll scene. All were pop ballads, two composed by the absent Norman Petty – 'Moondreams' and 'True Love Ways', for which Holly provided the melody, based on his favourite gospel song 'I'll Be All Right'. 'Raining In My Heart' was composed by Nashville writers Felice and Boudleaux Bryant, writers of many hits for the Everly Brothers, while the fourth track had only been offered to Holly earlier that day by Paul Anka, with whom he had toured earlier that year. This was 'It Doesn't Matter Anymore'.

That session indicated one route that Buddy Holly's career might have taken in 1959 if the fatal plane crash had not occurred. A different direction was signposted by the final demo recordings of his own compositions. These six tracks were made by Holly at his New York apartment where he lived with the Puerto Rican-born Maria Elena Holly (née Santiago), whom he had married in Lubbock in August 1958.

The best known of the six songs is 'Peggy Sue Got Married', a witty "follow-up" to Holly's first solo hit. The other songs were the pensive 'Learning The Game', the plaintive 'What To Do' and 'Crying Waiting Hoping', 'That's What They Say' and 'That Makes It Tough'. The songs represented continuity with his rockabilly and rock 'n roll songs but showed a new dimension to his songwriting. They were presented simply with voice and acoustic guitar, and overdubbed after Holly's death by a small group and backing singers assembled by Coral producer Jack Hansen.

3 On Stage, 1956–1959

Performance venues and systems in popular music can be categorized as single shows or "one-night stands", residencies, circuits and tours.

The least prestigious is the single show, unlinked to others, typical for the kind of neophyte performers Holly and his associates had been for the two or three years before 1956. These one-night stands would have included one-off events organized by high-school students, teenage birthday parties, publicity events for stores or showrooms and opportunistic shows at cafes or drive-ins.

In the mid-1950s, Buddy Holly had several residencies – regular weekly shows at the same venue on the same day each week. At first these were live radio shows, including the Buddy & Jack and Buddy & Bob Sunday afternoon slots on KDAV. In 1956, there was the weekly residency for Buddy Holly and drummer Jerry Allison to play a Saturday dance at the American Legion Youth Center.

Circuits of venues are generally associated with specific genres of music and consist of similar-size venues in a circumscribed geographical area. For example, the "chitlin' circuit" of the United States was a series of venues in cities with large African-American populations. Describing the role of Buffalo, a division of Don Robey's Duke/Peacock records empire, Nelson George wrote: "From St Louis over to Atlanta down the coast to Miami and New Orleans, back over to Atlanta, and down the coast to Miami and New Orleans again, and then back over to Houston, Buffalo Booking dominated the Southern wing of the chitlin' circuit. Consistent sellers like [Bobby] Bland and B B King easily did over 300 dates a year" (George 1988: 34). In West Texas, Ellis Amburn writes of Buddy & Bob with Larry Welborn playing the "West Texas honky tonk circuit" where "one night in San Angelo they were heckled by oilfield roustabouts in the audience" (Amburn 1995: 32). San Angelo was a town over 100 miles south-east of Lubbock. Honky tonks were roadhouse clubs that featured the proto-rockabilly honky tonk country music sound associated with such artists as Floyd Tillman and Webb Pierce.

Table 1: Buddy Holly tours and residencies 1956–1959

	Start date	Title	Type	Length of tour	Holly/Crickets place on bill	Headlining act
1	Jan '56	Hank Thompson	C&W regional	unknown	Last of 8	Hank Thompson
2	April '56	Sonny James	C&W regional	Unknown	Last of 5	Sonny James
3	July '56	Hank Thompson	C&W regional	15 days	Last of 8	Hank Thompson
4	July '57	R&B tour	E. Coast chitlin' circuit	28 days	Last of 7	Clyde McPhatter
5	August '57	Holiday of Stars	R&R package New York residency	14 days	4th of 12	Little Richard
6	September '57	Biggest Show of Stars 1957	R&R national package	85 days	Unknown of 15	Chuck Berry
7	December '57	Holiday of Stars Xmas Show	R&R package New York residency	14 days	4th of 12	Fats Domino
8	January '58	Everly Brothers tour	R&R package East Coast	17 days	4th of 14	Everly Brothers
9	February '58	Lee Gordon's World Hit Parade	R&R package Australia	6 days	3rd of 5	Paul Anka
10	February '58	Big Gold Records Stars	R&R package Florida	6 days	3rd of 4	Everly Brothers
11	March '58	Buddy Holly and the Crickets	Variety tour England	25 days	Top of 4	Buddy Holly and the Crickets
12	April '58	Big Beat Show	R&R national package	40+ days	Unknown of 13	Chuck Berry
13	July '58	Summer Dance Party	Mid West	10 days	Top of 2	Buddy Holly and the Crickets
14	October '58	Biggest Show of Stars 58	North East states and Canada	18 days	Unknown of 13	Frankie Avalon
15	January '59	Winter Dance Party	R&R package Mid West	25 days	Top of 6	Buddy Holly and the Crickets

Joe Mauldin, Buddy Holly and Jerry Allison on stage
Redferns/John Rodgers. Reproduced by permission of Getty Images.

Finally, the pinnacle of live performance in all forms of popular music was the tour – a single sequence of daily shows covering one region or all of part of the country. While Buddy Holly had given dozens of performances with his various groups between 1953 (when he was 16) and 1955, all these had been discrete gigs or weekly residencies at specific venues within West Texas, mostly in Lubbock itself. In 1956 he moved into a new phase of his career, where his successive recording contracts with Decca in Nashville and Coral/Brunswick in New York were paralleled by an ascent into the world of tours, first in the Southern states during 1956, then nationally and internationally in 1957 and 1958. Record releases, touring and associated radio and television appearances combined to construct Holly as a leading figure in the fast-developing sphere of rock 'n roll.

Between January 1956 and his death just over three years later, Holly took part in 15 tours of North America, Australia and England, and two residencies at venues in New York (numbers 5 and 7). Table 1 shows them in chronological order. There are few indications of the size of the audiences to whom Buddy Holly played, but it has been reported that the *Big Beat Show* tour (number 12 in the table) played 68 shows in 37 cities to over 350,000 people (Lewis with Silver 1982: 148). Based on that number, it is probable that over one million people would have heard him perform on these tours.

The first three tours were aimed at regional audiences for country music. Despite the disappointments of the Decca sessions, Buddy Holly's "discoverer", Eddie Crandall, was able to get Buddy and his group a support slot on short tours led by country singer Sonny James and western swing and honky-tonk bandleader Hank Thompson.

In January and September 1956, Holly and group went on tours of the southeastern states headlined by Hank Thompson. He was already acquainted with Thompson's band, which frequently played in Lubbock. Both tours included several supporting acts in addition to Thompson, and Buddy's group had to accompany other singers. For the September tour the group was expanded from a trio (Holly, Guess and Curtis) to a quartet, including Jerry Allison on drums.

One of the singers on the January tour was George Jones, who much later would become one of the biggest stars in country music. While Buddy's group provided rock 'n roll backings for another member of the troupe, Glen Reeves, Jones at this time was resolutely opposed to the new music. According to one source, the backing musicians told him he'd like rockabilly if he could do it, and would occasionally trick him by changing their four-square country rhythms into a rockabilly beat while Jones was singing. One night, Jones took up the challenge and turned in a polished rockabilly performance (Goldrosen and Beecher 1996: 39).

In April 1956, Jones actually made a recording (as Thumper Jones) in a rockabilly style. Whether or not this incident was a catalyst for that shift, it encapsulates the continuing tension between the conservative tendencies of the country music mainstream and Holly's determination to follow Elvis Presley into rock 'n roll.

The Sonny James tour was a package show that also included Faron Young, Tommy Collins and Wanda Jackson, who would soon be recognized as the leading female rockabilly singer. The tour visited the south-eastern states of Louisiana and Florida. Holly's group, billed as Buddy Holly and the Two-Tones, was a trio with guitarist Curtis and double-bass player Don Guess.

As well as opening the show, the group was expected to provide backing for some of the other acts. The three-week tour took place in April and early May. It coincided with release of the first Decca single which coupled 'Blue Days, Black Nights' with 'Love Me', the only two songs played by Holly's group in their short opening set, although the touring had no discernible effect on sales.

In his autobiography, the English rock 'n roll and pop singer Tommy Steele described seeing Buddy Holly perform as part of what he called a "Grand Ole Opry Travelin' Show" in the port of Norfolk, Virginia. Steele was then a merchant seaman who sat through the show until:

> After about an hour a boy walked on to the stage. He was about my age, six feet tall and wore massive horn-rimmed spectacles. He played an electric Gibson guitar and, like everybody else that night, he played country. He sang three songs but in the middle of the third, he did something that to my ears was remarkable. He changed the rhythm and what had been a forlorn someone-done-me-wrong song suddenly went into a beat and style that shook my soul. For the first time in my life, I was listening to rock-and-roll and it was being played by a fella called Buddy Holly. (Steele 2006: 238–9)[1]

After the second Thompson tour of 1956, Buddy did not tour again until July 1957. In the intervening six months he divided his time between local shows in West Texas and the intensive recording sessions with Norman Petty. A snapshot of his professional situation in October 1956 was provided by an article in the *Lubbock Avalanche-Journal* on "Lubbock's 'Answer to Elvis Presley' ". It mentioned the first Decca single and included a final paragraph on Buddy's activities as a live performer. If not precisely accurate, this description sums up the stage reached by Holly and his two-piece "orchestra" shortly after his 20th birthday:

> A booking agent has kept Holly and his orchestra fairly busy with one-night stands, about 200 miles apart. While he has presented stage performances mostly, Holly takes a special interest in playing for the American Legion Youth Center, 2nd St and College Ave, which had an attendance last Saturday of

about 350 and is increasing attendance weekly. He has also
toured with Grand Ole Opry shows. (Fairbairns 1956)

In the final 18 months (550 days) of his life (August 1957 to the beginning of
February 1959), the focus of Holly's activity moved to live performance. The
trigger for this intensive activity was the success of the singles 'That'll Be The
Day' and 'Oh Boy!' by the Crickets and 'Peggy Sue' by Buddy Holly. The first
entered the US pop charts in August and the others in December 1957.

During that 18-month period, Buddy was on tour for over 250 days, sometimes playing two or even three shows a day. On every overseas gig in Australia and Britain he did early-evening and late-evening performances at each
venue, even squeezing in three shows at the Sydney Stadium and cinemas in
the English towns of Ipswich and Nottingham.

The fourth tour by Buddy and his musicians (Allison, Mauldin and Niki Sullivan on second guitar) coincided with the rise up the charts of 'That'll Be The
Day'. Consequently, the group was billed as "The Crickets". It involved week-
long residencies at three of the country's leading theatres catering to African-
American audiences, the Howard in Washington, DC, the Royal in Baltimore
and the famous Harlem Apollo in New York. All were described as "jewels of
the chitlin' circuit" by Nelson George (George 1988: 50). The remainder of the
artists on the bill were all African-American. Top of the bill was proto-soul
singer Clyde McPhatter, followed by R&B singer Edna McGriff, blues guitarist and singer Otis Rush and doo-wop groups the Cadillacs (famous for their
1955 hit 'Speedoo') and Lee Andrews and the Hearts.

Biographer Ellis Amburn says that this booking "was a managerial gaffe of
colossal proportions on the part of Norman Petty" who "delivered the Crickets into the hands of Irving Feld, the tour promoter" and claims that black
audiences "might be out for the scalps of any honkies [sic] who dared show
up on their stages" (Amburn 1995: 83). His account loses some of its persua-
sive power by introducing the testimony of the black actress Lesley Uggams
who, Amburn says, "throughout 1957 [had] been buying Buddy's records"
(1995: 89) when the only release to date during that year had been 'That'll Be
The Day' by the Crickets a few weeks earlier.

John Goldrosen concurs that the booking was an error and states that the
Crickets were added to the tour because its promoter had wrongly assumed
they were a black group, presumably because of the sound of their record
and/or because there had been a black vocal group called Dean Barlow and

the Crickets (Goldrosen and Beecher 1996: 70). However, this group of Crickets had split up in 1956 after lead singer Dean Barlow began a solo recording career (Groia 1983: 86), a fact that makes it very unlikely that Holly's group could be mistaken for them, especially by industry professionals such as tour promoters.

On the other hand, the historian of black American music Brian Ward cites the fact that 'That'll Be The Day' had sold well to black listeners and argues that this booking was deliberate (Ward 1998: 115). This view is supported by chart evidence. 'That'll Be The Day' (issued on Brunswick, a label associated with black music) entered the *Billboard* chart of Top 15 Best-selling R&B singles (which was based on estimated sales to African-American record buyers) at the end of August 1957, reaching a peak position of number 2 and staying in the chart for 11 weeks. African-American audiences would also have heard a cover version of 'That'll Be The Day' by veteran black vocal group the Ravens who had released it as the B-side of their single 'Dear One' on Argo, a label belonging to the Chicago-based Chess Records.

The Crickets were by no means the only white artists to appear on this R&B chart in the mid-1950s. Elvis Presley, Carl Perkins and Jerry Lee Lewis also figured there in 1956–7, as did West Texan rockabilly singer Buddy Knox with the Petty-produced hit 'Party Doll'. Like Holly, Perkins and Lewis were to tour with packages including both white and black acts playing to integrated audiences except in Southern cities where segregation was still enforced. The difference for the Crickets was that all the performers they were booked to perform alongside were African-American, as was the vast majority of the audience.

Buddy Knox and his group the Rhythm Orchids were also sometimes booked to play with black artists. Knox's fellow singer Jimmy Bowen recalled being booked to headline a gig with Little Richard in Detroit: "Before the curtain went up, I peeked out and saw that we were the only whites around and had to face an audience primed for serious R&B. The moment they saw a quartet of white kids and their rockabilly gear, the energy of the place sagged with a collective gasp of disbelief" (Bowen with Jerome 1997: 55).

Knox resolved the situation by persuading the promoter to change the running order, so that his group went on before Richard, when Knox told the audience his band's set would be brief. The Crickets managed sometimes to get a better response from R&B audiences, even if they had to mimic R&B artists to do so. According to Niki Sullivan, the group was "made to feel at home" in Washington but the Harlem Apollo audience was more difficult to please:

> The first time we went on it was a weekday matinee. They opened the curtains and Buddy stepped towards the mike and there was this large black woman in the front row who said "It'd better sound like the record!" You could have heard a pin drop. And after we got through I don't think five people clapped. The same thing on the evening show, and the next day – nothing. The third day, we did our first song and got no response again. So Buddy turned round and said, "Let's do Bo Diddley". And we went into 'Bo Diddley', cutting up and working our butts off. I was dancing around in a big circle, going through a bunch of gyrations, and Buddy was all over the stage, and Joe B was bouncing that bass back and forth and I've never seen Jerry work harder on those damn drums. And when we finished that song, the people just went bananas. From then on we were accepted at the Apollo. (Goldrosen and Beecher 1996: 70–71)

This was perhaps the *Mach Schau* moment for Buddy Holly. Those two words were shouted at the Beatles by a club-owner in Hamburg when their lack of stage movements had failed to galvanize the German audience in their first days at the Kaiserkeller in 1960. As a result, the Beatles worked up a stage act full of movement and humour that would colour their music throughout the next decade. In Holly's case, the "bunch of gyrations" was remarked on by many eyewitnesses of his stage act during the remainder of his brief career.

On August 30, the Crickets were back in New York to take part in an Alan Freed show at the Brooklyn Paramount Theatre, the *Holiday of Stars*. Freed was the disc jockey often credited with inventing, or at least promoting, the term rock 'n roll, and his show reflected the range of artists appealing to American teenagers under that generic label. For the remainder of their touring career, Holly's groups would be unequivocally recognized as at the leading edge of rock 'n roll music.

There were 14 acts on the bill, with the Crickets fourth from the top. Above them were the headlining Little Richard and his Band, the Del Vikings, a vocal group with both black and white members and a recent big hit, 'Come Go With Me', and the Moonglows, an African-American vocal group who were Freed protégés. Appearing before the Crickets were vocal groups (Cleftones,

Diamonds, Five Keys, Tune Weavers, Mickey & Sylvia) and solo singers (Larry Williams, Jo-Ann Campbell, Ocie Smith, Jimmy Rodgers), all backed by Freed's pit band, led by saxophonist Sam "The Man" Taylor.

The Crickets and Little Richard were the only artists to provide their own backing, and the Crickets were the only ones to rely on amplified guitars to fill the auditorium. They carried over their energetic stage show from the Apollo in order to capture audience interest. According to Philip Norman (who does not give his source), by now Buddy had emancipated himself from the influence of Presley, although whether the stage moves were "cheerfully self-mocking" may be doubted – this feels more like a British trait than a Texan one:

> Buddy sang in a sidelong posture at the principal . . . stand-mike, his left leg planted firmly forward as if he were about to take a stride on a roller-skate. In the wilder rock 'n roll numbers, he would start to "cut up" – not with the self-conscious slinkiness of those who borrowed their body-language from Elvis, but in a cheerfully self-mocking way, swinging his Stratocaster around on its strap, snarling, whooping and Rebel-yelling, crouching double to sing a chorus into the low-level mike beside Joe B. Mauldin's bass-fiddle, even slithering across the stage on his knees to the detriment of his new stone-grey slacks. If the stage were particularly wide, he always took care to visit each corner regularly for a few seconds' communion with the "bad" seats. (Norman 1996: 165)

The artists booked for the *Holiday of Stars* were required to play up to seven shows a day, beginning at 11 am and finishing at 2 am. After each show, the audience was cleared out to make way for the next crowd, each member of which had paid one dollar. Apart from Little Richard, no act got to play more than three songs before giving way to the next group or soloist.

After a week with Freed, Buddy Holly and the Crickets set off on an 85-date "integrated" tour with ten African-American acts and only three other white ones. Despite the preponderance of black artists, this tour, titled *The Biggest Show of Stars for 1957*, was targeted at the rock 'n roll audience that comprised white, black and Hispanic youth. Many of these artists were "stars" of the pop chart as well as the R&B one. Among them were the 14-year-old sensation Frankie Lymon and the Teenagers (with their current hit 'Goody Goody'),

Chuck Berry, the Drifters, LaVern Baker and Clyde McPhatter, the only artist apart from the Crickets to have played the previous chitlin' circuit tour. The other white acts were Jimmy Bowen, the Everly Brothers and the precocious Canadian songwriter and singer Paul Anka with his quintessential teen pop anthem 'Diana'. When the show reached the West Coast in October, several acts left the tour and others joined. Among these was Eddie Cochran, who quickly became friends with Holly.

Earlier, the white acts had been withdrawn from five concerts in Georgia, Tennessee, Alabama and Louisiana because segregationist laws in those states prevented African-American and white performers sharing the same stage. In an interview with Chip Deffaa, the African-American singer LaVern Baker gave a graphic description of playing to segregated audiences on this tour:

> Some of them had the blacks upstairs, whites downstairs; some of them had a rope in the middle – white on one side, black on the other side. Some places we had to do two shows: white first show, black second show . . . and so many of our white fans wanted to come to us and they couldn't. And with the Everly Brothers, I saw a [black] girl actually cry one night because the police wouldn't let her across the ropes: she just wanted an autograph. (Deffaa 1996: 197)

The Biggest Show of Stars for 1957 was one of the pioneering "package tours", on which promoters packed in as many acts with current hit or potential hit records as could be practically managed. Several of the least prestigious artists would be given time for only one or two songs, while the biggest stars of this "biggest show" would be rationed to four at most, as the Crickets were. Included in their set was 'Peggy Sue', the new single by Buddy Holly that entered both the pop chart and the R&B chart as the tour drew to a close in November 1957 and stayed there for three months. According to sources quoted by Ellis Amburn, the set also included three cover versions: Fats Domino's 'Blueberry Hill' and two Chuck Berry songs, 'Roll Over Beethoven' and 'Brown Eyed Handsome Man' (Amburn 1995: 97).[2]

From the perspective of the 21st century when most pop and rock tours feature only one or two acts, the package tour can seem a bizarre concept. But it had a logic derived both from the history of American entertainment and the structure of US broadcast and film media in the 1950s. At the end of the 19th century, the dominant showbusiness institution was vaudeville. A typical vaudeville bill, presented in a theatre, included up to a dozen "turns" ranging from musical performers to magicians, jugglers, dancers and comedians. Each act would last for a maximum of 10 or 15 minutes. The first continuous vaudeville show opened at the Boston Bijou in 1885, running from 10 am to midnight with standing tickets priced at 10 cents and seats at 15 cents (Sanjek 1988: 17). This format was carried over into the touring tent shows or "tent repertory" shows. Singers as far apart as Bessie Smith and Jimmie Rodgers began their careers in such shows, which toured the South in the period between the two world wars. Country music historian Bill Malone commented:

> The tent-rep show brought to rural America a touch of vaudeville, including everything from magicians, acrobats and trained bears to Irish tenors, Swiss yodelers and dancing-girls. These organizations, transported by horse-drawn waggons in the early days, would move into a rural community, stake out their tents, hold nightly shows that might run as long as a week, and then move on to another excited community . . . my father remembered a tent show which, just before World War I, lingered for a week in his rural home community of Galena, an East Texas village near Tyler so small that it could not be located on the map. (Malone 2002a: 6)

The rock 'n roll package shows, then, inherited the format made familiar to American audiences by vaudeville and the tent show. The package shows also acted as a complement to the main media distributor of popular music: local radio. Just as the new disc jockey shows aimed at teenage audiences provided a swiftly moving sequence of records by different performers, the package shows offered a similar sequence but with the added value of the presence and visual display of the performers. The wave of rock 'n roll films, beginning in 1956 with *Rock Around The Clock*, also adapted the vaudeville format in their presentation of musical performances, although these had to be, often very tenuously, linked to a narrative or plot.

By, 1957, however, the development of networked television posed a challenge to the "unique selling point" of the package shows. On August 5 of that year, the ABC network decided to broadcast *American Bandstand* to 67 affili-

Poster for the Australian tour. Note the separate billing for The Crickets and Buddy Holly.

Redferns/GAB Archive. Reproduced by permission of Getty Images.

ate stations across the country. This teen pop show, hosted by Dick Clark, had previously been available only in the Philadelphia area on WFIL-TV since 1952. Its main components were the lip-synching by singers and groups of their current record releases accompanied by dancing by teenagers recruited from local high schools. The show was broadcast from 3.00 pm to 4.30 and on August 26 the Crickets performed 'That'll Be The Day' on the show – the record had entered the Top 100 two weeks earlier. The group made their second appearance on *American Bandstand* in October 1958, with three Crickets' tracks, 'Think It Over', 'Fool's Paradise' and 'Heartbeat'.

The world of concert and tour promotion and booking was essentially conservative, and the initiative to organize racially mixed rock 'n roll package tours was seized by relative newcomers to this region of showbusiness. One was Alan Freed, but the instigator of *The Biggest Show of Stars for 1957* was one of Freed's main rivals, Irvin Feld, of whose career one historian has written that it "illuminates how one could rise with the crest of the tide, bringing rhythm 'n' blues to fruition and then catching the new wave carrying rocknroll" (Ennis 1992: 180).[3]

The Feld tour finished in late November. Buddy Holly and the Crickets, now a trio because Niki Sullivan had left the group after the tour, returned to New York for a two-week season starting on December 24, promoted by Alan Freed at the 3,600-seat Paramount Theater in New York's Times Square (number 5 in Table 1). Titled the *Holiday of Stars Twelve Days of Christmas Show*, this was another package show, but with a majority of white acts, including Jerry Lee Lewis, Eddie Cochran and Danny and the Juniors, plus the Everly Brothers and Anka – although top of the bill was Fats Domino. There were up to six shows a day, interspersed with a B movie which served to move each show's audience out to make way for the next crowd. Buddy Holly and the Crickets were fourth on the bill, after Domino, Lewis and the Everly Brothers. They had a 20-minute spot to play about six songs including their three recent and current hits, unlike another Lubbock act, Terry Noland, who opened the show with one song, 'Patty Baby' (Amburn 1995: 119).

Almost immediately after the Paramount shows, several of the acts including the Crickets went straight on to a 17-date tour of the eastern seaboard headlined by the Everly Brothers, again promoted by Irvin Feld. This time, all but one (the Rays whose current hit was 'Silhouettes' / 'Daddy Cool') of the ten acts were white. They included Paul Anka, Danny and the Juniors and the Royal Teens, fresh from their debut hit 'Short Shorts'.

In late January and early February, Holly and the Crickets undertook their first overseas tour, to Australia (tour number 9 in Table 1). This was the third tour of that country by American rock 'n roll acts, following visits in 1957 by Bill Haley and Little Richard. The six-date, eleven-show tour was promoted by Lee Gordon, a leading impresario, as *Lee Gordon's World Hit Parade*. The other acts joining the tour were Paul Anka (top of the bill), Jerry Lee Lewis and Jodie Sands and local rock 'n roll star Johnny O'Keefe.

Two weeks after their return, the trio took part in a short *Big Gold Record Stars Tour* of Florida. On the six-city tour, they were featured alongside Jerry Lee Lewis, the Everly Brothers and Bill Haley and the Comets. The Everlys were provided with local backing bands, but at one show the Crickets provided the accompaniment instead of an inexperienced trio of high-school students. A newspaper reviewer provided a glimpse of Buddy's stage act presenting "a touch of humor . . . as he struts around the stage bobbing his head back and forth to the rhythm of the music" (Amburn 1995: 141).

In March, the trio of Holly, Allison and Mauldin made a 25-day tour of England, playing two shows on each night and three in two cities. Unlike Australian fans, British youth had been given the opportunity to see a series of American rock 'n roll performers in the year prior to this visit. Bill Haley and the Comets had been the first to tour, followed by Frankie Lymon and the Teenagers, Freddie Bell and the Bellboys, Charlie Gracie and Paul Anka. Buddy Holly and the Crickets, however, were the first guitar-led band to tour, and the quality and volume of Holly's playing made a great impression on English audiences. Keith Goodwin's review in the *New Musical Express* of the opening show at the Trocadero, Elephant and Castle in South London was typical:

> Without doubt, the Crickets are the loudest, noisiest trio
> I've ever heard in my life. They completely overpowered the
> 13-piece Ronnie Keene Orchestra in relation to the volume
> of sound produced. Everyone loved the group's spirited lusty
> rock 'n roll style and they went for Buddy's easy-going natu-
> ral stage personality in an equally big way. (quoted in Frame
> 2007: 323)

The tour was booked by the New York agent Manny Greenfield and one of London's leading showbusiness agencies, run by Lew and Leslie Grade. The show was in the tradition of vaudeville or variety, with the Crickets as the only rock act. The others were ballad singer Gary Miller, pop harmony singers the Tanner Sisters, the Ronnie Keene dance orchestra with singer Lynne Adams and a juggling act. The compere was a young comedian, Des O'Connor.[4] Speaking to a journalist, Buddy expressed his surprise: "Back home we tour with other rock 'n roll acts but here we're with jugglers, ballad singers, a jazz band and a comedian; a real cross-section of show biz" (Ingman 2008: 15).[5]

Holly's stage act was described by Jim Newcombe who attended a show at the Philharmonic Hall in Liverpool:

> During guitar breaks Buddy whooped and hollered encour-
> agement to the others and the sound was incredibly strong.
> Buddy danced first to Joe then to Jerry in a mixture of Chuck
> Berry's duck walk and Ronnie Hawkins's camel walk. He
> obviously had huge fun out of performing and frequently
> dropped on one knee playing his guitar held up high while
> Joe rode his bass in best Comets style. (Ingman 2008: 16)

As a bill-topping group for the first time in their career, the Crickets played up to ten songs in a 25-minute set. The "souvenir programme" for the tour gave the set list as:

That'll Be The Day	Oh Boy
Peggy Sue	Words of Love
Mailman Bring me no More Blues	
Every Day	I'm Looking for Someone to Love
Rock Around With Ollie Vee	
Almost Paradise [*sic*]	Not Fade Away

God Save the Queen

The last-named number – the British national anthem, which theatres and cinemas were required to perform at the end of every show – was performed not by the Crickets but by the Ronnie Keene Orchestra, which accompanied the other artists on the tour.

Despite the programme list, eyewitness accounts assembled by John Ingman show that what the band actually played was a mixture of their own hits and those of other rock 'n roll singers: "About nine numbers were fea-

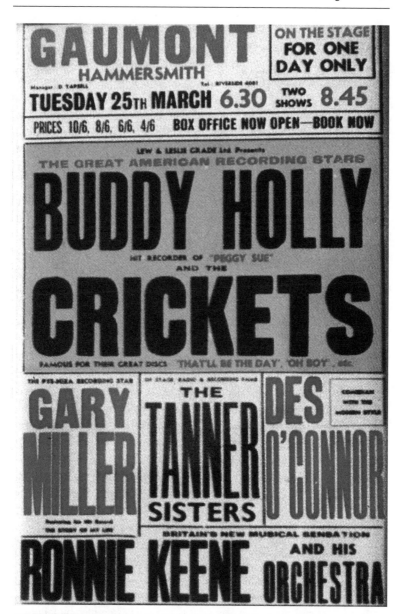

Poster for the UK tour

Redferns/GAB Archive. Reproduced by permission of Getty Images.

tured with the hits of 'Oh Boy!', 'Maybe Baby', 'Peggy Sue' and 'That'll Be The Day' ever present. Originally they opened with 'That'll Be The Day' but soon moved that to the finale with a fast version of 'Everyday' usually opening the routine" (Ingman 2008: 14).[6]

Little Richard's 'Ready Teddy', Gene Vincent's 'Be-Bop-A-Lula' and Jerry Lee Lewis's 'Great Balls Of Fire' were included in most shows, while other songs by Richard ('Lucille', 'Long Tall Sally', 'Rip It Up', 'She's Got It', 'Tutti Frutti'), Lewis ('Whole Lotta Shakin' Goin' On'), Elvis Presley ('Jailhouse Rock', 'Good Rockin' Tonight') and the Drifters via Presley ('Money Honey') were performed at least once on the English tour.

While in Britain, the group appeared in two television shows including the leading light entertainment programme *Sunday Night at the London Palladium*, where they played their three big hits. While some future British rock musicians saw the band live, many others were transfixed by this broadcast – for example, Hank Marvin of the Shadows: "[I] couldn't work out how they got the sound until I saw them on the Palladium" (Ingman 2008: 17).[7]

Three days after they flew back from London, Buddy Holly and the Crickets joined their second and last full-scale national package tour, Alan Freed's *Big Beat Show* (number 12 in Table 1). There were 13 acts plus an orchestra led by saxophonist Sam "The Man" Taylor. Like earlier tours organized by Freed and his rival Irvin Feld, the bill mixed African-American and white acts, established stars and those at the very start of their career. Leading the six black acts were Chuck Berry, Frankie Lymon and Larry Williams. Jerry Lee Lewis vied with Berry to top the bill, with Buddy Holly and the Crickets, Danny and the Juniors (currently enjoying their first hit 'At The Hop') and Jo-Ann Campbell among the other white rock and pop artists.

In contrast to their lengthy sets on the English tour, Holly, Allison and Mauldin were limited to only three or four songs in the 40 cities where the tour was scheduled to play during April and May. The *Big Beat Show* tour encompassed 19 Eastern and Midwestern states and several cities in Eastern Canada, but it came to an abrupt end when it reached the 7,000-seat Boston hockey arena on May 3.

Boston had a reputation for racism but this was an integrated audience for an integrated tour. Trouble began when an audience member ran on stage during the performance by the Diamonds and many others started dancing in the aisles. After order was restored by Alan Freed and the police, dancing broke out during Jerry Lee Lewis's set. It was stopped by police. Chuck Berry's act was also interrupted. Sources differ as whether this was the result of fans again getting up to dance or of missiles thrown by white gang members. The house lights were switched on and the police announced that the show would not resume until everyone had returned to their seats. According to his biographer, when Freed commented not unreasonably from the stage that "it looks like the Boston police don't want you to have a good time", the audience "erupted" (Jackson 1991: 192–5). After police closed the show and ejected the audience, running battles broke out on the street. The remainder of the tour was cancelled. Freed was soon indicted for incitement to riot and lost his job at the New York station WINS.

After a break of two months, Holly made a short Midwest tour with his own band and a western swing group led by guitarist Tommy Allsup and featuring Earl Sinks as lead vocalist. Sinks would join Jerry Allison's Crickets group in 1959. Once again it was organized by Irvin Feld's General Artists Corporation. This *Summer Dance Party* of 11 concerts during July visited small towns in Indiana, Illinois, Michigan, Iowa, Minnesota and Wisconsin where local bands would open the show. It was the first time that Joe Mauldin played a Fender electric bass guitar instead of his acoustic double bass and he reverted to the acoustic instrument soon afterwards.

The reason Holly accepted this regressive move in his career was financial. By mid-1958, his relationship with Norman Petty was at breaking point. Holly was receiving very little money from Petty and he took the unprecedented step of retaining the cash payments made by venue owners on this tour. Previously he had sent performance fees to Clovis for Petty to bank.

In contrast to the brief sets played by the band in the auditoria of the package tours, these shows were actual dances at holiday resorts. The musicians were expected to perform between eight o'clock and midnight, with Holly and the Crickets often playing two 45-minute sets, as they had in the days before they became international recording stars.

In October, Irvin Feld once again booked Holly and the Crickets for his *The Biggest Show of Stars for 1958 – Autumn Edition*. This wound its way though Canada, the Great Lakes and the eastern seaboard, playing every night between the 4th and the 19th of the month. On this tour, the four-piece group (Holly, Allison, Mauldin and guitarist Tommy Allsup) was augmented by backing singers, the Roses.

It was another racially integrated tour, with the 14 acts split equally between white rock 'n roll and pop singers or groups and black R&B groups and soloists. For the first time, Buddy Holly was part of a package tour headed not by the "old guard" of rock 'n roll pioneers but by newer white teen pop singers, namely Frankie Avalon, Jimmy Clanton and Bobby Darin. Like the Crickets a year earlier, these singers had recently had their first chart hit, which was enough to win them a place on the package tour. Avalon was a product of the Philadelphia pop scene of which *American Bandstand* was an integral part, and had achieved two Top 10 hits ('Dede Dinah' and 'Ginger Bread') earlier in the year. Clanton, from New Orleans, and his Top 10 hit 'Just A Dream' on the local Ace label had booked his passage on the *Biggest Show*. As recounted in Chapter 2, Bobby Darin's first hit 'Splish Splash', in June, had led to Holly's recordings of two of Darin's songs.

Almost all the other acts involved were neophytes (the black vocal group the Olympics had their debut hit in July with 'Western Movies', for example, and Dion and the Belmonts in May with 'I Wonder Why'). The only artist with whom Buddy had previously toured was the R&B star Clyde McPhatter. According to David Bigham of the Roses, "all of our venues were packed with screaming fans. The lineup of the tour was so broad that there was music for all to enjoy. The best venue was Montreal, as it was the largest facility and was packed to the rafters" (Stewart interviews).

The final tour

That tour ended in mid-October in Richmond, Virginia. For the next three months, Buddy was in a state of enforced idleness in New York, with no money coming in.

According to Maria Elena Holly, the Puerto Rican secretary from Southern Music whom Holly had married in Lubbock on August 15, he used this time to acquaint himself with New York's vibrant music scene, particularly the jazz clubs and folk venues of Greenwich Village. Buddy also took flamenco guitar lessons and showed an interest in training at the Actors' Studio, home of the fashionable method acting style (Amburn 1995: 202–7; Norman 1996: 263).[8]

During this time he tried to make a definitive break with Norman Petty and hired the Everly Brothers' lawyer Harold Orenstein to assist him in disentangling his contractual relationships with the manager, producer and songwriter.[9] The deadlock between Holly and Petty continued into 1959 and it was only for financial reasons that he agreed to headline yet another Feld/ GAC package tour. The *Winter Dance Party* was scheduled play some 25 dates through the Midwest, beginning at George Devine's Million Dollar Ballroom in Milwaukee on January 23. It was to be a scaled-down package, with just five acts, four white and one Hispanic. According to Goldrosen, this was the result of "a national economic recession and to changes in rock 'n roll music itself, the big package shows had declined in size and strength over the previous year and were becoming more [racially] segregated" (Goldrosen and Beecher 1996: 139).

True to the Feld and Freed model, two of the acts had broken into the charts only recently. These were the Texas disc jockey and songwriter J. P. Richardson a.k.a. the Big Bopper and the Los Angeles Chicano teenager Ritchie Valens. The Big Bopper's novelty number 'Chantilly Lace' had been a Top 10 hit in the autumn of 1958 while Valens's plaintive ballad 'Donna' was a current hit as the tour began. The other acts on the bill included Dion and the Belmonts (with whom Holly had toured extensively in 1958) and a newcomer, Frankie Sardo.

Buddy Holly had tried to persuade Jerry Allison and Joe Mauldin to side with him in the schism with Norman Petty, but his former backing musicians eventually decided to remain with Petty. Therefore, Buddy needed a new group for this tour. He brought to New York Tommy Allsup, drummer Carl Bunch, formerly of West Texas band the Poor Boys (whom Holly had seen recording in Clovis) and Waylon Jennings, a Lubbock friend who worked mainly as a radio disc jockey. Jennings was to play bass guitar, an instrument with which he was unfamiliar. Buddy taught him the bass lines of the hits at the New York apartment.

The tour began inauspiciously. Carl Bunch recalled that: "We were over an hour late due to problems with the bus and the weather. I remember very clearly Buddy asking just as we pulled up, 'What time is this eight o'clock gig going to get started?' We had to set up on stage in front of an angry crowd and we ended up starting about two hours after we were supposed to" (Stewart interviews).

There were continuing problems with bus breakdowns, eventually leading Buddy to decide to charter the light plane whose crash caused his death. On the bus, the native New Yorker Dion nicknamed them 'Bloody Holly and the Rickets' while the Texans retaliated with 'Moron and the Bellhops'. Bunch explained these good-natured insults by saying "you couldn't be culturally more divergent than Dion and me" (Stewart interviews).

As the only instrumental group on the tour, the three Crickets provided backing for other singers. The show was opened by Frankie Sardo, followed by Dion with his hits 'Runaround Sue' and 'Teenager In Love', the Big Bopper ('Chantilly Lace') and Ritchie Valens (whose 'La Bamba', the B-side of 'Donna', was now climbing the chart). And "when Buddy came out, it was almost like God had walked out on stage" (Bunch; Stewart interviews).

Holly's set of about eight songs began with the Billy Grammer pop-country hit 'Gotta Travel On' before turning to the solo hits and Crickets hits. As on the British tour, these were interspersed with songs first recorded by other artists. Each night, the set included a selection from 'That'll Be The Day', 'Everyday', 'Maybe Baby', 'It Doesn't Matter Anymore', 'True Love Ways', 'Heartbeat', 'Peggy Sue', 'Oh Boy!', 'It's So Easy' and cover versions of 'Brown Eyed Handsome Man', 'Whole Lotta Shakin' Goin' On' and 'Be-Bop-A-Lula'. The encores were generally 'Not Fade Away', 'Rave On' and 'Bo Diddley' (Norman 1996: 320). Even if some performances included the new ballad recordings, the choice of cover songs by Chuck Berry, Jerry Lee Lewis, Gene Vincent and Bo Diddley shows Holly's continuing commitment to classic rock 'n roll.

A set list for the gig at Fournier's Ballroom, Eau Claire Wisconsin shows that he played 'Gotta Travel On', 'Peggy Sue', 'That'll Be The Day', 'Heartbeat', 'Be-Bop-A-Lula', 'Whole Lotta Shakin' Goin' On' and 'It Doesn't Matter Anymore'. At his final show, at the Surf Ballroom, Clear Lake, Iowa, the first half consisted of brief sets by Frankie Sardo, the Big Bopper and Ritchie Valens. After the interval, Dion and the Belmonts sang several hits before Buddy appeared. This time, he also played 'Everyday' and 'Rave On', followed by 'Brown Eyed Handsome Man' with Valens and the Big Bopper. The show ended with a reprise of 'La Bamba' by Valens (Goldrosen and Beecher 1996: 143).

Having worked with him on this tour, Waylon Jennings's valedictory verdict on Buddy Holly's performances was given to John Grissim in 1969: "When he came on stage he'd get applause because he was Buddy Holly, but it wasn't five minutes before he had the house completely captured . . . he didn't jump around too much . . . there was excitement in his singing. He knew how to communicate from the stage to the people . . . Hank Williams, Johnny Cash and Ray Charles have it . . . but few others ever do" (Grissim 1970: 73).[10]

Jennings was affected particularly strongly by Holly's death. He and Allsup had been offered a seat on the small plane chartered by Buddy to fly to the next gig of the tour, but they gave up their places to Richardson and Valens respectively. The events leading up to the fatal accident have been told in considerable detail by Amburn and Norman, who even pored over the lengthy accident report filed by the United States Civil Aeronautics Board. The more laconic United Press International despatch dated February 3, 1959 summarized the story:

Clear Lake, Iowa

Three of the nation's top rock-'n-roll singing stars – Ritchie Valens, J. P. (The Big Bopper) Richardson and Buddy Holly – died today with their pilot in the crash of a chartered plane.

The singers, members of a rock-'n-roll troupe touring Midwest cities, died because they wanted to make a fast hop between dates so they could get their shirts laundered.

Following an appearance before 1000 fans at Clear Lake last night, they chartered a plane at Mason City Airport, two miles east of here, and took off at 1.50 AM for Fargo, North Dakota. Their four-seat single engine plane crashed minutes later.

The plane skidded across the snow for 558 feet. Holly, 21, was found twenty feet from the wreckage. Valens, a 17 year old recording sensation hailed as 'the next Elvis Presley' was thrown forty feet. Valens, from Pacoima California, was rapidly becoming one of the hottest singing talents in the country. His first record, of a song he had written called 'Come On, Let's Go', was released last summer and made him famous.

The wreckage and the bodies were not discovered until long after dawn. The other members of the troupe, including singer Frankie Sardo, 'The Crickets' and 'Dion and the Belmonts' made the trip by bus. Although grief-stricken, their performance tonight in Moorhead, Minn. took place as scheduled.

(quoted in Laing 1971: 37)

Understandably, the Crickets and other musicians wanted to abandon the tour, which was scheduled to continue for a further 13 days. Nevertheless, the tour continued at the insistence of Irvin Feld, who promised a bonus to Tommy Allsup and the other Crickets. This was never paid, according to Carl Bunch.[11] At Moorhead, Waylon Jennings sang Buddy's songs. For the remaining six shows of the tour, West Texas singer Ronnie Smith of the Poor Boys was drafted in as singer with the Crickets. Also joining the tour were Jimmy

The crash was front-page news

Redferns/GAB Archive. Reproduced by permission of Getty Images.

Clanton and Frankie Avalon. Local singer Bobby Vee and his high-school group the Shadows were added to the show at Moorhead only.

The Crickets had been promised they could leave the tour to attend Buddy Holly's funeral but this promise was not kept by Feld and GAC. The funeral took place at the Tabernacle Baptist Church in Lubbock on February 7 and was attended by over 1,000 people. Bill Pickering, the principal backing singer on Crickets records, sang the hymn 'Beyond The Sunset' and a record of Buddy's favourite black gospel song 'I'll Be All Right' was played.

4 The Recordings, 1955–1959

Introduction

In the two years between his first meeting with Norman Petty and his death, Buddy Holly recorded just under 50 songs, some of which were issued under his own name and some under that of the Crickets. A small number were not released until after his demise.[1] These are almost all of the recordings upon which his reputation rests and this chapter is a commentary on them.

The recordings fall into four groups. Firstly, Buddy Holly sang the lead vocal on 16 tracks released under the name of the Crickets. Ten were released on singles during 1957 and 1958 and the remaining six appeared only on the album *The Chirping Crickets*. All were produced by Norman Petty either at his Clovis studio or at a military base near Oklahoma City. The second group of recordings are the 19 "solo" releases produced by Petty with two exceptions ('Rave On' and 'That's My Desire') and issued as by Buddy Holly with "instrumental accompaniment". These were also made in Clovis, contemporaneously with the Crickets tracks.

The third and fourth groups of recordings were made in New York and issued, mostly posthumously, as by Buddy Holly. The third group are the six tracks to come out of studio sessions held in late 1958, on which Holly was accompanied by Dick Jacobs's Orchestra and Chorus. The final group of tracks consists of the six song demos of new compositions made by Holly in his New York apartment in December 1958.

One immediate reaction to many of Buddy Holly's best records has been a feeling that they are very simple compared with later rock music and even much music of the late 1950s. In fact, this simplicity is an effect of the careful integration of a very small number of instruments and voices into the overall sound, an integration that was new to rock 'n roll. Charlie Gillett summarized Holly's contribution in his magisterial history of rock, *The Sound of the City*: "Of all the Southern singers who came into pop music through rock 'n roll, Buddy Holly seemed to have the widest vision, the keenest sense of what was possible in just over two minutes for a guitar-playing singer with a basic framework of guitar, bass and drums embellished by backing vocals and various keyboards" (Gillett 1996: 97).

This chapter explores the words, structures and sound of these songs that Holly recorded. It concludes with an examination of the meanings ascribed to Holly's recordings by various critics, scholars and biographers.

Of the 47 songs discussed here, a little more than half (25) were wholly composed or co-written by Buddy Holly. The remainder were divided between songs co-written by Norman Petty and writers other than Holly (10) and compositions from outside the Holly–Petty network (12), mainly cover versions of titles already recorded by other rock 'n roll singers. Table 2 summarizes this information for the four groups of recordings.

Table 2: Composers of songs recorded by Buddy Holly

Composers	Crickets	Solo	NY studio	NY apartment	Total
Holly and others	8 (1)	10 (1)	1 (0)	6 (6)	25 (8)
Petty and others	5	4	1	0	10
Outside writers	3	5	4	0	12

In the first line of Table 2, the parentheses indicate the number of songs credited to Buddy Holly alone, although several others credited to Holly–Petty can reasonably be supposed to be wholly or primarily written by Buddy. According to John Goldrosen, Norman Petty had said that "usually, Holly wrote the music for a song and brought it to Clovis, where he (Petty) wrote the lyrics".[2] Goldrosen comments that "in at least several instances, this was clearly untrue" (Goldrosen and Beecher 1996: 62).

One such instance concerns the first songs recorded by Holly at Petty's studio. 'That'll Be The Day' and 'I'm Looking For Someone To Love' had already been written by Buddy Holly and Jerry Allison before the 1957 recording session. However, when they were published and released as a single, Norman Petty also had a composer credit. In contrast, the Decca version of 'That'll Be The Day' was credited to Holly and Allison when it finally appeared on an album in 1958, and the lyrics of the Clovis version had been written out by Holly in a notebook before this recording was made. The music of both versions was identical.[3]

In other cases, Petty at best made minor changes to a song and a defence of Petty's practice would need to be based on a "before and after" comparison of the songs. It can readily be admitted that Petty's arrangements and studio inspirations must have contributed strongly to the overall sound of the tracks, but such input should not affect the copyright status of the song itself, unless it includes significant additions or alterations to the lyrics, the music or both.

Although it does not concern a song composed by Holly, there is one significant "before and after" example that shows how a lyric could be changed after a song was brought to the Clovis studio. This is the words of 'Oh Boy!', the second big hit for the Crickets. It had been written by two West Texas musicians known to Petty: Sonny West and Bill Tilghman. Their song was called 'All My Love' when it reached Petty.

In their book on Holly, Ralph and Elizabeth Peer reprint the words of both 'All My Love' and 'Oh Boy!' to support their view that, as well as the title, "the lyrics were also changed, considerably altering the meaning of the song" (Peer and Peer 1972: 25). The only significant change is the replacement of the line "I'm gonna have some fun tonight" by "I'm gonna see my baby tonight", presumably a decision by the prudish Petty to eliminate any implication of sexual misconduct.[4]

There is some further evidence of Petty's revision of songs composed by Holly and his circle. Leading Hollyologist Bill Griggs has asserted that Norman Petty was responsible for the lyrics of 'True Love Ways' (with Buddy writing only the music) (Stewart interviews) and Jerry Allison conceded that 'Take Your Time' was co-written at Clovis by Petty, Holly and himself, citing the fact of "Buddy not liking the line that Norman came up with about 'Heartstrings will sing like a string of twine'" (Goldrosen and Beecher 1996: 98). Goldrosen also reported Jerry Allison's account of the creation of 'Everyday': the drummer credited "the melody and most of the lyrics to Holly, with Petty having some role in rearranging the order of phrases and verses" (1996: 78).

The composition of approximately half of the Crickets and solo tracks was credited to varying combinations of Holly, Petty and Jerry Allison, with occasional credits for Bob Montgomery, Joe Mauldin and C. W. Kendall Jr, a Dallas pianist with Trini Lopez's group the Big Beats. Kendall's credit may be connected with the fact that he is the pianist on Holly's recording of 'Little Baby'. Buddy is credited as sole writer of 'Lonesome Tears' and 'Words Of Love'.

Of the six songs recorded in New York studios in 1958, only 'True Love Ways' was a Buddy Holly composition, co-written with Norman Petty who was the sole composer of 'Moondreams'. The final group of songs in Holly's career were all composed by Holly alone and recorded with only an acoustic guitar backing, forming the basis for two later sets of overdubbed versions.

The composer category "Petty and others" is made up of songs credited to Norman Petty and other, mainly West Texas, musicians. This category includes the breakthrough Crickets hit 'Oh Boy!' and 'Rave On', both credited to Petty with Sonny West and Bill Tilghman, plus 'You've Got Love' and 'An Empty Cup', two songs co-written by Petty and Roy Orbison. 'Heartbeat' was credited to Bob Montgomery and Norman Petty, while 'Come Back Baby' was written with Fred Neil.

The third composer category of "outside writers" beyond the Holly–Petty networks includes Crickets and Holly solo cover versions of R&B or rock 'n roll songs first recorded by Elvis Presley ('Baby I Don't Care'), Little Richard ('Send Me Some Lovin'' and 'Ready Teddy'), Bobby Darin ('Early In The Morning' and 'Now We're One') and Chuck Willis ('It's Too Late'). The Crickets also recorded 'That's My Desire', an overwrought 1931 ballad by Helmy Kresa and Carroll Loveday, which had been revived several times, by Frankie Laine in 1947, by Dion and the Belmonts and by black vocal group Earl Lewis and the Channels in 1957. Of the New York studio tracks, 'It Doesn't Matter Anymore' was given to Holly by its composer Paul Anka and 'Raining In My Heart' was supplied to him by Felice and Boudleaux Bryant.

This survey of the varied sources of Holly's recorded repertoire raises the question of the authorship of recordings in the rock 'n roll era. While the innovations of the 1960s and beyond have led generations of listeners and critics to attribute authorship variously to recording artists (especially the singer-songwriters), producers (from Spector to Rubin) or even to composers (Bacharach and David, for instance), the issue was seldom considered in this way in the 1950s.

However, through analysis of the four key contributions of composer, singer, instrumentalist and producer, it is instructive to consider the "authorship quotient" of some of the main performers in rock 'n roll. At one end of the authorship spectrum would be Chuck Berry, who was self-contained in three of the four aspects (he wrote sang and played lead instrument) and at the other Elvis Presley, whose contribution was almost invariably as a vocalist only, although he sometimes received a credit as co-writer. In between these poles, Fats Domino obviously sang but only co-wrote some of the songs he recorded with his producer/arranger Dave Bartholomew and played the highly recognizable piano although most solos were taken by saxophone players.

Where does Buddy Holly fit in this authorship spectrum? The complexity of his recording career meant that some tracks found him rivalling Berry in his contribution of song, voice and guitar solos while on other occasions he was "reduced" to the status of Elvis, that of a singer of compositions by others while making no contribution as an instrumentalist. This contrast is most stark in the two sets of New York tracks. In the studio with a session orchestra and without his guitar, he was a vocalist only. On the apartment demo tapes he was the model singer-songwriter, although that appellation had not yet been invented. Sometimes, commentators have hailed his overall contribution as that of a complete author, but it is necessary to recall that the only constant across all these recordings was his presence as the lead singer, and that he composed or part-composed only around half of the songs he recorded in 1957–9. By excluding the six apartment tapes demos, the proportion of songs involving Holly as composer falls from 53% to 46%.

Song words

In this section, the language of the songs recorded by Holly is discussed through discourse analysis (modes of address and the use of pronouns); poetics (the linguistic tropes and effects) and thematics (the content or subject matter of songs – their signifieds). This is followed by comments on the verse and chorus structures of the songs.

The words of any song establish a mode of address: the position of a subject who is making the utterance and whose words are performed by the singer. The subject or protagonist identifies her or himself by the use of the first person. The first person is usually singular but it can be plural, or both – as in the gospel or protest song 'We Shall Overcome': "Deep in my heart I do believe / We shall overcome some day". In all of Buddy Holly's recordings the protagonist uses the first person singular, a stance sometimes signalled in the song titles such as 'I'm Gonna Love You Too' and 'I'm Looking For Someone To Love'.

Popular song lyrics can have two broad types of protagonist: the narrator and the participant. A protagonist-narrator is typically found in ballads and other songs from (or influenced by) folk traditions. When Bob Dylan wrote 'The Lonesome Death Of Hattie Carroll', the protagonist narrated the story of her death at the hands of William Zansinger from the outside. Relatively rare examples of narrated lyrics in popular songs are the Beatles' 'She's Leaving Home' and 'Eleanor Rigby'. In the Holly *œuvre*, the only lyric presented, at least partly, from the viewpoint of a narrator is one of Holly's last compositions, 'Peggy Sue Got Married'. Here, the protagonist combines elements of the narrator role, when he seems to be commenting on the current pop scene as he sings "you recall a girl that's been in nearly every song", with elements of a participant role when he discloses that "I just heard a rumour from a friend". It is at that point that some listeners will make the link with Holly's role as participant in 'Peggy Sue' where he sang "I need you girl, I want you Peggy Sue" and hear the protagonist of the later song as the now disappointed protagonist-participant of the first one.

The protagonist-participant is inside the narrative presented by the song words. To borrow a term from film and video studies, he or she is inside the diegetic world of the song, while the narrator is extra-diegetic. The participant is similar to a character in a novel or play; indeed, in musical theatre, this is literally the case, as with such Lloyd Webber songs as 'I Don't Know How To Love Him' (Mary Magdalene about Jesus in *Jesus Christ Superstar*) or 'Don't Cry For Me Argentina' (Eva Peron addressing the nation in *Evita*). In Holly's recordings, the words of 'Peggy Sue' and almost all the other songs set up the singer as an active participant in a romance scenario. This is the case from the earliest track 'That'll Be The Day' ("you say you're gonna leave me / I know it's a lie", etc.) to New York apartment songs such as 'That Makes It Tough' ("time goes by, I'll still remember you").

These last examples exemplify a further element of the song lyric: the fact the protagonist's utterance is generally directed to an addressee, a second person identified as "you". The exceptions to this rule are lyrics that take the form of a dramatic monologue or soliloquy, a strategy often found in compositions by singer-songwriters and very occasionally used in the Holly *œuvre*.

In most of the love songs of Holly and the Crickets, the addressee is unambiguously identified as a current, future or past lover. This is the case with the majority of Clovis Crickets and solo tracks and with all six New York studio recordings. In 'Everyday', the protagonist-participant hopes that "love like yours will surely come my way", while in 'Oh Boy!' he boasts "all my love all my kissing / you don't know what you've been missing". So it is with 'Words Of Love', although this lyric contains an interesting twist as the participant puts words into the addressee's mouth in the last line, in a kind of ventriloquism:

> Hold me close and tell me how you feel
> Tell me love is real
> Words of love you whisper soft and true
> "Darling I love you"

In that final line, "you" is a reference to the protagonist himself: he turns the monologic lyric into a near dialogue or duet.

The addressee is not always signified through the use of the second-person pronoun ("you"). In popular song lyrics, the addressee may be named, although only 'Peggy Sue' takes this form in the Holly *œuvre*. In other songs, the addressee is identified as "darling" (e.g. 'Listen To Me') or, frequently, "baby" ('Little Baby', 'Come Back Baby').

In some of these love songs, the addressee is not the lover herself but some third person to whom the protagonist-participant is imparting information, or asking for advice or assistance, about his love affair. Five, or about one-quarter of the Buddy Holly solo songs produced by Norman Petty, have a different mode of address to the direct statement to the beloved. This is a much higher proportion than is found in the songs recorded by Holly and his musicians as the Crickets.

'Mailman Bring Me No More Blues' shifts the (former) lover into the third person ("she wrote me only one sad line") with the mailman taking up the position of the second-person addressee. Bob Montgomery's song 'Heartbeat' has a similar structure with "my baby" as third person and the protagonist's statement addressed to his own "heartbeat", which is interrogated over its irregular behaviour – 'why do you miss when my baby kisses me?' In 'Valley Of Tears' (first recorded by Fats Domino), the protagonist asks to be led to the place of despair ("I want you to take me to the valley of tears"). The addressee is possibly some New Orleans equivalent of the boatman who rowed the dead across the river Styx in Greek mythology.

A handful of the songs are what I have called dramatic monologues or soliloquies. In the Crickets repertoire, 'It's Too Late' and 'An Empty Cup' lack an addressee in the sense that the second-person pronoun is absent from the lyric. In these songs, Holly sings "It's too late – she's gone" and "she was to meet me / we had a date". Among the Holly solo songs produced by Petty, the Little Richard song 'Ready Teddy' has no specified addressee, unless we hear "Teddy" as the actual name of a (male?) addressee rather than a convenient serendipitous rhyme word.

While those three songs are by "outside" writers, two of the six apartment tapes compositions by Holly himself have this soliloquy format. 'What To Do' asks what the participant-protagonist can do "now she doesn't want me" while 'That's What They Say' is a musing on the advice given by a third-person-plural group: "I only know that what they say / has not come true for me". And, while the second-person pronoun appears in these lyrics, as in the example from 'Words Of Love', it refers to the participant himself, as the third-person group address him: "you just keep waiting and love will come your way / that's what they tell me / that's what they say".

There are further variations on this pronoun structure in the Holly repertoire and in popular songs in general. "You" in particular is capable of great abstraction or ambiguity. Like "I" it is genderless; therefore an addressee could be a female or male lover. This pronoun is also the same for singular and plural and there is a further ambiguous "you", what might be called the first-person "you". This occurs where the utterance may actually be describing the protagonist's own experience rather than that of a separate person, or may be describing both, in the same way as the archaic pronoun "one". The lyric of the New York apartment song 'Learning The Game' can be heard as a soliloquy where the singer addresses himself – perhaps in addition to an external singular or plural addressee – as "you" ("when you love her and she doesn't love you / that's when you're learning the game").

When the protagonist of 'Love's Made A Fool Of You' sings "When you're feeling sad and blue / You know love's made a fool of you", who is being addressed as "you"? This second person seems to be gendered as male in the line "you know love makes fools of men", and we might suspect that it is an objectification of the protagonist himself. It might be a soliloquy in which he addresses himself, it might be a statement addressed to a different (male) person or it might be a "you" that is linking the two in their common experience.

The ambiguous status of the addressee in 'Well All Right' is different. The protagonist of the lyric is concerned to valorize the authenticity of teenage romance against what "people say", that "those foolish kids can't be ready / For the love that comes their way". The protagonist calls on the addressee to "let people know / about the dreams and wishes you wish' and asserts that he and the addressee together "we'll live and love with all our might". Therefore the second person could be the protagonist's partner, or one or more members of the wider generational group. This song lyric is also notable for being one of the few sung by Holly where there is a clear identification of the protagonist as a member of the younger generation ("those foolish kids").

A final variant use of the second person in song words occurs when the "you" of the song shifts within the lyric between the beloved and another person or persons. In 'Peggy Sue', for example, the protagonist-participant sings in turn to two different addressees. In the first part of the song, "if you knew Peggy Sue" is sung to an individual or crowd of people who are not acquainted with the beloved, but there is a later shift to addressing the beloved in "Peggy Sue, oh how my heart yearns for you". Such shifts are not uncommon in popular songs, although this is almost the only example in Holly's recorded *œuvre*.

In a contrast to earlier groups of songs, only two of the six New York apartment tapes songs – 'That Makes It Tough' and 'Crying, Waiting, Hoping' – are addressed by a protagonist directly to a beloved. In addition to the complex modes of address in 'Learning The Game' and 'Peggy Sue Got Married', in 'What To Do' the love object has become "she" rather than "you" and the lyric takes the form of a soliloquy. Finally, 'That's What They Say' is another soliloquy in which the third-person referent ("they") is identified as conventional opinion or the doxa. These features of the majority of this group of songs lend support to the view that it marked a significant progression in Holly's songwriting craft.

The linguistic dimension of a song includes not only this discursive structure, but many rhetorical features (rhyme, assonance, metaphor, etc.) also found in lyric poetry. Among the leading rhetorical figures of song words are various types of rhymes, repetition of rhymes and phrases and homonyms. Such figures are found less frequently in modern(ist) poetry (i.e. it is free verse rather than rhymed), perhaps because song words are closer to speech than to writing.

The most important of these figures in Buddy Holly's work (and arguably in popular music in general) is rhyme. In his study of Elvis Costello, Dai Griffiths highlighted the complexity of the work done by rhyming by citing a 12-category typology developed by T. V. F. Brogan in a study of lyric poetry (Griffiths 2007: 197). While some of these categories are very specific to written language (e.g. the relationship between sight-rhymes and sound-rhymes), others are pertinent to song words. Among these are the number of syllables that make up a rhyme; the lexical category of the rhyming words (nouns, verbs, etc.); the degree of closeness of the sound match in a rhyme (perfect or half rhymes); the position of the rhyme in the line (e.g. internal rhymes); and further complication of sound patterning in rhyme words, such as assonance or alliteration. The following discussion of rhyme in the songs recorded by Buddy Holly draws on some of these categories, as well as others, such as the frequency of rhyming in a song lyric.

'Peggy Sue' has the highest such frequency, containing five perfect one-syllable rhymes centred on the second word of the title. "Sue" is made to rhyme in the song with "knew", "blue", "true" and "you". "Sue" is repeated 14 times in the song and "you" eight times, contributing to a total of 26 rhyme words in a track lasting 2 minutes 29 seconds. The lexical categories of the rhyme words also range from a proper noun ("Sue") and pronoun ("you") to a verb "knew" and two adjectives ("blue", "true") .

The title of 'Maybe Baby' is an example of a double-syllable rhyme where the sound of one syllable – the second – is repeated exactly. The lyric of this song relies on this and the parallel phrase of the second verse – "funny honey" – for much of its linguistic dynamic. This rhyming strategy has a clear echo of Leiber and Stoller's 'Money Honey', a 1953 hit for the Drifters. The rhyme structure of the Holly's song is even more complex, however. There are additional separate single-syllable rhymes in verse 1 ("you"/"true"), verse 2 ("care"/"prayer") and the middle eight ("sad"/"glad" and "me"/"see"). The latter pair distantly echo the second-syllable rhymes of "may-be ba-by", and within the two verses there are much closer single-syllable rhymes linked to the title phrase. Thus, verse 1 closes with "maybe baby I'll have you for me", where "me" again links to the second syllable sounds "be" and "by". In contrast, verse 2 closes with a rhyming link to the first-syllable sounds. The line is "maybe baby you will love me someday", with "day" echoing the "may" of "maybe" and the "ba" of "baby".

Other songs use half, part or near-miss rhymes. 'I'm Looking For Someone To Love' rhymes "long" with "wronged"; 'Mailman Bring Me No More Blues' has "mine", "line" and then "time"; 'Everyday' has "closer"/"rollercoaster" , "faster"/"ask her", "longer"/"stronger"/"long for"; in 'I'm Gonna Love You Too', the part rhymes are "things"/"sing"/"ring". 'Lonesome Tears' has "cried"/"goodbye" and "a-lone"/"home". A double-syllable part rhyme between "foolish" and "you wish" is used in 'Well All Right'.

The most awkward of these is the pair of lines attributed to Norman Petty in 'Take Your Time': "Heart strings will sing like a string of twine / if you take your time". Leaving aside the semantic confusion (how can twine "sing"?), "twine" is a missed rhyme with "time", but there is also a trio of unhappy internal rhymes in "strings", "sing" and "string"

A homonym is a signifier that can have two or more meanings. The frequency of this trope can be quite high in the lyrics of so-called Broadway songwriters that preceded or were contemporaneous with the rock 'n roll era. In contrast, homonyms are rare in 1950s rock and the Holly repertoire is no exception, with only two significant examples.

'Take Your Time' has a complex and perhaps confused play on the words 'time' and 'take' in the lines "take your time and take mine too / I've got time to spare". The phrase "take your time" meaning "do not hurry" is deconstructed so that the reiteration of "take" shifts its meaning to "appropriate" and the second iteration of "time" makes it into a material object (such as money) rather than a temporal flow.

'Not Fade Away' includes the lines "my love bigger than a Cadillac / I try to reach you but you drive me back". The placing of "drive" picks up the automobile reference as well as the additional sense of "drive back", meaning to repel the advances of the lyric's protagonist.

There is a relatively small incidence of imagery and metaphor in the lyrics of the 47 songs recorded by Holly. 'Peggy Sue' is at degree zero in this respect with words that are almost free of metaphor. In its lyrics, the protagonist confesses that he "loves" and "needs" Peggy Sue, that his heart "yearns" for her and also tells her she is "pretty". The absence of metaphor leaves the lyric to rely almost wholly on the conventional and clichéd lexicon of romantic discourse. The dominant terminology is that of direct denotation of affect or feeling: in 'True Love Ways', for example, Petty's lyrics evoke shared emotions through the terms "sigh", "cry", "joys", "care". The only statement approaching the condition of metaphor is "I feel blue", but even this use of "blue" is a hallowed cliché rather than a metaphor that energetically links two spheres of discourse.

Even when metaphors, similes and metonymic figures are employed, the poetics of these love lyrics are mostly highly conventional. The religious imagery frequently found in romantic discourse can be found in 'Maybe Baby' where the lover is told "you never listen to my prayer" and 'Last Night', whose protagonist tells his lover that he "prayed to the lord above to guide and protect you". The words of Felice and Boudleaux Bryant's 'Raining In My Heart' are powered by a pathetic fallacy, an extended conceit making a homology between rain and tears; Norman Petty's title for 'Moondreams' also links natural and psychological phenomena. The idea of a lover "hooking" the object of his or her desire like a fish – "I'm gonna do my best to hook ya" – is present in 'You're Gonna Love Me Too'. In the same song, the phrase "You're gonna hear those bells ring" is a rare metonym – the ringing church bells standing for marriage.

Two figures of speech are taken from mechanical vehicles. In 'Everyday', love gets closer by "going faster than a rollercoaster" and the protagonist of 'Not Fade Away' compares his ardour to a prestigious luxury automobile: "my love bigger than a Cadillac / I try to reach you but you drive me back".

Another metaphorless strategy, at least on the surface, is the insertion of what could be called reality effects, to create a feeling of verisimilitude. In many songs, the setting for the tableau or fragment of a love story remains abstract: there are no specifications of person, time or place by name. But some songs add these, giving "you" a name and even including the names of "real" places. If 'Peggy Sue' is the only song to insert a "real world" name, several other lyrics of the Holly *œuvre* provide a detailed backdrop as part of the protagonist's statement. In 'Oh Boy!', the time of day is characterized by the line "stars appear and shadows [are] fallin'", in support of the refrain, "I'm gonna see my baby tonight". Time is also a feature of Roy Orbison's song 'An Empty Cup', which is almost painterly in its description of a typical small-town setting. The setting is a "drive-in" where the protagonist had arranged to meet his girlfriend. He had "a date at seven / I dreamed of heaven / now it's way past eight / she just drove by / with another guy".

Elsewhere, two songs evoke details of teenage leisure culture. There is the "rockin' band" and "movie-show" of 'Baby I Don't Care', a song by Leiber and Stoller, composers who frequently added such effects to their lyrics. And a New York apartment song lyric, 'What To Do', looks back on the "record hops", "soda shops" and "walks to school" of a lost Edenic period of "all the happy times we had". An earlier leisure culture is portrayed in the scene of the "gypsy band" in the 1930s song 'That's My Desire'.

'Peggy Sue Got Married' is a very rare example of intertextuality, that is of specific links to other song texts or cultural artefacts. Not only does this lyric reference Holly's own earlier song, but it is surely also a *hommage* to Hank Ballard's Annie series of songs and his own recording of 'Midnight Shift'.

Modalities of the love song

Thematically, almost all of the recordings considered here are love songs enacting various attitudes and phases of heterosexual relationships. Recently, some attempts have been made to separate this category from "songs about sex", and there may be some value in such efforts, particularly when considering songs composed in the later parts of the 20th century and the early 21st century. However, with the exception of novelty items using *double entendre* to brag about sexual prowess (e.g. 'Sixty Minute Man' by the Dominoes) and a limited number of songs expressing direct sexual desire (notable for their banning by radio, etc.), this process of separation is pointless in considering songs of the 1950s, since any such expression of sexuality was sublimated in the linguistic conventions of romantic discourse, notably the word "love" itself and even the inherited sense of "desire".[5]

The romantic scenarios or tableaux established by the lyrics of love songs might be mapped onto a generic narrative typology of love affairs or relationships, with three phases: before, during and after. "Before" would include scenes or moments of courtship and moods of anticipation or anxiety; "during" is the celebratory and euphoric phase of an achieved romantic relationship; and "after" is the period of loss and accompanying moods of desolation or anger, etc.

The lyrics of the songs recorded by the Crickets are split almost equally into the three categories. Six songs present a scene of courtship and mood of anticipation (e.g. "Maybe baby I'll have you" and "you're gonna give your love to me" in 'Not Fade Away'), and four are set in the context of an achieved relationship, including the two big hits 'Oh Boy!' and 'That'll Be The Day', although both lyrics intimate of anxiety about the future of the affair. The remaining six lyrics enact scenes of loss and desolate moods (for example, 'It's Too Late') although one of them, 'I'm Looking For Someone To Love' (a Holly–Petty song), sets up a different emotional resonance, as the protagonist expresses defiance of the beloved's decision to leave him: "if you're not here my baby / I don't care / because I'm looking for someone to love".

The scenarios or tableaux presented in the solo Buddy Holly love songs differ from the songs of the Crickets in their much higher proportion of anticipatory ("before") and celebratory ("during") scenes. Almost half of the solo songs are of the celebratory type. These include 'Words Of Love', 'Listen To Me', 'Heartbeat', 'Little Baby' and 'Well All Right'. Only three of the Holly solo song lyrics present a scene of loss and mood of depression. All are by "outside" writers: the severely lachrymose 'Valley Of Tears', 'Mailman Send Me No More Blues' and 'Come Back Baby'. Among the songs of anticipation, 'Everyday' and 'Wishing' contain an element of fantasy in their hopes for the future while the words of 'Peggy Sue' are suffused with anxiety about the future of the relationship.

All six New York studio recordings are love songs, but only 'Moondreams' depicts the anticipatory phase of courtship found in the earlier phases of Holly's career. Three songs are celebratory expressions of an achieved relationship, notably 'True Love Ways' with its vision of a life-long satisfaction, but arguably the two most emotionally potent of this group of tracks are songs of loss: 'Raining In My Heart' with its binary contrast of the external environment ("not a cloud to spoil the view") and internal affect (the oddly archaic phrase "oh, misery, misery") and 'It Doesn't Matter Anymore' whose sorrowful verses ("you left me here to sit and cry") contradict the unconvincing stoicism of the title line.

Of the songs on the New York apartment tapes, 'Peggy Sue Got Married' treats the theme tangentially, unless the listener chooses to hear it as an expression of disappointment and loss sung by the protagonist of 'Peggy Sue'. The advice dispensed to the protagonist of 'That's What They Say' concerns the anticipation of courtship ("you just keep waiting and love will come your way"). None of this group of songs is celebratory; 'Learning The Game', 'That Makes It Tough', 'What To Do' and 'Crying, Waiting, Hoping' are all tableaux of loss.

Sound

This section of the analysis shifts from the words to the sound, using song structures as a bridge between the two. The structure of the songs composed by the Holly circle is generally conventional. Many follow the classic pop pattern of the alternation of A and B sections, sometimes with a third section leading back to a concluding segment taken from A or B or both. Numerous songs by Holly's and Petty's circle of writers – among them 'Heartbeat', 'Well All Right', 'Look At Me' and 'Peggy Sue Got Married' – are of the A–A–B–A form, where A is the verse and B the "middle eight" or bridge.

However, the performance of the songs often belies this conventionality. The A and B sections are often brief, because they consist of only four or eight bars, or because of the swift tempo of the playing and singing. This creates a sense of constant flow rather than a sequence or series of sections. The feeling of flow is accentuated by the frequency with which rhyme or half-rhyme syllables (and even the refrain) occur in many songs. A similar effect is created by the alternation of one- or two-bar guitar fills with each short sung line of a verse.

The primary feature of the sound of these recordings is Buddy Holly's voice. The vocal stance in the performance of a song, whether in real time or on record, can be understood as poised at or between two poles. At one pole, the confidential stance is achieved on record when the singer's mouth "is placed nearer the listener's ear by means of mike positioning and volume level in relation to the accompaniment . . . this reflects the actual/imagined distance between two persons (transmitter and receiver) in an intimate/confidential dialogue" (Tagg 1981: 14). The contrasting vocal stance is the declamatory, which reflects a greater distance between the singing voice and listener, one that is typical of more public forms of dialogue.

These two types of stance can be mapped onto genres of popular music. The confidential is typical of the love song or the singer-songwriter genre, while the declamatory is more often found in R&B, rock 'n roll and narrative ballads. Unlike crooners (who favour the confidential mode) or R&B shouters such as Little Richard (confined to declamatory performances), Buddy Holly uses the full range of vocal stances between the outright declamatory (on 'That'll Be The Day', for example) to the almost whispered confidential (a primary example is 'Words Of Love').

In a much (and perhaps over-) quoted essay, "The Grain of the Voice", Roland Barthes made a crucial distinction between the pheno-song and the geno-song of vocal performances. The pheno-song is made up of elements that are "in the service of communication, representation, expression"; the geno-song is "that apex or depth of production where the melody really works at the language – not at what it says but at the voluptuousness of its sound-signifiers" (Barthes 1977: 182). Insofar as the vocal stance serves to communicate the mood established by the lyrics, it helps to constitute the pheno-song of the Holly recorded *œuvre*. But this always co-exists with a range of vocal embellishments or ornaments that mainly function as geno-song, as vocal grain.

What is the relationship of Holly's voice to the sense and the mood of the song words? How far is he concerned with "delivering" the "message" of the lyrics, acting out their emotional implications? And how far is the vocal performance a "phatic" one, conveying the grain of his voice irrespective of the demands of the song words?

The anthropologist Bronislaw Malinowski was the first to use the term "phatic communication". He was drawing attention to a social function of language to signal friendship or at least a lack of enmity, irrespective of the immediate semantic content of an utterance or a gesture. Examples of phatic communication can be polite greetings ("pleased to see you", "how are you?" etc.) or, in media discourse, the almost ritualized nods of the head that television interviewers use to signal understanding of, or sympathy with, an interviewee's statement.

Phatic communication in a performance can take the form of a dialogue with the audience, as when a singer comes on stage to say "Hello London", calling forth the response "Hello!!" from the audience. The idea of phatic communication can be extended to encompass those idiosyncratic elements of individual vocal style called "the grain of the voice" by Barthes. When these features are dominant in a vocal performance by Holly, the primary effect on a listener is a recognition that this is Buddy Holly singing. A vocalist who is held up by critics as an ideal interpreter of a song will have a different primary effect on the listener, providing her with an understanding of, or empathy with, the song's semantic or emotional content. The use of the adjective "primary" here is a recognition that the phatic dimension of a performance almost always co-exists simultaneously with the communicative one. The question, then, is: which of these dimensions is dominant in any particular listening experience?

Some authors have recognized Holly's apparent prioritizing of the vocal grain and contextualized it. Gillett points out that Holly's ability to "pick on any word and play around with how it could sound and what it could mean" was a feature of the singing of African-American artists he admired such as Jimmy Reed, Clyde McPhatter, Fats Domino and Mickey and Sylvia, adding that 'Holly made the technique standard for white singers too" (Gillett 1996: 98). More apocalyptically, in *Mystery Train*, Greil Marcus numbered Holly (with Harmonica Frank, Clarence Frogman Henry and Bob Dylan) as among the "rock 'n roll vocal contortionists . . . whose mission in life seemed to be the wilful destruction of the mainstream tradition of popular singing and the smooth and self-assured way of life it was made to represent" (Marcus 1977: 13).

Many of the embellishments found in Holly's recordings are melismatic in character – they elongate a single syllable so that it covers two or more beats. The simplest form of melisma is produced when a singer holds the same note for an extended period, something frequently used to signal the finale of a vocal performance, often as a gesture of technical or natural ability. In the 12-bar blues 'Mailman Bring Me No More Blues', several final phonemes are stretched in this way as the original note is held for a further two beats.

However, this simple melisma is rare in Holly's recordings. Instead, there are different forms of complex melisma, where the original phoneme sound is transformed or mutates through certain types of repetition. The slow ballad 'Listen To Me' includes "me-hee" and "say-hay" where the second phoneme is both different to, and articulated to, the first, thus both extending it and becoming a variation of it.

A renowned example of complex melisma occurs in 'Peggy Sue', where the final repetition of the syllable 'Sue' is extended over six beats (or two bars) of the song, heard by Norman as "a six-syllable schoolyard taunt" (Norman 1996: 142). But here the melismatized syllable is also chopped up into separate "oo" sounds in different rhythmic groups.

Another of Holly's vocal techniques is the use of sequences of wordless or asemantic phonemes in the interstices between verses made up of semantically conventional sounds or between verse and instrumental solo and sometimes as the introduction to a song, or its coda. There is a "paradigm shift" between syllables that signify semantically as well as phonetically and these syllables that are solely phonetic in their signification.

On 'Words Of Love', each of the three verses is concluded with a short sequence of "hmm" sounds that is somewhere between singing and humming. 'I'm Gonna Love You Too' provides an extreme example of this vocal motif. The introductory section consists of almost 16 bars of Holly singing the syllable "ah" to the melody line of the song. The section is followed by the sung phrase "you're gonna love me too", two more lines beginning with the second-person pronoun and then the title line of the song.

The introductory section of 'I'm Gonna Love You Too' can be heard either as a discrete unit (which might instead have been played on guitar) or as an extreme melisma with the "ah" sound resolving into the first syllable of the song title ("I'm") which Holly sings in a slight Texan accent, so that it emerges as a sound somewhere between "I'm" and the broad Southern version, "Ah'm". The vocal ornamentation here is thus liminal, on the borderline between melisma and wordless singing, or a combination of the two.

The third and fourth vocal techniques to be mentioned were clearly learned by Buddy Holly from the singing of Elvis Presley. The first of these is the use of spoken lyrics, found in the Holly repertoire on 'Listen To Me' and delivered over a muted guitar solo. The other Presley-esque technique is a sudden shift in register, usually from high to low. This is evident on the Holly version of 'You're So Square (Baby, I Don't Care)', a song written by Leiber and Stoller for Elvis to sing in the film *Jailhouse Rock*. Holly's recording faithfully follows Presley in dropping an octave to achieve a growling effect for the title phrase 'Baby I Don't Care', an effect intended to signify sexual interest or desire. That register shift is found on several other tracks, including 'Peggy Sue' where the song title at different points is the site of a similar downward shift but also an upward shift to a very brief kind of falsetto yelp.[6]

'Peggy Sue' also includes a different type of shift from Holly's "normal" vocal register and accent into a higher voice but also a different intonation that might be compared with the slightly infantilized tone taken by an adult talking to a child or pet animal. Greil Marcus once claimed that Holly's versions of the "crazy shifts from high to low . . . sounded funny" whereas with Elvis they "sounded frightening" (Marcus 1977: 175). While Marcus's hero worship of Elvis makes this comparison seem exaggerated, Holly's modification of the register shift in 'Peggy Sue' certainly diverges from Presley's über-erotics. Michael Hicks underlines this point by attributing to Holly "a technique that allowed weaker singers to vary their vocal expression". Borrowing the term from Jonathan Cott, Hicks defines this "baby talk" as "a soft high-pitched, crisply enunciated, frontally resonant singsong – a kind of nasal cooing", citing in particular the fourth verse-line of 'Peggy Sue': "I love you, Peggy Sue / with a love so rare and true" (Hicks 1999: 4).

The final element in this inventory of Holly's geno-song is what has sometimes be seen as his "trademark" ornamentation, the so-called "hiccup" or "hiccough" effect. Philip Norman picks out 'Look At Me' as a "gently hiccoughing ballad" (Norman 1996: 183), while Alan Mann cites the "stuttering treatment of the initial 'Well' in 'Rave On'" as "unprecedented in mainstream pop" (Mann 2009: 134).

The *Collins Dictionary* defines "hiccup" as "a spasm of the diaphragm producing a sudden breathing in of air resulting in a characteristic sharp sound". The "characteristic sharp sound" described (metaphorically) as a hiccup is produced by Holly in the third line of 'Look At Me' and signified here by ^. Holly sings "say say ^ look at me and tell me", with the curt sound attached to the repeated "say" taking the form of a heavily curtailed repetition or extension of the "y" sound of "say" cut in a much higher register, gesturing towards falsetto. This para-falsetto dimension of the vocal ornamentation links it to the yodel, an important part of the set of vocal effects deployed by older country singers with whom Holly was familiar, such as Hank Williams.

Barbara Bradby describes this feature of Holly's singing as "the clipped pronunciation of the first or last consonant of a word or syllable, slightly separating it from the vowel sound that succeeds or precedes it" (Bradby 2002: 89). This is consistent with the more precise definition of the technique as "aspirated glottal stop". While the hiccup is an involuntary sound derived from a breathing malfunction, the glottal stop (a term derived from linguistics) is an element of spoken dialect in which a consonant sound in the middle or at the end of a word is erased or compressed. Discussing Holly's version of this effect, when the vocal bands are pressed so tightly together that air pressure from the lungs is resisted, Maury Dean writes, "to aspirate the glottal stop, the compressed air is released in a quick puff", producing such a sound as the "wo-uh-ho" heard in 'Peggy Sue'" (Dean 1973: 245–6).

One necessary feature of the tracks issued under the name of the Crickets is the existence of the supporting voices to Holly's lead. This was the "proof" that these records featured a vocal group and not a solo singer. As we saw in Chapter 2, for this purpose Petty usually overdubbed the three harmony voices of the Picks a few days after the main vocal recording had been made.

The Picks' voices are precise but not improvisatory. In contrast to the melisma-based variations of Holly's lead, they sing key syllables and phrases in clipped style. As such, their role was downplayed in my earlier book on Holly: "In contrast with the ingenuity of gospel choirs and the black vocal groups of the '50s, members of these white groups [such as the Picks] all sang the same part and were firmly subordinated to the named singer out in front. Their roles were limited" (Laing 1971: 51–2).

This negative view has been challenged by Barbara Bradby, who distinguished the three "roles" of the chorus's part in 'Oh Boy!' as echo, beatless word and wordless beat. The echo is the immediate repetition of Holly's iteration of the title phrase, something that occurs 12 times in the song. The "beatless word" is an open vowel sound "aaah" used as a background accompaniment to the lead voice or a guitar solo. The "wordless beat" is the rhythmic singing of the non-signifying syllables "dum de dum dum" that combine with a (non-echoing) "oh boy" to simulate the "Bo Diddley" rhythm used in this recording (Bradby 2002: 72).

While examples of these vocal roles can be found in other Crickets recordings, I am inclined to revert to my earlier assessment of the lack of harmonic creativity in the vocal arrangements, presumably chosen by Norman Petty. What might have been achieved can be heard on the album of cover versions of Buddy Holly songs recorded in Nashville in 1996 by Connie Francis.[7] Her producer Stuart Colman included the Jordanaires on backing vocals, taking the role played by the Picks and others in the 1950s. The Jordanaires, of course, were the white male backing singers who had worked frequently with Elvis Presley. They provide for Francis the polyphonic variety that was lacking in the original recordings.

If there is a close relationship between song words and song non-words in Holly's singing, the same is true for the interface between the voice and his guitar playing on many of the recordings. Just as the voice seems to be ever-present on each track, so the guitar is ubiquitous, whether playing lead phrases or providing a constant rhythmic undercurrent. Generally, the guitar solos reiterate something that has gone before, rather than introducing something new into the song. Sometimes, these roles are reversed. On 'Words Of Love', a series of guitar arpeggios opens the track, from which the voice seems to emerge as the same guitar lines take a background role. At the close of the song, the vocal line dissolves back into the repetitive, hypnotic guitar part.

John Goldrosen has noted this highly integrated nature of the instrumental passages of many Holly recordings. He comments specifically on the three four-bar sequences of the "instrumental chorus" of 'That'll Be The Day'. The first is dominated by "the blues runs of Holly's treble strings, falling in pitch and then returning upwards in the fourth bar to a crescendo which Allison supports with a heavy triplet rhythm on drums and cymbals". In bars five to eight, this sound gives way to "the stand-up bass, bass drum and bass guitar strings" but returns in the final sequence with "perfectly timed and syncopated phrases" (Goldrosen and Beecher 1996: 52).

Another feature of the guitar playing is the manipulation of tempo and of timbre. The dynamic guitar sound of 'Peggy Sue' was achieved by accelerated tempo and imaginative recording techniques, as Gillett pointed out: "Holly strummed his guitar very fast, sixteenths, all on the down stroke, with the guitar close-miked to pick up the sound of the plectrum on the strings" (Gillett 1996: 98).

There has been widespread recognition of the originality of Holly's playing, although little unanimity about where the originality resides and where it originated. The British skiffle star Lonnie Donegan described his guitar playing as "a fingering electric style. The only fingering you could see in Europe at that time was Spanish or classical. Buddy was like a one-man orchestra" (Leigh 2003: 59).

Some authors have traced the origins of Holly's guitar style either to his early experiences as a bluegrass banjo player (Carr and Munde 1995: 123) or the "brush and broom" technique used by country groups in West Texas. This was analyzed by Irwin Stambler and Grelun Landon, who wrote:

> He would hit the note, which was the "broom" and then "brush" his fingers across the chord. For example, a guitarist might pluck the G string, or the D string, then strum the G chord (This type of playing is also used in many Johnny Cash arrangements). This technique of note and strum is much simpler than the fancy runs of an artist like Jimmie Rodgers. Holly's material combines a Jimmie Rodgers–Leadbelly feeling with heavy guitar sounds out front and a pronounced beat underneath (Stambler and Landon 1971: 120).

The particular tonal quality of the Fender Stratocaster is an essential component of the recorded sound. Despite the importance of both country music and R&B in Holly's musical evolution, the guitar motifs typical of each genre are generally absent from his recordings. Instead, there is a denotative clarity to the sound, deriving from the single-coil pickups of the Stratocaster and from its design concept as a solid-body electric guitar. Steve Waksman emphasizes the importance of the sound of the electric steel guitar for the Stratocaster concept. The new guitar was intended to "capture 'pure string vibration'" and thus to create a "clean" sound "that had sustain and a lack of feedback" (Waksman 1999: 46).

Apart from the six apartment tapes songs, all the tracks under discussion include a rhythm section of double bass and drums, occasionally supplemented by rhythm guitar. The creative contribution of Jerry Allison's drumming to Holly's recordings is not always given full recognition by critics and biographers. But, in Gillett's words, Allison was "a drummer who thought as freely as he did himself, who was happy to try out new patterns, play just on tom-toms, or whatever fitted with the rhythm set by Holly's voice and with the mood set by his voice" (Gillett 1996: 97). Jerry Allison acknowledged his debt to African-American music by adapting the Bo Diddley beat as the basis of the rhythm of 'Not Fade Away' and 'Oh Boy!'[8] Elsewhere, Allison's contribution to 'Maybe Baby' was adapted from Little Richard's hit 'Lucille'.

One feature of Allison's recorded work was his willingness to abandon the standard drum set in order to "fit in" with vocal rhythm and effect. The use of a cardboard box on 'Not Fade Away' and hand–knee claps on 'Everyday' has already been mentioned. But, even where conventional percussion was used, Allison applied imagination to his role in the overall sound. One classic case is 'Peggy Sue'. Michael Hicks describes how the "fragility" of the baby-talk vocals "contradicts the dark, incessant tom-toms underneath" (Hicks 1999: 4). But the drumming itself involved two contrasting sounds, as Albin Zak has shown. Zak has analyzed how two drum sounds, "wet" (or ambient) and "dry", alternate as the sound of an ambient chamber is alternately switched on and off, and interact with other levels of the sound of 'Peggy Sue'. According to Zak:

> In the introduction, the contrast between the two simply appears as a novel sonic effect. As the track progresses however, each takes on a specific association: the ambient drums are associated with the voice, the dry ones with the instrumental sections of the arrangement. Furthermore, rather than simply mirroring the song's form, the interplay between the two drum sounds follows its own course, its own rhythm. In the first verse, the ambient drums play throughout; in later verses the dry drums often intrude between vocal phrases, interrupting the sonic cohesion of the voice's accompaniment and introducing a secondary level of articulation into the track's narrative structure. (Zak 2001: 81–2)

Lonnie Donegan told an interviewer that, on the British tour, Joe Mauldin "had the most perfectly hit bass sounds, filling the hall" (Leigh 2003: 59). However, this impact was generally not re-created on record. Although his instrument was sometimes miked up by Norman Petty, Mauldin's sound was often crushed between Holly's electric rhythm guitar and what Donegan described as Allison's "one-man percussion unit". On many of the most famous tracks, for instance 'Peggy Sue', the bass line is barely discernible and its sound merely adds to the thickness of the rhythm. It becomes audible when Holly is playing rhythm guitar part and his vocals are mixed down. An example is 'I'm Gonna Love You Too' and the end of 'Everyday', when the bass plays a wrong note. Mauldin was unusual among young rock 'n roll musicians in 1957–8 in choosing not to play electric bass guitar (the first Precision bass had been launched in 1951). By not switching, he contributed to the different sound of Holly's records and the absence of a clearly delineated bass line on many of them.

Buddy Holly has often been described as the first of the rock 'n roll generation to record with strings. Only four tracks include a 12-piece string section as part of the accompaniment: 'It Doesn't Matter Anymore', 'Moondreams', 'Raining In My Heart' and 'True Love Ways'. All come from the New York studio sessions when the session musicians included violinists, cellists, viola players and even a harpist.

On 'True Love Ways', the strings often act as the equivalent of backing singers, echoing the melody of the phrase just sung by Holly. The track includes a tenor saxophone, blowing phrases in among the string sound. 'It Doesn't Matter Anymore' and 'Raining In My Heart' both feature the *pizzicato* (plucked) sound that was to influence future pop song arrangers. Like 'True Love Ways', the latter song has the strings playing "fills" after vocal phrases, though here they most resemble the role of the guitar parts on earlier Holly tracks, bowing brief arpeggios scored by Dick Jacobs. 'It Doesn't Matter Anymore' has the most elaborate polyphonic string arrangements.

A Holly structure of feeling?

In my analysis of Holly's vocal style, I have implied that the peculiarities of his singing constitute an excess of expression, beyond the requirement to portray the emotional content of the song words. However, Jonathan Cott, Barbara Bradby and the biographers (John Goldrosen, Philip Norman and Ellis Amburn) have in different ways argued that Holly's recordings contain or embody something like a particular "structure of feeling", to use a term of the culture critic Raymond Williams. According to Williams, in any historical moment or period:

> In the living experience of the time, every element was in solution, an inseparable part of a complex whole. And it seems to be true, from the nature of art, that it is from such

> a totality that the artist draws; it is in art primarily, that the
> effect of the totality, the dominant structure of feeling, is
> expressed and embodied. (Williams and Orrom 1954: 21)

To a large extent, the biographers hear Holly's voice enacting the affective cues of the lyrics. Writing of 'Listen To Me', Goldrosen says that the voice "breathes life into the words, varying and moulding the tone of the lyrics and lending them a tense, urgent emotion". He goes on to generalize about Holly's role as a singer, that "he provides the listener with a friend who has shared his [sic] experience and can express it in a general but quite realistic fashion" (Goldrosen and Beecher 1996: 99). Here, Buddy comes across as a counsellor to his listeners.

Philip Norman also finds a confessional element in 'Look At Me', which he describes as "a gently hiccoughing ballad . . . typically blending self-confidence and uncertainty" (Norman 1996: 183). For his part, Ellis Amburn decodes a philosophy of love in the songs. He writes of 'Everyday' that it "dwells on the youthful belief that love is right around the corner" and its message is "that love is not so much a revelation, or something you fall into, as it is a gradual unfolding". Amburn adds a directly autobiographical dimension, claiming that 'Everyday' "also embodies Buddy's dogged faith that Echo, the 'good girl' of every boy's fifties dreams, or a girl very much like her, would eventually become his wife and the mother of his children" (Amburn 1995: 75).

Amburn quotes from the analysis of Holly's songs by Jonathan Cott, the author of the Holly chapter in the first edition of the *Rolling Stone Illustrated History of Rock & Roll*. Cott asserts several things about Holly's structure of feeling. He writes that through a "shy coy ingenuous tone of voice", Holly "perfectly, almost obsessively, communicated in song after song his joyful acceptance of 'true love ways', his indivertible expectation ('crying, waiting, hoping') of someday finding a love 'so rare and true' " (Cott 1981: 77). This romantic optimism is psychologically rooted in wish fulfilment – Cott perceptively cites the repetition that is a feature of the songs (and most pop songs) as a mechanism to achieve this wish fulfilment, comparing the Holly stance to that of ritual.

Cott also claims that Peggy Sue is "the first rock 'n roll folk heroine (Chuck Berry's Johnny B. Goode is her male counterpart)". He suggests that, through the complete lack of detail in the song, Buddy "colluded with his listeners, suggesting that they imagine and create Peggy Sue for him" (and presum-

'Oh Boy!' sheet music cover

Redferns/GAB Archive. Reproduced by permission of Getty Images.

ably for themselves). While this is a somewhat weak argument, Cott points out that the figure (or at least the name) of Peggy Sue crops up in several other songs of the late 1950s and early '60s: 'Splish Splash', 'Queen Of The Hop' (both Bobby Darin), 'Ooh My Head' by Ritchie Valens (like Darin, an occasional associate of Holly) and in the Beach Boys' 'Barbara Ann'. There, however, she is "discarded for a younger rival" according to Cott. The song words are 'Tried Peggy Sue / But I knew she wouldn't do'. Cott is keener on the sequel to Peggy Sue, calling its lyric a brilliantly constructed equivocation whereby the confirmation that Peggy Sue (his object of desire in the earlier song) has married someone else is postponed until the "inexorable last stanza", after which she "vanishes, like Humbert Humbert's Lolita, into the mythology of American Romance".

He finds it "tempting to imagine the idea of Peggy Sue permeated all of Holly's compositions . . . to view all of Holly's recordings as a synchronic rather than diachronic structure . . . as one long song" (Cott 1981: 80). Cott points out Holly's espousal and transformation of "baby talk" in such songs as 'Maybe Baby', 'Oh Boy!' and 'Rave On', which reveals "the child inside the man" and his ability to signify a pubescent or adolescent persona, "the insouciance of a choirboy who doesn't realise his voice is changing".

In her commentary on 'Oh Boy!' (Bradby 2002), Barbara Bradby picks up and develops this insight. She sees in Holly's music the expression of a new "identity of male adolescent independence" but for her this is achieved more through the formation of a strongly homosocial "buddy group" than idealized heterosexual romance. Rather than concentrating on lyrics or Holly's vocal embellishments, Bradby's very detailed analysis of 'Oh Boy!' focuses on the relationship between lead vocals and backing vocals (which she calls the "chorus") and on a rhythmic conflict within the track.

Bradby's observation that the chorus provides three distinct types of vocalization has already been mentioned. In her interpretation of the role of the chorus she adds that songs such as 'Oh Boy!' conduct "an internal dialogue between different voices" so that "two male voices address simultaneously each other and a woman" (2002: 63). The address to the woman is inscribed in the song words ("you were meant for me") but Bradby's additional insight is to hear the relationship between Holly's voice and the choral work by the Picks as an equally, if not more, important element of the song. This is established in part by a suggestion that there is a kind of homonymic dimension to the word "boy". Its manifest meaning is as an exclamation denoting excitement, in which place it could have been substituted through a commutation test[9] by some equivalent term such as "gee" or "gosh". But the term "boy" also carries its primary meaning outside the song of a young male.

Bradby hears this meaning as co-present when the dialogue between lead voice and chorus takes place in the song. Thus, when the second line of the song "you don't know what you've been missing" is followed by an exchange of the phrase "oh boy" between Holly and the Picks, there is an ambivalence of address that introduces "mutuality of admiration/desire on the part of the two 'boys'" (2002: 84). That is, we can hear the claim about "what you've been missing" as a momentary expression of same-sex attraction. Bradby points out, however, that "this 'literal' homosexual address is immediately contradicted by the conventional hearing of 'when you're with me' as addressed to a woman" (2002: 84).

Bradby's perception of a homosocial stance momentarily shading into an expression of homosexual desire in the structuring of the symbolic relationship between lead voice and backing vocals opens up an area for speculation about the performative sexuality of male rock 'n roll singers. Tim Riley has confidently opposed the presentation of masculinity in Elvis Presley's singing to the working out of "the feminine side of masculinity" in Little Richard and Buddy Holly. The two singers were "unashamed of their feminine side, whether for reasons of sexual preference (Little Richard) or self-conscious opposition to the tough-guy standard (Holly or [Roy] Orbison)" (Riley 2004: 28).

Riley's discussion implies a triangular relationship between Presley (heterosexual and masculinized), Holly (heterosexual and feminized) and Little Richard (homosexual and feminized). And, in reality, Holly was a link between the other singers, in the sense that he was friendly with both – with Presley in Lubbock in 1955 and with Richard in Lubbock and on tour. One of the two reported incidents involving Holly and Richard is of interest here. As recounted by Richard to his biographer, it concerned a dressing-room party at which Buddy Holly was engaged in sexual intercourse with a female friend of Little Richard with Richard himself watching and masturbating. The action ended when Holly was due on stage, giving the anecdote its punchline – "he came and he went" (White 1985: 87–8). The neatness of this phrase emphasizes that there is room for doubt over the veracity of the tale – Richard is not always a credible witness. But the structure of the three-way relationship (whether actual or fantasized) linking heterosexual and homosexual desires can be seen as strikingly similar to Bradby's assertion of the way a similar triad operates in the interaction of singers in 'Oh Boy!'.

Jonathan Cott's recognition of "baby talk" in Holly's music is also transformed in Barbara Bradby's article. Using the psychoanalytically based contrast between the symbolic and semiotic elements of language first proposed by Julia Kristeva (where the semiotic sphere is "bound up with musical features that continually recall the rhythms and melodies of pre-verbal communication with the mother" (2002: 70), Bradby locates the semiotic dimension in the structure and rhythm of children's songs. She finds this "on beat" rhythm in sections of 'Oh Boy!', where it conflicts with the syncopated beat of other parts of the record, until in the final section of the song a resolution is found when the phrase "makes everything right" is articulated to the correct, children's, rhythm.

Bradby locates the presentation of gender and desire in the recording as a structure of feeling created in the historical specificity of Holly's era, when "rock 'n roll represented new, sexualised gender identities for the teenagers of the late 1950s". This Holly song, she writes, "addresses those who have not had sex" (2002: 64), and "addresses precisely the moment of initiation into adult sexuality", noting that in this connection "the discourse of rock has proved to be a crucial rite of passage for several generations" (2002: 68). There is no suggestion that Buddy Holly's music was unique in expressing this essence of post-World War II adolescence, but the reference to the relevance of rock discourse to "several generations" offers an insight into why the 1950s music of Holly and his rock 'n roll peers might continue to resonate half a century on.

5 After the Day the Music Died: Memorializing

Premature deaths in popular music

In April 1975 the British music magazine *Let It Rock* asked the rhetorical question "Is there Rock after Death?" as an introduction to a series of articles dealing with premature demise in popular music. Buddy Holly occupied a prominent place on the magazine's cover, alongside Sam Cooke, Otis Redding, Brian Jones, Jimi Hendrix and Janis Joplin. In the music industry, the cynical view that death is a good career move was already common currency by that time and American trade papers in the 1950s noted the commercial impact of premature death.

Following the accidental death of R&B star Johnny Ace in December 1954, *Billboard* reported that the event had "created one of the biggest demands for a record that has occurred since the death of Hank Williams just over two years ago. Orders for his new recording 'Pledging My Love', began to pour into the Duke/Peacock diskery in the same amounts as the large diskeries usually receive for a new record by a big pop artist" (quoted in Salem 1999: 159).

Just over four years after the plane crash, the sudden and shocking death of Holly, Valens and the Big Bopper inspired similar editorializing by *Variety* magazine writer Mike Gross. Under the headline "Album Sales Keep 'Em Alive", he wrote in 1963:

> Immortality comes easy in the record business. If there are enough masters in the morgue or tapes in the vault, the "death rattle" goes on perpetuating the performer, and, very often, filling the record company coffers . . . This disk-after-death activity came into the spotlight again this week with release of a "new" LP by Buddy Holly, called *Reminiscing*, on the Coral label . . . Holly . . . continues to build new teenage fans. Some wonder if he would be as popular today

if he hadn't died, while others say that the Holly image has
remained constant and will continue to attract the juvenile
disk buyer because his "young sound" stays the same ... At
any rate, the Coral boys are pegging their merchandising and
promotion techniques on Holly as though he were a "living"
act. (quoted in Goldrosen and Beecher 1996: 150)

Death and sound recording

Gross's reference to "disk after death activity" highlights the fundamental
way in which recording and death have been linked since the invention of
the technology. In its first account of Edison's demonstration of recording, the *Scientific American* linked it with death: "nothing can be conceived
more likely to ... arouse the liveliest of human emotions than once more
to hear the familiar voices of the dead" (*Scientific American* 1877a). A month
later, another article in the *Scientific American* specifically mentioned singing voices: "the voices of such singers as Parepa and Titiens will not die with
them, but will remain as long as the metal in which they may be embodied
will last" (*Scientific American* 1877b).[1]

In his study of the cultural origins of sound reproduction, Jonathan Sterne
links this idea of the immortality of the voice with the parallel technology
of chemical embalming that "opened up a whole field of cosmetic possibilities for the presentation of the dead to the living". Sterne argues that this
technology contrasted with competing methods of embalming "concerned
with interiority, with preserving the body in its original form". The chemical
method was instead aimed at preserving "the appearance of the body and its
potential to perform its social function" and the implied logic in preserving
the voices of the dead was identical in that it involved a "disregard for the
preservation of the voice in its original form, instead aiming for the preservation of the voice in such a form that it may continue to perform a social
function" (Sterne 2003: 296–7).

The "social function" performed by the voices of dead popular musicians
is a complex one, encompassing commercial, historical and psychological
dimensions. In the following discussion I have distinguished between the
functions of memorialization (discussed in this chapter) and representation
(discussed in Chapter 6).

Memorialization and representation

To memorialize an individual is to provide reminders of their life and to fix its place in the past, in history; the process of representation adds to that life through the creation of new artefacts or events that seek at different times and in various contexts to (temporarily) fill the space created by the absence of the individual, to provide new signifiers for the dead artist. In what follows I have assigned for analytical purposes a large number of features of Holly's posthumous career into one or other of these categories. However, as will become clear, many of these practices or products contain elements of both memorialization and representation.

Holly's posthumous career has been the combined and often conflictual and contradictory product of a variety of human and institutional agencies in an actor network that established itself after February 1959. It should be emphasized that such a network is not assembled through a single directly conscious act, although one can see that elements of the network were – a prime example was the formation of fan clubs to perpetuate the memory of Buddy Holly. On occasion, though, there have been direct attempts within posthumous careers to annex or determine the overall direction and space of action of network participants. This can be seen in the role of Elvis Presley Enterprises (EPE), the company set up by the Presley estate to oversee, regulate and monetize as much as possible of the posthumous career (O'Neal 1996).

Despite the efforts of EPE to exercise a kind of panoptic control, David Wall has argued that the posthumous career needs the "celebrity culture" nurtured by fan groups and others outside that control to ensure the dynamism of the career because "too much restriction through over-zealous control could effectively strangle the celebrity culture by killing off sensibilities of personal ownership and affiliation" (Wall 2003: 35). The Presley case, however, stands at one end of the spectrum of posthumous careers in popular music. The careers of some deceased artists have, in contrast, been almost wholly unmanaged. One example is the fate of Janis Joplin's music since her death in 1970. There has been no organization, commercial or fan-based, to keep her name and her recordings in circulation and to implant her achievements securely in the popular memory (official or unofficial) of popular music. In particular, Joplin has been ill served by her biographers.

Buddy Holly's posthumous career has been steered not by a single dominant organization equivalent to EPE, but by participants in a relatively diffuse network. Among this posthumous network's participants have been family members, musical collaborators and others who had been members of the networks that precipitated Holly's formative years and his professional career. But many new actors – individuals, institutions and technologies – were to play important roles in the posthumous career network's twin functions of memorialization and representation.

Eight faces of memorialization

Barry Schwarz has written that the process of remembering the deceased can be divided into chronicling and commemoration:

> The events selected for chronicling are not all evaluated in the same way. To some of these events we remain morally indifferent; other events are commemorated, i.e. invested with an extraordinary significance and assigned a qualitatively different place in our conception of the past . . . Commemoration celebrates and safeguards the ideal. (Schwarz 1982: 377)

In an analysis of newspaper coverage of four "pop deaths" more recent than those of Holly and Presley (John Lennon, Kurt Cobain, Tupac Shakir and Jerry Garcia), Mazzarella and Matyjewicz use frame theory to conclude that the media play an important role in creating "collective memory" and a mythology of the artists as "'icons' of a generation or era" (Mazzarella and Matyjewicz 2002).

In the case of Buddy Holly (and many other deceased stars), memorialization or commemoration, and the formation of collective or public memory, has taken a wide range of forms since his death. At least eight types of memorialization and their practitioners can be identified. These have been:

- Tribute songs (songwriters and musicians – including Holly collaborators – record companies, DJs and listeners)
- Reissued recordings (record company compilers, music publishers, fan clubs, listeners)
- Fans and fan clubs (enthusiasts, organizers, musical collaborators)
- Biographies and journalism (writers, publishers, interviewees, readers)
- Canonization (industry institutions, writers and academics, reader and listener polls)

- Iconography – photos, stamps, etc. (state institutions, photographers, copyright law)
- Monuments and museums (state institutions, fan clubs, sculptors and artists, curators and collectors)
- The "death" of rock 'n roll (writers, critics, historians)

Each of these is discussed below.

Tribute songs

Almost immediately following the demise of Hank Williams on New Year's Day 1953, songs "describing the event or commemorating his career made their appearances on jukeboxes and radio shows" (Malone 2002a: 243). The same was true of the aftermath of the death of Johnny Ace two years later.

Country music historian Bill Malone lists the titles of four tributes to Williams, ranging from reportage ('The Death of Hank Williams') to religiosity ('Singing Teacher In Heaven' and 'Hank Williams Will Live Forever') and a direct address ('Hank, It Will Never Be The Same Without You') (Malone 1985). According to Ace's biographer, "more than half a dozen tribute records were released, and at least two of them were covered by other R&B labels" (Salem 1999: 162). Here the religious tone was most prominent in, for example, Varetta Dillard's 'Johnny Has Gone', which claimed that the quality of Ace's voice propelled him heavenwards: "An angel was listening, and called him above" (Salem 1999: 163–4).[2]

By 1959, then, the precedent has been set. There were eventually about a dozen tribute songs to one or all three of the plane crash victims and a further dozen that mention Buddy Holly among other dead rock stars (Goldrosen and Beecher 1996: 157). The first tribute song was 'Three Stars', composed almost immediately after the crash by "Tommy Dee" – actually a San Bernadino disc jockey called Tommy Donaldson.[3] It was a maudlin song with the chorus "Gee we're gonna miss you / Everybody sends their love" and a verse each for the three deceased. Eddie Cochran immediately recorded a version of 'Three Stars' but because his record company could not find a way to donate royalties to the bereaved families, it was not released in 1959. The track was not available until 1966 in the UK and 1972 in the US.[4] Tommy Dee's own version became a Top 10 hit and there was a cover version by Ruby Wright (Collis 2004: 150).

No other tribute song was recorded until the British vocalist Mike Berry recorded Geoff Goddard's 'Tribute To Buddy Holly', produced by Joe Meek in

1961. Geoff Goddard had composed hits for British actor John Leyton and his 'Tribute' shared the supernatural ambience of Leyton's biggest hit 'Johnny Remember Me': Goddard claimed to interviewers that he was inspired to compose the song when he had dreamed of Buddy after attending a séance (Repsch 1989: 116). Like many in the British music industry, Meek was an ardent admirer of Holly. Louis Barfe is one of several authors to note that the date of Meek's suicide was "eight years to the day after the death of Buddy Holly" (Barfe 2005: 231).[5]

Although he was not a slavish imitator, Mike Berry's singing owed much to Holly's vocal mannerisms. Berry was to become a frequent performer at Holly memorial events in the latter part of the 20th century.

Unusually for a sub-genre that is always centred on the immediate aftermath of a death, Holly tributes have continued to be written and recorded up until the first decade of the present century. There have been songs by his family and associates. Holly's mother wrote 'Buddy's Song' for Bobby Vee to record in 1963. The lyrics included the titles of ten songs recorded by Buddy and borrowed the melody of 'Peggy Sue Got Married'. *Holly's House* (1980) was an album by Buddy's siblings and their children. It included a song called 'Buddy Holly And The Crickets' sung by Larry Holley and composed by Robert Cooke and journalist William Bush. Larry's daughter Sherry is a semi-professional singer, one of whose albums was called *Looking Through Buddy's Eyes*.

Among those who played with Buddy, Waylon Jennings was the first to write and record a tribute ('Old Friend', 1976) and Sonny Curtis was inspired by his sense of outrage at the version of Holly's life portrayed in the film *The Buddy Holly Story* to write 'The Real Buddy Holly Story', which he recorded for Elektra in 1979. Carl Bunch recalled in doggerel his performances as the last tour continued without Buddy:

> I was there when they said the music died
> And I stood by and watched Waylon cry
> When we sang 'It Doesn't Matter Anymore'
> And I remember just like yesterday
> All the music that we used to play
> And it makes my heart beat just like it did before

John Pickering and the Picks emphasized his (and the Holley family's) roots in Southern Baptist theology with the mawkish 'Buddy Holly Not Fade Away'

(1984): "Mama raised him in the church / And Buddy Holly is at home with God". And a contemporary of Holly's, Buddy Knox, recorded 'I Named My Little Girl Holly', a song composed by one Lee Jackson.

Among other tribute records are those by Bennie Barnes ('Three Gold Records In The Snow'), rockabilly singer Ray Campi ('Ballad Of Donna And Peggy Sue'), Loretta Thompson ('Buddy, Big Bopper And Ritchie') and Hershel Almond ('The Great Tragedy'). Country songwriter David Allen Coe's 1986 song 'A Country Boy (Who Rolled The Rock Away)' linked Holly's name with those of Hank Williams and Elvis Presley in a three-person hall of fame.

Some British tributes have been composed and recorded since the 1980s. Singer-songwriter Harvey Andrews's 'Please Don't Get On The Plane' includes the advice "take your time / Like the words of the song you just sang". English country singer Terry Clarke told journalist Spencer Leigh that he was recording in San Marcos, TX, when he looked out of the window and thought of Buddy Holly, finding inspiration to compose 'Buddy's Waiting On The Flatland Road'. The same 1990 album included 'Lubbock Calling' in which Clarke emphasizes a link to the pivotal figure in a later generation of the city's musicians: "The ghosts have got it right / Buddy Holly's singing to Joe Ely tonight".

The prolific British songwriter and producer Mike Batt was responsible for Alvin Stardust's 1984 Top 10 hit 'I Feel Like Buddy Holly'. This was not a tasteless reference, but was so titled because the lyric had the protagonist quoting lachrymose hits of the past including 'Raining In My Heart' and Paul McCartney's 'Yesterday'. A transatlantic collaboration between Bobby Vee and Tim Rice was responsible for 'Whatever Happened To Peggy Sue?' in 2002, and, most recently, 'Mirror Door', a Pete Townshend composition from The Who's 2006 album *Endless Wire*, included a litany of 19 musical inspirations including "Elvis, Buddy and Eddie C".

Reissued recordings

Apart from albums containing previously unreleased or overdubbed tracks (to be discussed in Chapter 6), there have been numerous "greatest hits" or "best of" Buddy Holly albums issued in the past half-century. Interviewed in 1998, a Lubbock-based collector and dealer had amassed 196 different albums from all over the world (Kerns 1998). Goldrosen and Beecher's discography lists over 30 US albums and 50 issued in the UK alone between 1959 and 1995 (Goldrosen and Beecher 1996: 190–7). A television-advertised *20 Golden Greats* album was a number 1 hit in the UK in 1978, as was an almost identical release on CD in 1993 (*Words Of Love*).

These reissue albums were mainly restricted to tracks that had been released during Holly's lifetime, with the occasional addition of items first released in the 1960s having been overdubbed by Norman Petty or Coral Records' Dick Jacobs. But alongside them has been a strand of historically minded compilations that sought to construct a discographical chronology and to ensure the release of all variant versions of Holly recordings. This would create a different kind of representation of Holly as a serious artist, an image often accorded to jazz or classical figures, but seldom to those prominent in any form of popular music.

The principal figures in this process were two British fans, John Beecher and Malcolm Jones. Their nationality was not a quirk of fate but a reflection of the longer-lasting popularity of Holly in Britain in the 1960s. In the ten years after Holly's death, there were a greater number of singles and albums released in Britain than in the US, and a greater number of hits. Between 1959 and 1969 eight Holly albums were Top 20 hits in Britain, while only two posthumously released albums entered the US Top 100 in that decade, reaching number 40 and 55 respectively (Goldrosen and Beecher 1996: 198).

The disparity between Holly's sales in the two countries has been attributed to the American company's indifference to his work. "If any major rock figure was ever worse served by his record company than Buddy Holly, I'd sure like to hear about it" wrote Chet Flippo in 1979 (Flippo 1979: 174), and the treatment of Holly's catalogue by the record company in the subsequent 30 years has continued to be mediocre. Among the company's misdeeds was the issue in the United States of a British compilation album that simply reproduced the sleeve note which referred to British hit singles!

John Beecher had been the driving force behind the British Buddy Holly fan club. Like Jones, he was working in the music industry, an important fact that assisted them in understanding the logic of Holly's recording career and in unearthing relevant material and information. Malcolm Jones had worked for the Fly and EMI record companies and had been of inestimable value to me when I was researching my first book on Holly in 1971.

The first attempts at a curated and scholarly account of Holly's recording career were made separately by Beecher and Jones in the 1970s. Beecher worked with the British branch of the record company, now renamed MCA, to secure re-releases of *The Chirping Crickets* and *Buddy Holly* albums as well as a more satisfactory presentation of some of the Petty overdubbed material.[6] Jones, meanwhile, compiled a five-LP set that was released in Britain by the mail-order company World Record Club in 1975 and included almost everything that had already been commercially issued.

However, neither of these projects was fully comprehensive and the two researchers joined forces to compile *The Complete Buddy Holly* issued by MCA in Britain in 1979 and in the US in 1981. This eight-LP set had over 130 separate tracks, including some juvenilia recorded at home, a number of radio and television interviews with Buddy and singles by Waylon Jennings and Lou Giordano produced by Holly. Even this did not quite live up to its title. *For The First Time Anywhere*, a 1983 album from MCA, provided ten tracks in their "original" versions that had only been available as overdubbed tracks to Beecher and Jones. In 2008, the US record label Geffen/Decca issued a two-CD 59-track selection called *Down The Line Rarities*, three tracks of which were described as "previously unreleased". These were also included in the 50th anniversary 203-track six-CD box set *Not Fade Away: The Complete Studio Recordings And More* released in 2009 by Universal.

Fans and fan clubs

The immediate impact of the plane crash was particularly sharp in Britain, where Holly had been the first major rock 'n roll star to tour since Bill Haley. The crash was front-page news in the *Daily Mirror*, then the biggest-selling daily newspaper. Young fans were devastated. A 12-year-old David Bowie had already told a school friend that Buddy had a better act than Elvis and, when the news came through, "David broke down in tears at school" (Sandford 1996: 19). Eric Clapton recalled that his school playground:

> Was like a graveyard, no one could speak, we were in such shock. Of all the music heroes of the time, he was the most accessible and he was the real thing. He wasn't a glamour puss, he had no act as such, he clearly was a real guitar player, and to top it all off, he wore glasses. He was like one of us. It was amazing the effect his death had on us. After that, some say the music died. For me it really seemed to burst open.
> (Clapton 2007: 21)

On the morning after the plane crash, an unnaturally subdued music class in Beethoven Secondary Modern School in West London was cheerily told by the music teacher, "Well, that wasn't much of a loss for music." A voice from the back of the class responded "Wait till Beethoven dies, and see how you like it" (Monaghan 2009).

Goldrosen and Beecher describe Holly and his wife personally answering fan letters in the months before his final, fatal, tour. No formal fan club was organized before the plane crash, but two important and influential organizations were set up in the years following his death. Their titles are significant. In the US, the International Buddy Holly Memorial Society was established by Bill Griggs in 1975; in Britain, John Beecher ran the Buddy Holly Appreciation Society during the 1960s.

Born in 1941, Griggs had been a Holly fan and memento collector as a teenager, seeing Holly and the Crickets perform in his home town of Hartford, CT. Griggs was inspired to found the society in part by his reactionary dislike of later musical trends. He told interviewer Dick Stewart that by the late 1960s he found music to be "turning real sour. The Beatles were doing strange things, acid rock was in and drugs seemed to be infecting the music. I turned back to the days when music was simpler – the 1950s – and rekindled my love for Buddy Holly and the Crickets" (Stewart interviews). The spark that prompted Griggs to found the fan club ignited in 1975, when he "was hosting my annual Rockandrollathon in my backyard, a get together of area record collectors, deejays and sometimes an artist or two . . . knowing of my adoration of Buddy Holly [a friend] remarked 'It's too bad we don't hear him on the radio anymore'. Another said 'Nothing in the fan or music magazines either'" (Stewart interviews).

Griggs began to publish *Reminiscing,* a newsletter and later a magazine. Publishing this and running the society was soon a full-time job ("a hobby turned into an infatuation turned into a business", he said). An initial Buddy Holly Convention was held in 1978, at which the re-formed Crickets performed. By the time the IBHMS wound down in the mid-1990s, it had 5,500 members in over 30 countries.

In 1981 Griggs and his family moved to Lubbock. Griggs subsequently published his pamphlet series *Buddy Holly Day By Day*, although he admitted to Dick Stewart in 2004 that there were still 21 days of Holly's life about which he could find no information. As well as listing performance and recording events, the booklets obsessively list the hotels Buddy stayed in while on tour, the flights he took, the cost of each item of stage clothing, and they reproduce almost 200 letters, receipts and cheques!

Griggs was heavily involved in a campaign to get official recognition of

Holly in Lubbock, and himself became a kind of arbiter of the various contro-versies and disputes of the post-mortem career. In the interview with Stew-art, he was more sympathetic than most towards Norman Petty's business arrangements and he remained neutral on the value of the biopic *The Buddy Holly Story*, although he had firm views on the three main biographies, pre-ferring that of John Goldrosen and showing hostility to Amburn's book.[7]

As well as chronicling Buddy Holly's life, Bill Griggs became one of the most fervent collectors of Holly memorabilia. To Philip Norman and a British film crew, he vouchsafed a view of the overnight bag carried by Buddy onto the final flight and its contents. It had been given to him by Buddy's brother Larry. Norman's choice of metaphor and simile is perhaps symptomatic of aspects of the fan-collector's mentality. He wrote that Griggs treated the "relic with almost religious reverence" as it "was unrolled from its plastic layers like a mummy's corpse being disinterred from its bandages" – the lurid imagery suggesting that the bag has become symbolic of Buddy's body itself (Norman 1996: 391).

Indeed, Norman's *tour de force* continues by quoting Griggs's conviction that "late at night, when I'm tapping on the computer . . . I suddenly get that feeling someone else is in the room. It seems to me that Buddy's standing there near my desk. He's wearing black slacks and the grey V-neck sweater he had on his English tour. And he always says the same thing: 'Thanks for what you're doing' . . . " (Norman 1996: 392).

John Beecher, Griggs's British counterpart, explained in his 1975 introduc-tion to the first version of Goldrosen's book that, only after the plane crash

> did I realize how much I had taken Holly and the Crickets for granted. Holly wore glasses of course, at least he had on tel-evision – but not on the *Buddy Holly* album cover. When the Crickets had toured England there were three of them, but there were four on the *Chirping Crickets* cover. So I began try-ing to find out a little more, and in doing so discovered there were many other fans who weren't going to forget Buddy Holly. There were no fan clubs for Holly and the Crickets at this time, so I started one.[8] The response was incredible and within a few months the membership was second only to the club for Elvis Presley. (Beecher 1975: 8)

In 1961, Beecher was called upon to give his (and the society's) seal of approval to Mike Berry's recording of 'Tribute To Buddy Holly' by its producer Joe Meek. He and a number of fan club members attended a performance at Meek's studio by the singer Mike Berry and his group the Outlaws. Beecher was impressed, later telling Meek's biographer, "It *did* sound like Buddy Holly and the Crickets" (Repsch 1989: 119).

Both the British and American organizations eschewed the lesser nomenclature of the "fan club" in favour of a more dignified stance. This may have reflected the organizers' wish to differentiate themselves from the association of fan clubs with teenage female fans. Certainly, there was a masculine bias in Holly fandom. Buddy's mother told Goldrosen that, following her son's death, "90 percent of the letters she received were from men" (Goldrosen and Beecher 1996: 87).

During one of the New York residencies, Don Everly had noticed the gendered character of Buddy Holly's appeal to audiences. He told an interviewer that 'Young girls would fill up the audience in the early shows [i.e. those in the morning and afternoon]. As it progressed to the evening, it filled up with men and if you were getting a lot of girl reaction, like screams and things, it would start to wane . . . But Buddy Holly was an exception – would go over more on those evenings where there was a bigger male audience" (Goldrosen and Beecher 1996: 87). Jerry Allison added that this appeal to male audience members was doubly important when "teen idol" singers got too much "girl reaction": ". . . it seemed like the boys liked us better – you know, with some of the idol-type groups, the boys would be turned off because their chicks would be saying, 'Oh, look at that'" (1996: 87).

Philip Norman wrote a 1988 play, *Words of Love*, which sought to explain Holly's appeal to young men. He explained that the play "contrasted the last hours in Buddy's life with the existence of a teenage boy like myself at sixteen, for whom his music is a respite from parental repression and dreary hopelessness" (Norman 1996: 20).

The reported predominance of men among Holly fans – contrasted with the appeal to female audience members of the Everly Brothers and others[9] – may be linked to what Barbara Bradby identified as "male narcissism" in 'Oh Boy!' which constructed "a male 'other' as audience, even when ostensibly addressing/desiring a woman" (Bradby 2002: 85). Bradby's reference is to the internal dynamic of the recording, but this insight might be extended to the actual "audience" for Holly's performances, on stage during his lifetime or on record then and after. This mechanism explains how the singer both inhabits and overrides the role of the participant-protagonist set up by the song words, and delivers a primary message to other men. It may also provide an explanation for the confusion felt by some (heterosexual) male fans of other male rock stars whose song words frequently express sexual desire for the addressee. The issue is discussed by Mark Duffett who reports male Elvis fans' fantasy construction of their hero as a brother (rather than a lover) (Duffett 2001).

Biographers and journalism

The Complete Buddy Holly album set was a kind of chronological account of Buddy Holly's recording career and the same narrative intention has informed much of the published writing about Holly. This written "archive" is an essential element of fixing the past and giving the memory of Buddy Holly a public and clearly defined form.

There have been at least half a dozen books about Holly beginning with my own 1971 volume in the *Rockbooks* series, which focused on the music rather than the "life". This was followed by the substantial conventional biography by John Goldrosen. The product of two years' research and numerous lengthy interviews, Goldrosen's book, in its various editions, remains the "gold standard" in Holly biography.

Goldrosen's work is carefully composed and, if anything, too even-handed in dealing with controversial areas of the career, notably the role of Norman Petty. The same cannot be said of the biography by Ellis Amburn, published in 1995. While Goldrosen seldom imagines himself inside the mind of his subject, Amburn has no such inhibitions. His Holly book was conceived as part of a "Texas trilogy" with biographies of Roy Orbison and Janis Joplin, and Amburn tries rather self-consciously to compare and contrast these three singers. While many Hollyologists disapprove of Amburn's more flamboyant speculations about Holly, his book contains some convincing speculation as well as some suppositions that seem off-centre. In particular, Amburn does not pretend that conservative Lubbock was sympathetic to Holly's rock 'n roll, a view that seems to me to be difficult to contradict.

The most recent full-scale biography was by British author Philip Norman, whose principal pop biography is of Elton John and who has published lesser studies of the lives of the Beatles, John Lennon and the Rolling Stones. Norman's book added little new information to that provided by the other biographers and the Holly fan club researchers. Even though the author had access to financial records from the Norman Petty estate, he seemed more fascinated by the (unsubstantiated) rumour that a teenage liaison might have resulted in Holly being the father of an unacknowledged child.

Canonization

Substantial biographical publications such as those of Goldrosen, Amburn and Norman have been an essential part of the process of winning an exalted position for Buddy Holly in the history of popular music. In recent years, the established past of the music has increasingly been referred to as a "canon" of recordings and musicians and the procedure by which an album or artist was admitted to this "canon" as "canonization". A special issue of the journal *Popular Music* was even devoted to the topic and in 2008 the first book on the "rock canon" was published (Wyn Jones 2008). In his introduction to the *Popular Music* issue, Motti Regev claimed that "the cultural power of the popular music canon . . . resides in its unofficial status. There is no formal mechanism of canonisation" (Regev 2006: 2).

The idea of "canonization" originated in the Roman Catholic church where among its meanings was the extremely formal beatification of a mortal into a saint, who thereby joined the canon of saints. In the 20th century, the term was appropriated and applied metaphorically in the world of university literary studies. It described the contents of established curricula and examination norms which included certain authors (typically "dead white males") and excluded others, whose work was regarded as unworthy of study by those in control of English departments. As such, the association of the idea of control and definition of a canon with those holding power in an institution was carried over from its ecclesiastical origin.

In the further metaphorical shift, into popular music studies by, among others, Regev and the contributors to the special issue, this association of canonization with institutional control lost much of its relevance. Now the term was applied above all to the proliferating lists of "favourite bands" or top albums generated by circulation-chasing journalists or public relations people working for record store chains (von Appen and Doehring 2006). The sense of the institutional power and control that was associated with canonization by the church or the academy was missing. Readers of *Rolling Stone* or the *NME* were hardly a match for a college of cardinals or the faculty of Harvard or Princeton!

If canonization is to be a useful term in popular music, it should be applied more narrowly, to the actions or decisions of institutions that claim or are accorded prestige. One candidate for this role is the Rock 'n Roll Hall of Fame, established in the US in 1983 by a small committee of leading recording company executives including Ahmet Ertegun, Seymour Stein, lawyer to the stars Allen Grubman and *Rolling Stone* publisher Jann Wenner. A voting college of "more than 600 industry professionals" chooses artists to be inducted into the Hall of Fame from a list of candidates. To be eligible, artists must have had a "commercially released record" at least 25 years before the date of induction voting. The "industry professionals" also ensured that "non-performing inductees such as record company founders and songwriters" could be given membership of the Hall (Romanowski and George-Warren 1995: 863). In 1986, Buddy Holly became one of the ten founder-members of this Hall of Fame. The others were Chuck Berry, James Brown, Ray Charles, Sam Cooke, Fats Domino, the Everly Brothers, Jerry Lee Lewis, Elvis Presley and Little Richard – all still living apart from Holly, Cooke and Presley.

A more significant source of Holly's placing in music history is the conspectus of histories, dictionaries and encyclopedias that make up the notional reference shelf of popular music since the 1950s. Here, Buddy Holly's status has shifted as successive generations of historians have re-evaluated the rock 'n roll of the 1950s and its relative importance compared to the music of later decades.

During the 1960s, Holly was generally held to be one of the founding figures of that decade's rock music. Charlie Gillett's high estimate, dating from the 1969 first edition of *The Sound of the City* and retained in later editions, has already been quoted. In one of the first dictionaries of rock music, also published in 1969, the influential Australian-born US-based critic Lillian Roxon was hyperbolic in her praise, stating that he was "a figure so important in the history of popular music that it is impossible to hear a song on the charts today that does not owe something to the tall, slim bespectacled boy from Lubbock, Texas" (Roxon 1978: 254).

At the other extreme, in that same year, Nik Cohn's equally opinionated *Awopbopaloobop Alopbamboom* was published, subtitled "Pop from the Beginning". His title was taken from Little Richard's 'Tutti Frutti' which was a kind of yardstick for Cohn's judgments on bands and singers. Holly did not fare well. Cohn's comments began with an apparently even-handed comment that he "wasn't a hardcore rocker, being too gentle and melodic, and this eccentricity can be construed either as backsliding or progression". The use of the invidious term "eccentricity" was the cue for the assault to follow, that concluded with some sneering adjectival irony in the use of "noble":

> Not many white kids had the lungs or sheer hunger to copy Little Richard but Holly was easy. All you needed was tonsils. The beat was lukewarm, the range minimal – no acrobatics or rage or effort required. You just stood up straight and mumbled . . . in this way Buddy Holly was the patron saint of all the thousands of no-talent kids who ever tried to make a million dollars. He was founder of a noble tradition. (Cohn 1969: 46)

More recently, rock histories have mentioned Holly with respect but without enthusiasm. Reebee Garafalo's *Rockin' Out* gives him less than two pages out of 450 and seems most interested in the labels he recorded for (Garafalo 1997: 141–3). His name is mentioned only three times in the 40-plus pages devoted to "The Rock & Roll era" in the *Cambridge History of American Music*, on each occasion linked to others rather than presented as artist who made an individual contribution (Walser 2000). And, despite the fact that he was almost certainly the first rock 'n roll player to adopt the Fender Stratocaster, Holly is wholly absent from Steve Waksman's history of the electric guitar (Waksman 1999).

Iconography

It was 20 years before Buddy Holly was publicly commemorated in his home town "which continued to pay him little heed or honour" (Goldrosen and Beecher 1996: 173). It seems that the catalyst for a change in this attitude was the news that a Hollywood film was to be made of his life. A landfill site earmarked for development as a park was named after him hurriedly in 1978, to coincide with the opening of the biopic (Goldrosen and Beecher 1996: 173). In the early 1980s, Joe Ely organized annual outdoor charity concerts in this park, but the 1983 event was banned by the city council because of a "fear that the buffalo grass growing in the park would be damaged by the large crowds. The fact that live music was effectively banned from the park that bore Buddy Holly's name was an irony not lost on the Lubbock music community" (Carr and Munde 1995: 165–6). Later attempts to establish a regu-

The Lubbock statue by Grant Speed

Getty Images News/Ronald Martinez. Reproduced by permission of Getty Images.

lar concert or festival in memory of Holly himself were equally short-lived, though for different reasons. A Buddy Holly Music Festival was held in 1996 and 1997, but it was discontinued after a dispute with Holly's widow.

Following the naming of the park, the city council agreed to a site for a statue and a fundraising concert was held in 1979, featuring Roy Orbison and Bo Diddley as well as various current and former Crickets. The bronze statue itself, by sculptor Grant Speed, was unveiled the following year. Holly's biographer Ellis Amburn (whose book is enlivened by a relentless animus towards Lubbock, its city council and most of its population) contemptuously dismissed it with the phrase "as lifeless as the city that surrounds it" (Amburn 1995: 316–8).

Heavily rimmed spectacles and Stratocaster guitar were the two iconic objects of Holly's performances and his photographic image. The spectacles made a big impact. As late as 2008, the British comedian and former physician Harry Hill spoke in an interview of his choice of glasses to wear when he started his stand-up career in the 1990s: "the glasses were ones I had bought and worn when I was a doctor: I thought they were a bit Buddy Holly" (Lawson 2008: 33).

For some younger contemporaries of Buddy Holly, it was inspiration enough to find a rock star who wore spectacles with pride. Describing the future Elton John at the age of 13, his biographer commented: "he wore glasses not because he needed them but in homage to Buddy Holly, rock music's first four-eyes" (Norman 2000: 26). The future lead guitarist of the Shadows, Hank Marvin, said that on seeing the Crickets on a British television show "I knew I had to get my own Strat but that took a long time. My first move was to dump my specs and buy a pair with thick black frames" (Ingman 2008: 17).

By the 1970s, to wear heavy-rimmed spectacles had become an allusive gesture towards Holly and his iconic status. Discussing Elvis Costello, David Brackett has pointed out that "from the outset, Costello used artifice to create a distinctive image: adopting the most hallowed first name in the history of rock music and combining this with the visual image of Buddy Holly-turned-geek, the cover of Costello's first record attracted attention without having to produce a sound" (Brackett 1995: 162).

Holly's own spectacles were sought after by collectors and exhibitors of memorabilia. One pair was sold at auction in 1990 for $50,000. In 1994, the pair he was wearing at the time of his death was discovered in a sheriff's office in Iowa, "visibly scarred from the plane crash". They were given to Holly's widow who sold them to Civic Lubbock Ltd, a nonprofit arts body, for $80,000 in 1998 (Gunning 1998).

Holly was the first rock 'n roll star to play the Fender Stratocaster, with its revolutionary cutaway design. The Stratocaster had been launched in 1954, aimed primarily at the western swing and country music sectors. Holly bought his guitar in January 1956, for use at his debut recording session. Sonny Curtis, who also played this guitar on some of those early recordings, was using a "reissue" of that 1954 model when interviewed by Dick Stewart in 2004 because "you can get a variety of sounds by simply moving the toggle in mid-song if necessary, and since it is a solid body, it does not have a tendency to feed back, which means you can turn it up and blow the back out of a building if you want to" (Stewart interviews).

It was portrayed on the sleeve of the 1957 album *The Chirping Crickets*. Because of post-war import restrictions, American musical instruments were not on sale in Britain where would-be guitarists' "introduction to this guitar would have been through seeing Buddy Holly cradling a remarkable object on the cover of his LP *The Chirping Crickets*" (Foster 1997: 127–8). Eric Clapton saw Holly and the Crickets perform on a national television show, *Sunday Night at the London Palladium*: "that was when I saw my first Fender guitar. It was like seeing an instrument from outer space and I said to myself: 'That's the future – that's what I want' " (Clapton 2007: 19).

Holly's association with the Stratocaster became a feature of the provenance claimed for replicas of the 1954 model. An advertisement published in the late 1990s described such a "timeless classic. This reissue captures the feel of the Buddy Holly-era Strat. Its deep body contours, characteristic V-neck shape, vintage style hardware, classic colors, and aged plastic parts all lend authenticity . . . $489" (quoted in Ryan and Peterson 2001: 103).

The Holly profile with the trademark spectacles has also been utilized for postage stamps and paintings. In 1993 the United States Postal Service issued a set of three stamps honouring "music legends", featuring Holly, Presley and Otis Redding (O'Neal 1996: 166). Lubbock was probably the only city where first-day sales of the Holly stamp outsold Elvis (Amburn 1995: 331ff.).

Like other rock 'n roll singers, Buddy Holly has been the subject of works by "pop" artists. The English painter David Oxtoby and the Belgian artist Guy Pealleart created portraits of Buddy. The Oxtoby picture showed Buddy's head and shoulders and V-neck sweater emerging from a background composed of painted-over pages from US fan magazines (Sandison 1978: 27).

The issue of iconography and its commercial exploitation is complicated in the United States by the existence of a copyright in the image or likeness of an individual in the laws of many states (but not federal law). For many years Elvis Presley Enterprises has more or less successfully used such legislation to take control of the Presley souvenir industry (Wall 2003).

In the case of Buddy Holly, his widow benefited from a "Buddy Holly law" passed by the Texas legislature in the early 1990s. This granted "image rights" in his name and likeness and enabled her to license events using Holly's name and the marketing of souvenirs in that state only. By 1999, Maria Elena Holly had negotiated a 15% royalty on all sales of Holly merchandise at the Lubbock Buddy Holly Center. The centre was reported to be offering a wide range of branded products "from T-shirts and tote bags, to key-rings and mouse-pads". However, she turned down an offer of $50,000 and 15% of ticket sales for the annual Buddy Holly Music Festival. The festival went ahead but under the name Music Crossroads of Texas – West Texas Rock 'n Roll Festival (Kerns 1999). In a later dispute between the widow and the council, the Lubbock authorities decided to remove his name from the Buddy Holly Walk of Fame and the Holly memorial rather than pay a fee to Maria Elena.

Monuments, museums, memorabilia

Soon after Buddy's death, the Holley family erected a marble tombstone at Buddy's grave which contained an engraving of his face. This relatively modest monument was included among the 150 "celebrity tombstones" described by Elaine McCarthy in her guidebook *Morbid Curiosity* (McCarthy 2002). The family tomb became a place of pilgrimage for fans from all over the world.[10] In 2008, a British travel company, Dead Great Tours, organized a seven-night tour to Lubbock, Clear Lake and Cleveland, the home of the Rock 'n Roll Hall of Fame.

The 1980s brought a campaign for a Holly museum in Lubbock led by Bill Griggs and the Holley family. A local developer, who had bought Holly's guitar in a Sotheby's auction, offered $1 million for the use of the name "Buddy Holly" on a chain of hotels, for which he would build a "Disneyland-type" project celebrating Buddy. When this fell through because the various beneficiaries could not agree, the developer sold his collection of Holly memorabilia to the city of Lubbock in 1994. The council put to a vote a tax rise to build a home for the collection, which was narrowly lost. A temporary home for the memorabilia was found in 1995 at Texas Tech university. Perhaps in part compensation, in 1996 the city council voted to rename part of Avenue H, Buddy Holly Avenue. Also inspired by the Holly association, a Lubbock baseball team, the Lubbock Crickets, played their first games in the Texas–Louisiana League in 1995.

Eventually, the memorabilia became part of a permanent exhibition that opened in 1999 at a former railroad depot that was renamed the Buddy Holly Center and also housed an arts centre. The exhibition includes clothing, letters, photographs, handwritten song lyrics, a pair of Holly's horn-rimmed spectacles and a Fender Stratocaster guitar. His final Stratocaster guitar was bought by the city of Lubbock in the mid-1990s along with stage clothes and school exercise books, for $200,000 (Norman 1996: 388).

In 1991 some of Holly's possessions were included in a rock 'n roll auction at Sotheby's of New York. His Gibson acoustic guitar, including the leather cover he made for it, was bought by Gary Busey, star of the biopic, for $242,000. The sale also included his birth certificate, high-school diploma and some stage clothes.

The principal collectors of Holly memorabilia included a Lubbock businessman and Bill Griggs, the founder of his principal fan club. As well as bidding at auctions, Griggs contacted the New York optician who supplied Buddy's trademark spectacles and purchased a spare pair of tortoiseshell coloured frames made for Buddy in late 1958.

He even set out to find the Holleys' former home, a wooden house that had been moved outside the city limits in 1978 by an unknown purchaser. According to Philip Norman, Griggs "mobilized search parties of up to fifty fans, armed with photo-references of [its] covered front-end porch . . ." (Norman 1996: 389).

"Death" of rock 'n roll

Holly's death has often been presented as part of a larger metaphorical "death" – that of rock 'n roll itself. Peter Guralnick repeated what had become "a familiar litany . . . Elvis in the army, Buddy Holly dead, Little Richard in the ministry, Jerry Lee Lewis in disgrace and Chuck Berry in jail" (Guralnick 1971: 4). In what was a dominant paradigm in popular music historical writing in the 1970s and after, the music was supposed to have died after Presley's induction into the army, Berry's imprisonment, Little Richard's turn to sacred music, Lewis's "disgrace" and Holly's death, to be replaced by insipid teenage pop (Ennis 1992: 270, 408 fn 16). The refrain of Don McLean's massive hit echoed this rock critics' homily (probably the only hit to have set a critical nostrum to music).

It was not only critics that promulgated this death of rock 'n roll myth. Interviewed a decade after the plane crash, Waylon Jennings stated: "When Buddy died, rock 'n roll died. For quite some time. And the Beatles were the ones to bring it back" (Grissim 1970: 72).

In later years, this view of a "Fall" in popular music history has been frequently criticized by journalists and historians involved in "rehabilitating" the American pop music of the early 1960s, such as the work of the Brill Building songwriters (e.g. Emerson 2005). But if the "death of rock 'n roll" thesis is shorn of its judgmental elitism, it carries a certain explanatory power. It is possible to argue that rock 'n roll as it emerged in the mid-1950s was a formally limited style, permitting only a small number of variations. This position is supported by an analysis of the later career of those rock 'n roll stars who "survived" 1959. While Elvis Presley succumbed to the pressures exerted by Hollywood, RCA and Colonel Parker (and his own penchant for sentimental ballads), those who "kept the faith" seemed condemned to endlessly repeat their achievements of the 1950s. Thus, Domino, Berry, Little Richard and Lewis could be found 50 years on performing in an almost unchanged style (even if some had tried out other styles in the interim).

If, by 1959, rock 'n roll had exhausted its possibilities and was no longer capable of evolution, Waylon Jennings is in some sense correct. When the Beatles brought it "back" it was not as a revival but by integrating rock 'n roll's spirit, essence or influence into a new musical mode. Much the same thing occurred when the demise of punk was followed a decade later by the rise of Seattle's grunge bands whose new sound of the 1990s owed most to the legacy of a genre that had been "buried" by the New Romantics.

Buddy Holly, of course, occupies a unique position in the debate over the strange death of rock 'n roll. Because of his absence from "what came next", there has been an irresistible temptation to muse over what he might have done in the 1960s. Here, it is sufficient to say that his own musical position was both contradictory and enigmatic in relation to what with hindsight can been seen a seismic shift in American music at the end of the 1950s, as a new teenage pop music grew from both rock 'n roll and the showbusiness music that had preceded rock 'n roll.

If Holly was part of the "first generation" of rock 'n roll, he was by far its youngest member and one who was obviously influenced by the rest of that generation. But if it is not correct to see him as first-generation, neither was he primarily a member of the class of '58 and beyond who sang explicitly about and to teenagers as high-school students. We have seen that his brief period as a stalwart of package tours saw the hegemony of black R&B acts (from McPhatter to Domino) displaced by the white teen singers (Everly Brothers, Paul Anka, Frankie Avalon).

6 After the Day the Music Died: Presence and Representations

On the wall of a pub lavatory in Gateshead, there is a scrawled legend: "Buddy Holly lives and rocks in Tijuana, Mexico" (Cohn 1969: 46).

In the 1978 movie *American Hot Wax*, one of the leading characters is a young teenager, identified as the head of a 5,000-member Buddy Holly Fan Club. A huge yellow button reading "Buddy Holly Lives" decorates the fan's sports jacket (Goldrosen and Beecher 1996: 174–5).

> In Life, their names were linked for only a few cold, miserable weeks.
>
> In death, their names became a Trinity, as if carved into the same tablet of sacred stone.
>
> Ritchie Valens. The Big Bopper.
>
> Buddy Holly.
>
> Years later, we would look back with longing and say that the music has died.
>
> We should have known better.
>
> Prologue to *Buddy Holly is Alive and Well on Ganymede* (Denton 1991)

Memorializing fixes Buddy Holly in the past and in popular memory, but to represent (or re-present) him involves various ways of repressing his absence and making him present, however momentarily. They are different ways of demonstrating that "Buddy Holly Lives". The individual members of the actor network involved in the representational side of the posthumous career include musicians, producers, writers and actors; the institutional members include music publishers, record companies and the Holly estate. The elements of this dimension of the posthumous career are:

- Continuities – the Crickets and an apostolic succession
- "New" recordings (previously unreleased or overdubbed or "lost")
- Cover versions
- Copyists and tribute acts (including impersonators and lookalikes)
- Film and television representations (including documentaries)
- Stage representations (musical shows)
- Management

Bobby Vee with the Crickets

Redferns/David Redfern. Reproduced by permission of Getty Images.

Continuities

If a member of a popular music group dies or leaves, the remaining members may decide to continue the group career, claiming a continuity that transcends the absence of that individual. Sometimes, the succession process can become tortuous and litigious with competing versions of the same group claiming to be the original or authentic one, as has occurred with black vocal groups the Drifters and Platters where ownership of the name as a trademark has been a feature of legal disputes. On other occasions, the claim to continuity becomes increasingly tenuous when the claim is based on the current membership of one or more secondary members of a band.

All these issues are pertinent to the career of the Crickets after February 1959. The relationship of the group to Buddy Holly had been a complex one. At the beginning, Buddy was simply one member of the quartet, but an "unequal" one as the lead singer and lead guitarist. This was recognized after the success of 'Peggy Sue' established him as a solo recording artist. While the Crickets remained as a recording entity, the touring group was henceforward billed as Buddy Holly and the Crickets, with the latter implicitly relegated to the status of a backing group. This situation was most clear on the final tour when Holly recruited his "new" Crickets as his accompanists. On the other hand, the "original" Crickets (Allison, Mauldin and Sullivan) could stake a claim to be essential contributors to the Holly *œuvre* through their songwriting and contribution to the recorded sound (but not backing vocals, which were added by others).

After the fatal *Winter Dance Party* tour, the ownership of the name "The Crickets" was contested. According to drummer Carl Bunch, he and guitarist Tommy Allsup, both of whom had backed Holly on the tour, had planned to continue performing as the Crickets, but, faced with the threat of a lawsuit by Norman Petty, Jerry Allison and Joe Mauldin, they withdrew (Stewart interviews).

Because of the schism between himself and Buddy, Petty had already arranged to register the name of the group. Almost immediately after the plane crash, the Crickets relaunched a recording career under Petty's aegis, with Sonny Curtis on guitar and vocals and a new lead singer in Earl Sinks. They staked a claim to be the inheritors of the Holly legacy by releasing as their first single a new version of 'Love's Made A Fool Of You', a song already recorded by Holly as a demo intended for the Everly Brothers. The continuity was compounded by the fact that record was issued on Coral, like the previous Crickets records with Buddy Holly.

After 1960, the Crickets' recordings oscillated between re-presenting Buddy Holly's music and reinventing the group as an autonomous entity within contemporary pop or country music. In 1960, Coral issued the album, *In Style With The Crickets*. Almost all the tracks were new songs by members of the group, including the first recording of Curtis's 'I Fought The Law'.

The next album reasserted the group's claim to be the authentic successor to Holly and introduced another claimant. *Bobby Vee Meets The Crickets* (1962) teamed Holly's collaborators with the teenager who had compensated for Buddy's absence on stage at Moorhead in February 1959. It contained cover versions of three songs recorded by Holly and, in the same year, Curtis and Allison toured Britain on the *Bobby Vee Meets the Crickets* tour. They had previously toured in 1959 as the backing group for the Everly Brothers in the US, Britain and Australia, reprising a relationship that had been established with Buddy's participation on the 1958 Florida tour.

By 1961 Jerry Allison had broken with Petty and had settled in Los Angeles, having negotiated a recording contract for the Crickets with Liberty Records. Mauldin opted to remain in Texas, although he rejoined the band in 1977. Between 1961 and 1977, Allison was the only "original" member, guaranteeing the continuity with Holly, although Sonny Curtis was sometimes in the group with him.

The mid-1960s was a "contemporary" period which included British hit singles with Curtis's song 'My Little Girl' and 'Please Don't Ever Change' plus unimpressive cover versions of Beatles hits on *California Sun* (1964). Without Holly and often without Curtis, the group needed a lead singer and David Box and Buzz Cason briefly filled this role.[1]

In 1971, the Crickets went retro in an era of rock 'n roll revival with *Rockin' 50s Rock 'n Roll*, an album wholly devoted to re-creations of Holly songs, although three ('Everyday', 'Think It Over' and 'Maybe Baby') were run together in a "medley". In the mid-1970s, three albums (one called *A Long Way From Lubbock*) were made for the Philips group of labels that included 1950s songs by other rock 'n roll heroes (but not Holly) and newer material. At this time, the Allison, Mauldin and Curtis core of the group was augmented by pianist Glen D. Hardin (a sometime backing player for Elvis Presley and an occasional member of the Crickets since the early 1960s), as well as British musicians Ric Grech and Albert Lee.

After 1977, Allison and Mauldin maintained the Crickets as a working band, though not continuously. For five years from 1978, they and Curtis worked frequently on tour with Waylon Jennings. The link with this former Holly protégé re-emphasized their authenticity as representatives of Buddy Holly in his absence. In 1983, singer-songwriter Gordon Payne joined Allison and Mauldin as lead singer. He already had a distant link with Buddy, having been with Waylon Jennings's backing group the Waylors as a guitarist and singer. Payne brought new songs to the group on the album *T-Shirt* (1988). While his own vocal grain was quite different, Payne proved to be a skilful Holly imitator, switching easily to the nasal intonation and falsetto glottal stop effects (and just as easily to Bobby Vee's vocal trademarks when he sang 'More Than I Can Say'). As Alan Mann commented, Payne's arrival enabled the group to return "to playing a lot of Holly songs which they hadn't tackled for years" (Mann 2009: 229). This was evident from the trio's 1990 performance at the London Palladium, a concert issued by Rollercoaster Records on cassette two years later, where 13 of the 17 songs performed by the group dated from the 1950s. But this only foregrounded the question: was this group the living embodiment of Clovis 1957–8 or simply one of the better tribute bands to Buddy Holly? The latter interpretation was supported by the fact that the audience could be heard on the cassette singing along to 'Everyday', just as listeners to Björn Again or the Bootleg Beatles might.

Payne left the Crickets in 1994, after which time Allison re-formed a Crickets group for occasional events including two album sessions. The first was *Too Much Monday Morning* (1996), a collection of country-rock songs by various writers for which the core group was Allison, Mauldin, Curtis and Hardin. More considerable was the 2004 album *Crickets And Their Buddies*, another re-recording of the Holly-era classics with guest singers including Nanci Griffith, Eric Clapton, Vince Neal, Graham Nash and Waylon Jennings. The album is a pleasant enough experience, but one marred by the pun in the title which both recalled Holly and replaced him with some celebrity fans in what was little more than another of the series of similar "various artists" tribute records to numerous artists from the Beatles to Elton John that litter the release schedules of the last 20 years.

"New" recordings (previously unreleased)

A different form of post-mortem continuity with Holly's life was the decision to issue "new" recordings by Buddy Holly, thereby extending his recording career. These were to be drawn from tracks made by Holly but not issued during his lifetime. In John Goldrosen's words, such tracks were:

> scattered along the course of his musical career. Demos made in the days of the Buddy and Bob Show were in the hands of the Holleys, Bob Montgomery, HiPockets Duncan and others in Lubbock; sides cut during the period of Holly's Decca contract were in Decca's Nashville office or in the possession of Jim Denny's Cedarwood Publishing firm; Norman Petty had masters Holly had recorded before the break between them; and Coral had a claim on anything Holly had recorded during his period on the label. (Goldrosen and Beecher 1996: 150)

A very few of these tracks had already been completed and were waiting to be released at the time of his death. From the last New York studio session, there was 'True Love Ways' and 'Moondreams' (both issued in 1960). Among Petty's Clovis tapes there were the two tracks recorded by Buddy with saxophonist King Curtis. 'Come Back Baby' was issued unchanged in 1964 while 'Reminiscing' was overdubbed and became the title track of a "new" album issued in 1963. But the vast majority had originally been made privately and were never intended to be offered to the public or were "different" versions of tracks issued during his lifetime.

Six of these tracks were prepared for release in mid 1959 and at New Year 1960 by Dick Jacobs of Coral. These were the new songs sung by Holly to his own acoustic guitar accompaniment on the apartment tapes. Jacobs arranged for Holly's tapes to be augmented by piano, bass, lead guitar and drums plus the backing vocals of the male voices of the Ray Charles Singers (a white group with no relation to the soul music star). From the first overdub session, Coral issued 'Peggy Sue Got Married' / 'Crying, Waiting, Hoping' in July 1959 in the US, almost six months after 'It Doesn't Matter Anymore' / 'Raining In My Heart', the single that had become a big hit immediately following Holly's death. They were issued again with the other four apartment tapes tracks in 1960 on the album *The Buddy Holly Story Volume 2*.

The person chosen to prepare the remaining material for what became an intermittent programme of new releases was Norman Petty. Despite the split between Petty and Holly at the time of the latter's death, after some deliberation, the record company, his widow and his parents agreed in 1962 to allow Norman Petty a free hand in preparing further releases.

During the 1960s, Petty brought a total of 40 "enhanced" or overdubbed tracks to Coral to be issued under Buddy's name.[2] As Table 3 shows, these came from four main sources. Eight had originally been recorded by Buddy and Bob Montgomery in 1954–5 (A); nine were song demos recorded at Clovis in two sessions during 1956, one of which would later be re-recorded in Nashville (B); ten were committed to tape by Holly and Allison as a duo (probably at the Holley family home) at the end of 1956 (C); and eight had been taped at Buddy and Maria Elena's New York apartment (only one of these, 'What To Do', was among the six Holly compositions on the apartment tapes) (D). There were also a further six new recordings based on unreleased tracks cut at Clovis or a Lubbock radio station in 1956–8 (E). These tracks appeared on four albums issued between 1963 and 1969. These albums also included four tracks that had been issued during Holly's lifetime (F).

Table 3: Provenance of the tracks on the four "new" albums 1963–9

Album title/release date	A	B	C	D	E	F
Reminiscing, 1963	–	8	–	2	1	–
Showcase, 1964	–	1	5	1	3	2
Holly In The Hills, 1965	8	–	–	1	1	2
Giant, 1969	–	–	5	4	1	–
TOTAL	8	9	10	8	7	4

Key: A = Buddy & Bob 1954–6; B = Clovis demos 1956; C = Lubbock duo tapes 1956–7; D = New York apartment tapes 1958 (mostly cover versions); E = unreleased Clovis tracks; F = previously issued tracks

The principal method used by Petty was to "enhance" the sound of the previously unreleased material by overdubbing. This method of adding new sounds to an existing track had been used during Holly's lifetime, of course. But then the overdubs were of Holly's own singing and playing to produce a double-tracking effect, or of backing singers.[3]

In the overdubs created in the 1960s, Petty retained the original vocal track and added new instrumental parts, often "alongside" or on top of any existing accompaniment. While this could be a relatively unproblematic technical exercise in the case of tapes consisting of Holly and an acoustic guitar, a number of the enhanced tracks had originally contained drum and/or bass accompaniments. In these instances, Petty's tendency was to override the original playing with new versions, with mixed results.

The Fireballs with Jimmy Gilmer

Michael Ochs Archives. Reproduced by permission of Getty Images.

The overdubbing sessions were held at the Clovis studio between 1962 and 1968. The musicians used for almost all of these sessions were members of the Fireballs, a New Mexico group "discovered" by Petty who had recorded numerous instrumental numbers as well as an international hit, 'Sugar Shack', sung by their lead vocalist, Jimmy Gilmer. To establish the suitability of these musicians to play with Buddy, Alan Mann assures his readers that "their lead guitarist, George Tomsco, vividly remembers being introduced to Buddy Holly in Norman Petty's studio in September 1958" but adds that this was "the one and only time they met" (Mann 2009: 118–9).

Petty also stated in a sleeve note to one of the albums of this material that Tomsco's playing had "the same drive and freshness that was Buddy's" and that the Fireballs drummer, Doug Roberts, played with "even more drive than Buddy's drummer in those days", a claim that is not borne out by the overdubbed tracks.[4] In fact, on tracks where the original included Jerry Allison's drumming, the overdubbed version often has a cluttered sound as Roberts attempts to drown out Allison.

The first album of previously unreleased material was *Reminiscing* (1963). This brought together tracks originating from three sources between late 1956 and late 1958. As well as the title track produced by Holly himself in 1958, there were eight Clovis demo tracks from 1956. Six of these were made by Buddy, Jerry Allison, Don Guess and Sonny Curtis prior to the Nashville Decca sessions, while the rock 'n roll standards 'Brown Eyed Handsome Man' and 'Bo Diddley' were recorded in Clovis by Buddy, Larry Welborn and Jerry in December 1956. Thirdly, *Reminiscing* included two cover versions taped in late 1958 by Buddy with his acoustic guitar in the New York apartment. Everything on this album, even 'Reminiscing', which Holly had completed as ready for release, had been overdubbed.

The following year, the album *Showcase* was even more of a mixture. It included tracks from five sources. There was one more Clovis demo, five songs from the Lubbock duo tapes, one from the New York tapes plus the small-group demo of 'Love's Made A Fool Of You', a track made at a Lubbock radio station ('You're The One') and even two previously issued tracks from the Nashville Decca sessions. The next "new" album, *Holly In The Hills* (1965) contained eight of the surviving tracks from a single phase of Holly's career – the Buddy & Bob bluegrass and country recordings. But there were also two previously issued tracks that had not been issued on albums, plus a reworked 'Wishing', whose original had been on a single in 1963, and Petty's overdub of 'What To Do', one of the new songs from the apartment tapes, which had been issued in a Hansen overdubbed version five years earlier!

There was a gap of four years until the release of the fourth and final album of Petty's enhanced tracks. *Giant* (1969) was again made up from various sources, mixing material from the Lubbock duo tapes with apartment tapes rock 'n roll tracks and the unreleased Clovis recording 'You're The One', which had already appeared on the *Showcase* album.

In order to make the varied demos and private recordings suitable for the market, Petty and the Fireballs subjected all of them to a homogeneous modernizing process. This created a generic rock sound that occasionally recalled the Crickets' late 1950s approach but more often embodied a more contemporary, early 1960s, habitus, comparable to that of, say, Bobby Vee or even the Beatles. By doing so, Petty ignored the historically specific nature of most of the Buddy & Bob tracks by adding drums and electric guitars to what were derivative examples of bluegrass or acoustic country music, genres whose unwritten rules of ensemble formation excluded drums and, generally, amplified instruments of all kinds. Some of the overdubbed versions of the Lubbock duo rock 'n roll standards, which Jerry Allison said were played by Holly and himself at dances and had been originally recorded privately "just to see what [they] sounded like", were more successful, while Goldrosen asserts that three of the Clovis demo tracks on *Reminiscing* – 'Rock A Bye Rock', 'I'm Gonna Set My Foot Down' and 'Baby Won't You Come Out Tonight?' – are as Holly's group sounded "on the bandstand at a teenage rock 'n roll hop" despite the fact that the Fireballs' 1962 playing had been added to that of Holly's 1956 quartet (Goldrosen and Beecher 1996: 152).

Committed Holly fans were pleased to see these new items added to the Holly recorded *œuvre* (which almost doubled in size). The four albums and associated singles containing Petty's "new" tracks provided a certain momentum to the first decade of Holly's post-mortem career, particularly in Britain. There, both *Holly In The Hills* and *Giant* were Top 20 hits, and during 1963 three singles from the overdubbed material reached the Top 10. These were 'Brown Eyed Handsome Man', 'Bo Diddley' (number 2) and 'Wishing'.

Even if they loyally bought these releases, some fans were unhappy at the haphazard way the albums were compiled and sometimes dismayed by the overdubs themselves. Generally, the years have not been kind to Petty's efforts which can be compared with the colourization of films that had been shot in monochrome. What might have seemed "modern" in the 1960s has become archaic four decades on.

As has been discussed in Chapter 5, the next phase in the development of the posthumous recording career, beginning in the 1970s, was to belong to the discographers concerned with tracing the evolution of Holly's music. Norman Petty's approach to enhancement was the exact opposite of that historicizing vector.

Cover versions

A vital dimension of re-presenting a deceased artist and adding difference to a posthumous career is the recording by other musicians of songs composed or recorded by that act. The term "cover version" or simply "cover" has a relatively complex history in music industry discourse. In the pre-rock 'n roll era, the commercialization process was focused on songs as such. It was commonplace for unit sales of sheet music to exceed those of recordings of an individual hit song until the 1950s. When a new song was published, it was typical that several singers would make competing recordings of it. To this day, the term "cover" is used by music publishers and songwriters to describe the process of persuading a singer to record a previously unrecorded composition.

In the 1950s, however, "cover version" described a different phenomenon, in which a singer (or, more likely, a record company executive) was inspired to make a recording not by the song as such but by an existing recording of a song. What the cover version sought to do was to annex the appeal of the earlier recording, including aspects of its sound, the phrasing of the singer or the instrumental sound. Frequently, the annexation took place across genre and cultural boundaries: pop singers made cover versions of country or R&B hits, as when Tony Bennett covered Hank Williams's 'Cold Cold Heart' or Georgia Gibbs covered Etta James's 'Roll With Me Henry', renamed 'Dance With Me Henry'.

In Holly's posthumous career, cover version singers are the equivalent of a medium at a séance, enabling the absent voice to be re-called through their own. They are clearly separate from the imitators who appropriate recognizable elements of that artist's vocal style or instrumental motifs, and from the simulacra created by the impersonations by tribute acts, whose cover versions have a different aim – to substitute for the absent star.

There have been hundreds of cover versions in the half-century since Holly's death, with some songs (notably 'Oh Boy!', 'Everyday' and 'That'll Be The Day') attracting 50 or more versions. But, even before February 1959, several

Crickets and Buddy Holly tracks were covered by other artists at home and abroad. Contemporaneous versions of 'That'll Be The Day' were issued by black vocal group the Ravens (this is probably the only cover version of a Holly track by an African-American artist) and white singer Jeff Allen, and 'Peggy Sue' was covered by pop act Jackie Walker and country singer Rusty York. In Britain, the Crickets' 'That'll Be The Day' faced competition from Larry Page but the only cover version of 'Peggy Sue' was by Paul Rich on the budget price Embassy label, available only at Woolworth's stores.

After Holly's death, the motivation to make cover versions changed. In some cases, it was to acknowledge a debt or influence or even to associate the cover artist with the prestige of the absent star by integrating one or more of their songs into his or her own repertoire. As Greil Marcus has written, every cover version "becomes an opportunity to join the Grand Continuum of Rock 'n Roll History" (quoted in Gracyk 2001: 75).[5]

The rate at which cover versions were produced varied between historical periods. During the 1960s, it was mainly Holly's contemporaries who recorded his songs. These artists ranged from British Invasion beat groups to fellow Texas rockers and the occasional garage band or country act. The first performer to honour Holly with a whole album of cover versions was Bobby Vee, with *I Remember Buddy Holly* in 1963. This slavishly copied the arrangement of the original versions, even down to the male backing singers on 'That'll Be The Day' and the pizzicato strings on 'It Doesn't Matter Anymore'; but, according to one critic, "like Holly before him, he played with the songs, paying tribute in kind to Holly's inventive singing" (Hardy 1973: 149). In 1967, the female country singer Skeeter Davis issued her own album in tribute to Holly. *Skeeter Davis Sings Buddy Holly* was the first set of Holly cover versions by a female singer.

In Britain, Holly and Crickets songs had been an essential part of the repertoire of journeyman guitar groups playing local dances since the late 1950s. When an elite minority of such groups were signed to recording contracts in the early 1960s, the debt to Holly and the Crickets was acknowledged as cover versions were included among the tracks recorded as B-sides or as "filler" items for four-track EPs or 12-track albums. The Hollies recorded 'Take Your Time', the Searchers put 'Listen To Me' on their first album, Herman's Hermits covered 'Heartbeat', and Brian Poole and the Tremeloes recorded 'Someone Someone', a post-Holly Crickets song. The most commercially successful of these British Invasion cover versions was 'True Love Ways' by Peter & Gordon, a Top 20 hit in 1965.

The cover version relationship of both the Beatles and Rolling Stones to Holly was somewhat different. The Beatles performed, broadcast and/or recorded 11 songs by Holly or the Crickets, but only one ('Words Of Love' on the 1964 album *Beatles For Sale*) was released during the lifetime of the group. That song had been part of the repertoire of Lennon and McCartney's first group, the Quarry Men as soon as it was released in 1958. Other cover versions were regularly performed in Hamburg and Liverpool over the next five years. These included 'Mailman, Bring Me No More Blues', 'Crying, Waiting, Hoping', 'Reminiscing', 'That'll Be The Day', 'Peggy Sue', 'It's So Easy', 'Everyday', 'Maybe Baby', 'Think It Over' and 'Raining In My Heart'. And, if 'Words Of Love' was the only commercially released track in the 1960s, the Beatles' recording career was bookended by Holly tracks. Their first demonstration disc from 1958 included 'That'll Be The Day' and at their last recording session as a group in 1969, they ran through affectionate versions of 'Mailman, Bring Me No More Blues' and 'Not Fade Away' (Lewisohn 1988: 168).

The Holly connection of individual members of the Beatles continued after the group broke up. Apart from Paul McCartney's activities as Holly's music publisher, in recording tracks for what became his album *Rock 'n Roll*, John Lennon "wanted to record the songs with a stripped-down band, recreating the sound of Gene Vincent's Bluecaps or Buddy Holly's Crickets" (Williams 2003: 168).

The celebrity of the Beatles when they recorded 'Words Of Love' (and that of Eric Clapton and Steve Winwood when, as Blind Faith, they performed 'Well All Right' a few years later) is proof that Marcus's maxim could be reversed: by covering a song by an artist who was less famous, the Beatles enabled that singer to become part of "Rock 'n Roll History", or at least they revealed Holly's place to a new generation of listeners.

Commenting on the "striking sonic likeness to the original" of the Beatles' version of 'Words Of Love', Albin Zak notes that the group emulates both the "chiming guitar and the tone of Holly's voice" and that "the pat-a-cake effect of the eighth-note handclaps" is a reference to Holly's recording of 'Everyday'. He adds the significant point that "while the Beatles track is at one level a cover version of a Buddy Holly song, it is also a more extended allusion to Buddy Holly's sound" (Zak 2001: 27).

Almost the opposite is true of 'Not Fade Away' (1963), the only Holly/Crickets song to be recorded by the Rolling Stones. This version is an "extended allusion" to the Bo Diddley sound, emphasizing the "shave and a haircut, six bits" (Palmer 1996: 69) beat and adding tambourine, harmonica and maracas, instruments often to be found on Diddley's own records. The Stones' bass player Bill Wyman later wrote that "we brought the rhythm up and emphasised it. Holly played it very lightly. We just got into it more and put the Bo Diddley beat up front" (Wyman with Coleman 1990: 184).

In doing this, the Stones brought out the tremendous rhythmic debt owed to Diddley by Holly and Allison's original version, although they also accelerated the tempo from 90–95 to 115, as they did in many of their cover versions of R&B songs (Hicks 1999: 30). And, even if Keith Richards and Mick Jagger have at different times told interviewers of their admiration for Buddy, only one writer has discerned a Holly influence in the sound of the Rolling Stones. This was Iain Chambers, who claimed that their versions of Lennon and McCartney's 'I Wanna Be Your Man' and Bobby Womack's 'It's All Over Now' were "very "Hollyish'" (Chambers 1985: 66).

Apart from the special cases of the Crickets and Bobby Vee, there were few guitar band cover versions in the United States in the 1960s. Occasionally, a garage band would record a Holly song such as the Rogues' version of 'That'll Be The Day'. However, there was unexpected interest in Holly from the folk scene at its folk-rock edge. In 1966 Tom Rush cut a version of 'Love's Made A Fool Of You' and Phil Ochs confused his folk revival audience by performing a medley of Holly songs at a famous Carnegie Hall concert in 1970.

Another folk singer, Carolyn Hester, provides an example of a complex network of covers and influences leading from Buddy Holly. The Texas-born Hester was a leading figure in the folk revival but she met Holly at Norman Petty's studio in 1958. Holly and Jerry Allison played on tracks recorded there by Hester, including the Holly–Petty song 'Take Your Time'. Later, Hester performed Holly's 'Lonesome Tears' in a Greenwich Village club. In the audience was Bob Dylan who told Hester that Holly was one of his heroes and that he had attended the Duluth concert on the final tour. The resulting friendship led Dylan to attend a Hester recording session for an eponymous album on which Hester "thought I was taking a page out of Buddy Holly's book . . . we weren't rockabilly, we were folkabilly" (Unterberger 2002: 54).

In his own memoir, Dylan wrote of Hester: "that she had known and worked with Buddy Holly left no small impression on me . . . Buddy was royalty, and I felt like she was my connection to it, to the rock-and-roll music that I'd played earlier, to that spirit" (Dylan 2004: 277). Dylan has several times reiterated his admiration for Holly in interviews and in his 1998 Rock 'n Roll

Hall of Fame acceptance speech; and Michael Gray's *Bob Dylan Encyclopedia* lists the occasions on which Dylan performed versions of 'That'll Be The Day' and 'Not Fade Away' in concert. Gray even claims that "the way to encompass what Dylan has done via Holly is to say there's a strong positive level on which Dylan has effectively replaced him" (Gray 2006: 324–5).

Holly's songs benefited from the British rock revival of the 1970s with hit versions of 'Oh Boy!' by Mud and 'Heartbeat' by Showaddywaddy, while Denny Laine of Wings recorded an album of cover versions, possibly encouraged by his employer's ownership of the publishing rights to many of the songs. In the United States, new versions of Holly's songs came from a range of contemporary artists. The outstanding examples were Linda Ronstadt's 1976–7 hit versions of 'That'll Be The Day' and 'It's So Easy', which intriguingly inserted these old songs into the Los Angeles country-rock mode of which she was a key part (the Eagles were formed from her backing group). There were other covers by folk singers John Denver and Don McLean, who followed his 'American Pie' hit with recordings of several Holly songs on the 1973 album *Playin' Favorites*.

In more recent times, there have been fewer cover versions of Holly's songs. Several older musicians have acknowledged his influence on their formative years with albums of cover versions. In Britain, both the Hollies (1980) and Shadows guitarist Hank Marvin released such albums, and the 1980s synth-pop band Erasure included 'Everyday' and 'True Love Ways' on an album of *Other People's Songs* in 2003. The early 1960s teen-pop star Connie Francis recorded a dozen of his songs in Nashville in 1996. She gave a virtuoso performance of 'Peggy Sue' whose lyrics were revised by Sonny Curtis to take account of the gender reversal as the addressee of the song becomes a woman who has stolen the protagonist's man.

Buddy Holly has not been exempt from the fashion of creating various-artist albums of tributes to respected singers and performers. A 1989 album called *Every Day Is A Holly Day* featuring such acts as Willie Alexander and Chris Spedding was followed in 1995 by *Notfadeaway*. Issued by Holly's own record company, MCA, its participants included many current country acts including Waylon Jennings, Suzy Bogguss, the Mavericks and Mary Chapin Carpenter. A new-wave tribute album was issued by the French New Rose label two years later featuring such luminaries as Wreckless Eric. The most recent (and perhaps final) such tribute album was the Crickets' release from 2004 already discussed.

Copyists and influence

There is a continuum covered by the term "influence" ranging from singers that adopted one or more traits of Holly styles and more or less integrated them into a different music to those whose deliberate intention is to become a simulacrum of the singer and/or band – the so-called "tribute acts". One crucial difference between the two is the fact that tribute acts seldom make recordings: if they did so successfully, the result would be indistinguishable from the records by the "original" artist.

Aspects of Holly's music began to influence other popular music during his lifetime. 'Don't You Worry, My Little Pet', the B-side of 'To Know Him Is To Love Him', the late 1958 hit by Phil Spector's group the Teddy Bears, "began with a guitar intro that might have come straight off an old Buddy Holly record" (Williams 2003: 26). The pizzicato string arrangement of 'It Doesn't Matter Anymore' enthralled a young British bandleader called John Barry who adapted the sound for the theme to the British version of the television show *Juke Box Jury*, as well as 'Be Mine' by Lance Fortune and a series of records by Adam Faith, a singer who also adopted some of Holly's vocal mannerisms on such hits as 'What Do You Want?' A more direct imitator was Buddy Britten, who had got Holly's autograph on the 1958 tour of England. His chosen stage name proclaimed his allegiance and his claim to be the British Holly, a claim that he eventually relinquished to the more constant Mike Berry.

For tyro musicians, especially in Britain, Buddy Holly was often the place to start (a fact that perhaps supports Nik Cohn's dismissive view that Holly launched a thousand no-hopers). To take just a few examples: Brian Poole and the Tremeloes' repertoire "consisted almost entirely of songs associated with Buddy Holly and the Crickets, with Poole even wearing Holly-type spectacles" (Hardy 2001: 784); one of Britain's leading radio disc jockeys of the late 20th century recalled forming his first beat group in 1960: "we worked on our rudimentary skills in my parents' dining-room, four amplified young men in a confined domestic space, blasting the place out with enthusiastic versions of Buddy Holly hits" (Blackburn 2007: 56); and Mel Bush, an important concert promoter of the 1970s, "began by playing in a group at the age of fifteen. The group was called the Four Specs, and their repertoire was almost exclusively Buddy Holly numbers" (Gold 1976: 102).

The American equivalents of such neophytes can be heard on *Buddy Holly Days*, a compilation subtitled "30 Rare Buddy Holly Sound-a-likes". Most of

Buddy Britten, a British copyist

Redferns/Rick Hardy. Reproduced by permission of Getty Images.

the tracks were recorded between 1959 and 1964 by otherwise unknown singers, although there are Holly and Crickets connections through the inclusion
of items by Sonny Curtis, Earl Sinks, Ronnie Smith and Jack Huddle, whose
1957 piece 'Starlight' was made at Clovis and has guitar accompaniment by
Holly himself. The album is a compendium of hiccupping and adenoidal imitators, 'Peggy Sue' drumming and pizzicato strings.

In his book on 1960s music, Michael Hicks traces the influence of what
he terms Holly's dual vocal styles ("roar" and "baby talk") on singers such as
Mark Lindsay of Paul Revere and the Raiders and Mick Jagger of the Rolling Stones, who "took Holly's self-contradiction to a more profound level".
Hicks also notes the direct incorporation of "baby talk" singing on such hits
as Tommy Roe's 'Sheila' (1962) and the Kingsmen's 'Louie Louie' (1963) where
the lead vocal "subtly echoes Holly's baby talk" (Hicks 1999: 4–5).

Film and television representations

The 1970s was an era of rock revival in Anglo-American cinema and Buddy
Holly was fleetingly referenced in several films that sought to reanimate the
rock 'n roll era. In Francis Ford Coppola's *American Graffiti* (1973), a film set in
1962, Holly is the touchstone for "real" music as one character states "I hate
that surfin' shit; rock 'n roll's been going downhill since Buddy Holly died." In
the same year, the early days of British beat music were celebrated in *That'll
Be The Day*, a film whose title acknowledged the Holly influence on that generation of musicians, represented in the movie by Ringo Starr, Keith Moon
and Billy Fury. And, as the quotation at the head of this chapter shows, the
1978 film *American Hot Wax*, based on the career of Alan Freed, continued the
process by including an ardent fan with his "Buddy Holly Lives" button.

The Buddy Holly Story, directed by Fred Bauer and starring Gary Busey, was
released in the same year as *American Hot Wax*. Several projected films about
Holly had failed to materialize earlier in the 1970s, including one that actually
began shooting in 1975. Almost inevitably called *Not Fade Away*, this had been
based on a script by Jerry Allison which dealt solely with the experience of
the Crickets on the "chitlin' circuit" tour. According to John Goldrosen, the
"broader purpose" of this project was "to comment on race relations in early
rock 'n roll and the music's role in breaking down racial barriers". The film
was abandoned after the intervention of the Twentieth Century Fox studio
bosses who allegedly felt the film was "too serious in tone" (Goldrosen and
Beecher 1996: 165).

Gary Busey in *The Buddy Holly Story*

Hulton Archive. Reproduced by permission of Getty Images.

Both Holly's widow and his parents were unhappy with the script of *Not Fade Away*. Instead, they approved the proposal for a full-scale biography from the eventual producers of *The Buddy Holly Story*. John Goldrosen also sold the film rights to the first edition of his book to the producers, although he has stated that he was "not directly involved in the film's production" (1996: 168).

When the film was released, it proved to be an odd hybrid of "biopics" like those of *The Doors* (1991) with Val Kilmer as Jim Morrison and *Lady Sings The Blues* (1972) with Diana Ross as Billie Holiday and fictional films closely based on the lives of actual musicians, such as *The Rose* (1979) in which Bette Midler's character was a thinly-disguised version of Janis Joplin. While the central character was presented as Buddy himself, unlike *Not Fade Away*, where Holly, Mauldin and Allison were to be portrayed by actors, few of his real-life associates were among the characters presented on screen. Holly's drummer and bass player were fictionalized and there was no character (fictionalized or true-to-life) to represent the role of Norman Petty as producer: according to the film, Holly's hits were recorded in New York, not in Clovis!

The film was generally welcomed by newspaper critics. Vincent Canby wrote in the *New York Times* that "it may be argued that the film . . . reflects the essential simplicity of Holly's music, but that, I think, is to confuse simplicity with lack of technique, which is the manner of the film", but concluded that the film "comes alive only during the musical sequences, and these sequences, featuring Mr Busey's transformed country-boy, are so good, so full of energy, they turn the material that frames them into wood" (Canby 1978).[6]

On the other hand, many of Holly's former associates were deeply unhappy. In *Rolling Stone*, Chet Flippo summarized the view of the majority of Holly's network when he stated that "*The Buddy Holly Story* now stands as the official version of his life, but the movie does not seem to be about the real Buddy Holly" (Flippo 1978). Some years later, a strong attempt was made to supplant this "official version", through a 1986 documentary film financed by Paul McCartney's MPL company, which owned the rights to Petty's Nor Va Jak publishing catalogue. This included interviews with many of the Holly network including Allison, Vi Petty (by now the widow of Norman), Sonny Curtis, Tommy Allsup and Maria Elena Holly (Norman 1996: 18–21). The one-hour film was shown in Britain on BBC television and in the United States on PBS, the Public Broadcasting Service, and later issued on videocassette.

Although no more films were made featuring Holly himself, his song titles and his name have been attached to otherwise unconnected movies and television programmes. This process began as early as 1958 when *Oh Boy!* was borrowed for a short-lived British television music show produced by Jack Good. *Peggy Sue Got Married* was chosen as the name of the 1986 movie starring Kathleen Turner and Nicolas Cage (and with musical direction by John Barry), set at a high-school class reunion. *Heartbeat* is a long-running British drama series set in an idealized 1960s village. An instrumental version of the song is the series theme tune and one of the programme's stars, Nick Berry, had a British number 1 hit in 1992 with an insipid cover version.

An indirect link is found in British children's author Nigel Hinton's series of *Buddy* books. These feature a teenager whose Holly-loving former Teddy Boy father named him Buddy. The books were made into a television series in the late 1980s and one, *Buddy's Song*, became a 1990 British film in which Roger Daltrey of the Who played the father who was now the manager of his son's band. The boy Buddy was portrayed by Chesney Hawkes, son of a member of the Tremeloes, who had covered Holly's hits as Brian Poole's backing group.

Stage representations

The re-presentation of a deceased musician as a live performer can take three forms. The most conventional is the creation of a fictional version as a part to be played by a singer/actor in a stage musical of the artist's career. In rock music, this mode was pioneered in Britain in 1978 with *Elvis*, an opportunistic show created immediately after Presley's death by the television producer Jack Good and starring P. J. Proby. The Elvis formula was adapted for Holly's career in 1989 with *Buddy: The Buddy Holly Story,* which has had many thousands of performances in more than a dozen countries, including over 5,000 in London to audiences of over ten million. *Buddy* was conceived by British impresario Laurie Mansfield.[7]

Aware of the special affection of British audiences for Holly, evidenced most recently by the massive sales of a compilation in 1978, Mansfield commissioned a show based on Holly's career. The part of Buddy Holly was first taken by American actor Paul Hipp and other actor/singers took the roles of Ritchie Valens, the Big Bopper, Jerry Allison and Norman and Vi Petty among others. The show included over 20 songs and culminated in a re-creation of a concert from his final tour, described by Frank Rich in the *New York Times* as "a torrential simulation of a hard-driving yet senior-prom-sweet rock concert of the 1950s". Like his colleague Canby reviewing the biopic, Rich thought the musical sequences far superior to the dramatic segments. He described the latter as "a series of predictable, primitive vignettes – Buddy revolts against country music, Buddy wears his glasses on stage, Buddy gets married etc – in which actors announce events rather than inhabit them, like the androids in a Disney World pageant" (Rich 1990).

The second and increasingly pervasive re-presentation of dead (and living) singers is the "tribute act". While actors such as Hipp and Gary Busey sought to portray Holly on stage and screen, the primary purpose of tribute acts is to impersonate as closely as possible musicians or groups whose public appearances are either non-existent (such as Holly or Elvis Presley), unlikely to recur (Abba) or rare and expensive to attend (Pink Floyd). In his *Times* review of the stage show, Rich clarified the difference between portrayal and imitation:

> While no one will confuse the stand-in rock icons for their prototypes, Mr Hipp and his colleagues do have a youthful enthusiasm, a raw rock-and-roll talent and an obvious affec-

tion for the music that help diminish the ghoulish aura of
necrophilia that has given Elvis impersonations a bad name.
(Rich 1990)

In certain contexts, "impersonation" can constitute fraudulent or other
criminal behaviour. The legal status of the form of imitation purveyed by
tribute acts was established in a 1981 US court case involving a certain Larry
Seth, star of the "Big-El" show. While the court granted an injunction preventing the sale of souvenirs, it rejected the Presley estate's claim that Seth's
performance constituted copyright infringement because it "had no adverse
impact on the estate's economic interest, and also because of first amendment considerations" (Wall 2003: 41), the first amendment to the US consti-
tution protecting freedom of expression.

Using Jean Baudrillard's concept of "simulacrum", David Wall has discussed
three modalities of impersonation and simulation of Elvis Presley. These are
imitators and illusionists, translators and lookalikes. Of these, the first group
are mainstream tribute acts that attempt to provide "authentic performance
of the Elvis illusion" by substituting "signs of the real for the real". Of the
other categories translators include such figures as the Mexican Elvis or the
lesbian Elvis, who are creating "copies without originals", and lookalikes are
"hyperreal" in their adoption of fancy dress and their play with "symbols of
Elvis" (Wall 2003: 46–8).

Britain, in particular, has a thriving handful of imitators and illusionists,
Wall's first category of impersonation and simulation. Among these are a
group called Buddy Holly and the Cricketers, Marc Robinson and the Coun-
terfeit Crickets and Andy Wills. The Cricketers' punning name is a reference
to a publicity stunt on Holly's English tour when he posed with two leading international cricket players, and the group often performs at functions
held by sports clubs. One cricket team organizer praised the "truly wonderful
stage show", adding that he "was overwhelmed by their banter, quick-fire
humour and love of the game . . . All the cricketers on the circuit love them."
Like that group, Marc Robinson has an established career as an impersona-
tor, ranging from playing Holly in a touring version of *Buddy* to participation
in a lookalike competition organized by MPL and providing soundalike vocals
for a television commercial. He also devised two touring shows, *Rave On* and
Buddy and Friends, as well as playing in the 1950s tribute show *Rockin' on
Heaven's Door*.

Described by theatrical industry newspaper *The Stage* as "one of the country's best Buddy Holly tributes", Andy Wills is a member of the cast of Trevor Chance's Legends, "Blackpool's biggest summer season success story" with its "line-ups of past and present rock and pop legends". In this show, Wills's Buddy Holly follows Elvis and Bowie tribute acts on stage (Duke 2008: 21).

While some figures such as the British comedian Harry Hill with his Hollyesque spectacles may have elements of the hyperreal lookalike in their presentation, my research has uncovered no Holly translators (is there a lesbian Buddy anywhere?), except perhaps in literature where a secret service agent is described as looking like him in *A Catskill Eagle* by Robert Parker,[8] and he is exiled to outer space in the science-fiction novel *Buddy Holly is Alive and Well on Ganymede* by Bradley Denton.[9]

Finally, there have been a few attempts to circumvent the enforced absence of singers by finding a way to suspend the disbelief of an audience and persuade them that the actual artist has, in some sense, returned to the stage. A minor version of this practice was presented at a 2008 London concert commemorating the singer-songwriter Sandy Denny, on the 30th anniversary of her death. As the singers who had interpreted her songs gathered on stage and began to perform the final number, a back projection presented a film of Denny herself at the piano, silently playing and singing (Denselow 2008).

The most ambitious attempt to recreate a live performance by a dead star occurred in 1997 when an Elvis Presley 20th Anniversary Memorial concert was staged in Memphis. On stage was Elvis's regular band from the late '60s and '70s, the Memphis Symphony Orchestra and a gospel choir accompanying a projected video image of Elvis singing that had been edited from filmed performances between 1968 and 1973. The event was described by a reporter for the British magazine *Mojo*:

> To a portentous *Also Sprach Zarathustra*, a black stretch limo with police motorcycle outriders drives slowly across the floor of the auditorium. Ronnie Tutt's shuddering drums leads the band into the opening riff of 'C C Rider'. The noise is tumultuous. The limo disappears behind long black curtains side-stage. Seconds later the giant video screen flickers into life – and there he is . . . The King in his prime, with arguably the hottest band anyone ever had . . . Their synchronisation with a celluloid Elvis is almost beyond belief; especially when

he namechecks them and they each take a bow. (Barker 1997: 161)

We await a similar synchronization with a celluloid Buddy.

Management of the posthumous career

"Why I'll just go right on managing him!" This comment was attributed to Colonel Tom Parker when was asked what he would do after the death of Elvis Presley (Marcus 1991: xiv). While the career of a living artist is professionally directed (or misdirected) by a personal manager, a single entity may seek to control the direction of the posthumous career (e.g. Elvis Presley Enterprises) but more often there is a complex and multi-directional "actor network" of discrete and sometimes competing forces.

Elvis Presley Enterprises took decisive action to exclude rival claims on the proceeds of the career of "dead Elvis". The most important move was against Colonel Tom Parker who was pursued through the US courts. In a final out-of-court settlement in 1983, the executors of the Presley estate agreed to pay Parker $2m in return for Parker giving up all claims on future income from Presley's career. The money was actually paid by RCA records in exchange for the estate agreeing that RCA had exclusive rights in Presley's recordings. The Presley estate also bought Parker's collection of Elvis memorabilia in 1990 in competition with a Japanese company thought to be planning to open a Presley museum or show (O'Neal 1996: 73–4).

One focal point of posthumous management is copyright ownership and control, including (in the United States) copyright in the likeness of a person. Royalties from copyrights continue to flow after the death of the songwriter and performer. In contrast to the situation with Elvis Presley, a number of individuals and corporations have a continuing financial interest in Buddy Holly's posthumous career, and some have been in conflict with each other.

During 1957, Petty had taken control of all three aspects of Holly's professional career: publishing, recording and personal management. In later years, the principal focus of debates and controversies over his behaviour was to be the inclusion of his name as co-author on many songs recorded by the Crickets or by Buddy Holly. The majority view is that Petty was not entitled to claim to be an equal creator of the songs originated by Holly and his fellow musicians.

Petty had become the personal manager of the Crickets, at the insistence of the musicians themselves. In this capacity he dealt with requests for television and film appearances (turning down the latter), and, most importantly, became involved in the increasing number of national and international tours by Holly and the Crickets.

While modern music industry practice rejects such a concentration of influence and control of an artist's career in one person, it was not unusual in the 1950s. However, Petty was to be accused of abusing his position of power, notably in his failure to keep proper accounts of the finances of Holly and the Crickets. Petty was the sole conduit for publishing and recording royalties and for touring fees. He was also the sole signatory of the bank account into which these monies were paid and payments to the musicians were sporadic. For some months in late 1958 and early 1959, when he and Petty were estranged, Holly received nothing from Petty.

While there seems no doubt that Petty set up the business arrangements to unfairly (if not illegally) benefit himself, some pleas of mitigation have been entered by Bill Griggs and the biographer Philip Norman. Griggs has argued that Petty funded some extravagant spending by Holly and the others from the Crickets' account, leaving very little to be paid out in cash. Norman found convincing evidence that the failure to pay Buddy was the result of a lawsuit brought by the New York booking agent Manny Greenfield that froze the account administered by Petty. The agent, who handled the English tour in early 1958, claimed that he was due further fees for tours by Buddy and the Crickets later in that year (Norman 1996: 326).

As mentioned in Chapter 3, in the months before his death Holly had tried to break his business ties with Petty. Additionally, Holly was planning to broaden his own activities to include production and the ownership of his own record company to be called either Prism or Taupe.[10] Having produced Waylon Jennings's 'Jole Blon' in Clovis for Brunswick, he co-produced with Phil Everly two tracks by a young singer called Lou Giordano at the Beltone studios in New York at the end of September. These were intended to be issued by the putative label but they were eventually released as a single by Brunswick.

After his death, Holly's music continued to provide two main income streams – record royalties and songwriting royalties. The ownership and control of each was decidedly opaque. Norman Petty had originally taken ownership of the master recordings produced by himself of the Crickets and of Buddy Holly, but he had licensed these in perpetuity to the Coral and Brunswick record labels and their foreign affiliates. Initially, at least, the performer's royalties due to Buddy and the other musicians had been paid by the New York record companies to Petty. His lack of accounting for these monies was a main source of friction between Buddy and himself. Petty had made a similar arrangement regarding songs written or co-written by Holly. These were published by Petty's own Nor Va Jak company but administered by the major publisher Southern Music which passed on composer royalties to Nor Va Jak. In turn, this company was supposed to send royalties to the individual composers.

While Buddy Holly's estate passed to his widow, she immediately made his parents co-owners of future royalties with herself. There were also moves by the estate and the record companies to bypass Petty in the royalty flows, or at least to ensure that his behaviour was transparent.

The rights to Holly and Crickets recordings have continued to be controlled by the successor companies to the Decca, Coral and Brunswick labels. Ownership of the labels passed to the MCA corporation and later to the current owner, Universal Music Group, the world's largest record company whose parent company is the French-based conglomerate Vivendi.

MCA and Universal have been involved in disputes over royalty payments. In 1995, one claim by the Holley family was settled with an agreement by the company to increase the royalty rate to 15% from an average of 6.5%. Four years later, the family brought a legal action claiming that this agreement had not been honoured. A local newspaper quoted Larry Holley to the effect that "we know there have been many record sales, but very little has trickled down to us". Lawyers for the family claimed that the record company had behaved fraudulently as long ago as 1959 (Thomas 1999).

Like that of musicians, however, the life of sound recording copyrights is limited. At the time of writing, the copyright term in the United States was 95 years, but in Europe it was 50 years, meaning that most of the Crickets and Holly hit recordings are already out of copyright there.

A key player in the posthumous history of Holly as copyright creator is Paul McCartney through his MPL Communications company, formed in 1970 by Paul and New York attorney Lee Eastman, father of his first wife Linda. In 1975, MPL bought the Nor Va Jak catalogue from Norman Petty. Therefore, MPL owns the publishing rights to the compositions of Holly, Allison and Petty and, according to some sources, Holly's own rights as a songwriter, through a purchase from the Holley family. In order to promote Holly's catalogue, MPL organized an annual Buddy Holly Week in Britain for several years in the late 1970s. The events included a concert by the Crickets, special showings of *The Buddy Holly Story*, song contests and a Holly lookalike competition. Goldrosen and Beecher assert that such publicity "certainly helped lay the basis for the success of the *20 Golden Greats* album in 1978" (Goldrosen and Beecher 1996: 173). That album headed the British charts.

Finally, Holly's widow controls the use of his name and image for commercial purposes in Texas alone through her company Holly Properties. This followed the adoption of a so-called "Buddy Holly Law" by the state legislature in the 1990s. Her attempts to enforce her intellectual property rights led to conflicts with the Lubbock city authorities and Peggy Sue Gerron. In 2007, Maria Elena Holly requested a fee from Lubbock for the use of the name in Buddy Holly Terrace and the Buddy Holly Walk of Fame. Refusing to pay, the city changed the name of the latter to West Texas Walk of Fame. When Gerron published her memoirs in 2008 (Gerron and Cameron 2008), Maria Elena claimed the book was unauthorized and that it would harm Buddy's and her own reputation.

In his discussion of Elvis Presley's posthumous career, David Wall argues that it is vital that the unofficial or informal fan culture surrounding an artist exists in parallel and interaction with the commercial and legal intellectual property rights of EPE. Maria Elena Holly's actions seem to be aimed, albeit ineffectually, at disrupting any such circulation between right holders and others in the continuing career of her husband.

Conclusion: on the threshold

For Holly biographers and fervent fans, it has been impossible not to speculate or pontificate on what would have happened next if the plane crash had not occurred. Reports of his activities and ideas in the last few months of 1958 show him being recorded as a pop singer without guitar and with strings; writing songs in a mode that would later be called that of the singer-songwriter; taking steps to produce other artists; making plans for his own studio and label; and showing interest in acting, Latin music and jazz.

Depending on which of these tendencies is foregrounded, different authors have confidently or tentatively drawn conclusions about "what Buddy would have done next". While Robert Palmer focused on the pop singer and forecast a decline in Holly's significance, John Goldrosen, the most circumspect of biographers, states that "there is no way of telling where or how far Buddy Holly's expanding ambitions and interests would have taken him. When he died, Buddy Holly had not yet reached his peak – his career had only just begun" (Goldrosen and Beecher 1996: 132)

A more interesting issue for a concluding discussion is the nature of the longevity of Holly's posthumous career. Unlike the careers of Elvis or Jimi Hendrix, this one has no "larger-than-life" personality to power a legend, despite the best efforts of Ellis Amburn in particular to create such a divided soul. Instead, I want to suggest that the key factor is related to the impossibility of knowing what would have happened next, and that the suddenness with which his life ended left a sense that "Buddy Holly" would be forever standing on the threshold of something unknown and unforeseeable. Many of the outstanding features of Holly's career and music are homologous with the sense of liminality precipitated by this permanent uncertainty.

The sense of uncertainty associated with liminality was expressed directly by authors who summarized Holly's status at his death as "promising", such as the British critic and composer Wilfred Mellers who saw the plane crash as making the status of Holly's talent undecidable, as preventing us from knowing whether he would "progress". In his 1984 study of Bob Dylan, Mellers wrote that Holly "died too young . . . to prove whether the white adolescent ingenuousness of his quivery, even hiccupping, voice – charming in his first success, 'That'll Be The Day', and in the Mexican-tinged 'Tell Me How' – could combine with his snappy rhythmic sense to produce music of substance" (Mellers 1984: 106). Even Martha Bayles makes a partial exception for Buddy in her jeremiad against rock by calling him a "clever songwriter who died young and full of promise" (Bayles 1994: 149).

Among the commentators on Buddy Holly's music, the liminal theme can be found in several places. Authors who interpret his singing as the expression of specific forms of affect or emotion frequently find emotional uncertainty, tentativeness or even contradictory feelings. Jonathan Cott wrote of "indivertible expectation" and of "the child inside the man, the man inside the child" (Cott 1981: 77–8). Barbara Bradby's discussion of 'Oh Boy!' transposes the formal qualities of the recording into a representation of developmental stages, finding the protagonist of the song to be on the cusp between adolescence and adulthood.

While accepting the insights of these authors, I want to reject the tendency to find a homogeneity in the music and in the Buddy Holly presented to us through the music. In a very early work, I coined the term "creation-elation" to describe the ecstatic effect of Beatles' harmonies that exceeded the "message" of the songs they recorded, even to the extent of contradicting the composed emotion when they exultantly sang the word "misery" (Laing 1969: 122–3). In my earlier book on Buddy Holly, I tried to express the same idea in defining his singing as that of an *auteur* rather than a *metteur en scène*, borrowing the terms from film theory, where they were applied to different types of director: "Both auteur and *metteur en scène* work from a written text, but, whereas the latter does no more than faithfully transfer that text to the screen, the auteur gives it certain emphases which change its meaning" (Laing 1971: 58).

In this return to Buddy Holly, I am still struck by this effect, which now I can locate in the manipulation of the vocal embellishments, for example in those which I defined in Chapter 4 as operating on the borderline between melisma and wordless singing. Frequently, these are deployed not only, or primarily, in the service of the meaning of a song's words, but as sounds that signify a pleasure derived from creativity in itself. The best songs remain poised on the edge of something more than expression and it is this poise that helps to explain why Buddy Holly's work continues to exert its fascination and power.

Buddy Holly Timeline

1936
- (7 September) Charles Hardin Holley (Buddy Holly) born in Lubbock, Texas, fourth and last child of Lawrence and Ella Holley.

1941
- With his elder brothers he wins $5 in a talent competition.

1942
- Begins to learn violin.

1947
- Holly takes piano lessons.
- He enters J. T. Hutchinson Junior High School.

1948
- Has 20 lessons on steel guitar, then is taught guitar by his brother Larry.

1949
- Buddy makes a home recording of 'My Two-Timin' Woman' (Hank Snow).

1950
- Schoolmate Jerry Allison introduces Holly to the music of Fats Domino.
- Buddy begins making music with another schoolmate, Bob Montgomery.

1951
- Vision defects diagnosed – Buddy takes to wearing spectacles.
- Buddy enters Lubbock High School.

1952
- First Buddy & Bob home recordings, of country songs 'Take These Shackles From My Heart', 'Footprints In The Snow' and 'I'll Just Pretend'.

1953
- He writes in a term paper that "I have thought about making a career in western music if I am good enough."

- Buddy begins to listen regularly to the midnight show of R&B music from KWKH.
- (November) *Buddy & Jack Show* (with Jack Neal) on radio station KDAV.
- Buddy & Jack record two Neal compositions at KDAV.
- He writes to local high schools offering to play at fundraising events.

1954

- *Buddy & Bob Show* (with Bob Montgomery) on KDAV replaces the *Buddy & Jack Show*.
- Buddy & Bob perform risqué country song 'Too Old To Cut The Mustard' at a High School Parents Night event. 'Flower Of My Heart', performed with bass player Larry Welborn, is chosen as Class Song at school.
- First studio recordings at Nesman Studio in Wichita Falls.

1955

- (January) Elvis Presley's first appearance in Lubbock, with Buddy in the audience.
- (February) Elvis returns, Buddy & Bob open the show.
- (May) Holly graduates from High School.
- (June) Buddy & Bob again open for Elvis Presley show in Lubbock.
- (June) More recording at Nesman Studios, with Sonny Curtis on guitar.
- Buddy, Bob and Larry perform 'Down The Line' on the *Big D Jamboree* at Dallas radio station KRLD.
- (October) Buddy & Bob open for Presley show which includes Johnny Cash and Carl Perkins.
- (November) Holly's group opens for Bill Haley, Presley and Marty Robbins in Lubbock.
- (December) Robbins's agent Eddie Crandall asks Dave Stone of KDAV to send demos of Buddy to him in Nashville.
- (December) Buddy records four demo discs at KDAV to send to Crandall, who uses them to get a recording contract with Decca.

1956

- (January) First recording session in Nashville for Decca.
- (January) Holly and the Two-Tones make their first tour with Hank Thompson and other country artists.
- (probably March) First recording session at Clovis with Norman Petty.
- (April) Release of first single by Buddy Holly, 'Blue Days, Black Nights'.
- (April) Holly and the Two-Tones tour with Sonny James (Oklahoma area).

- (June) Holly and Jerry Allison write 'That'll Be The Day'.
- (July) Second Nashville recording session including 'That'll Be The Day'.
- (August) Holly and group again tour with Hank Thompson.
- (November) Third Nashville recording session.
- (December) Release of second Decca single, 'Rock Around With Ollie Vee'.
- (December) Holly and Allison record many tracks at Holly's home.
- (December) Recording at Norman Petty's studio ('Bo Diddley' and 'Brown Eyed Handsome Man').

1957

- (February to December) Numerous recording sessions at Clovis produced by Petty.
- Holly and the Three Tunes support the (chart-topping) Rhythm Orchids in Dumas Texas.
- (May) Release of 'That'll Be The Day' by the Crickets.
- (May) Recording of 'Not Fade Away' and 'Everyday'.
- (August) Three-week tour with Clyde McPhatter and other black artists (New York, Baltimore, Washington, DC).
- (August) 'That'll Be The Day' by the Crickets reaches number 1 in the US.
- (September–November) *Biggest Show of Stars for 1957* national tour (85 shows).
- (October) Recording session at Tinker Air Force Base, Oklahoma City, produced by Norman Petty.
- (November) 'Peggy Sue' reaches number 3 in the US.
- (December) After the tour, Niki Sullivan leaves the band.
- (December–January 1958) Alan Freed's *Christmas Holiday of Stars* (New York).
- (December) 'Oh Boy!' by the Crickets reaches number 1 in the US.
- (December) 'Peggy Sue' reaches number 6 in Britain.

1958

- (January) *America's Greatest Teenage Recording Stars* tour headed by the Everly Brothers (East Coast).
- (January) 'Rave On' recorded in New York.
- (January–February) Tour of Australia and Hawaii with Paul Anka, Jerry Lee Lewis, Johnny O'Keefe and others.

- (February) 'Take Your Time' and 'Real Wild Child' recorded at Clovis. The latter was sung by Allison and released as by 'Ivan'.
- (February) *Big Gold Records Stars* tour with Everly Brothers, Bill Haley and Jerry Lee Lewis (12 shows).
- (March) British tour (25 shows).
- (March) 'Maybe Baby' by the Crickets reaches number 17 in the US.
- (March–May) *Alan Freed's Big Beat Show* national tour with Chuck Berry and Jerry Lee Lewis and 10 others (42 shows).
- (June) 'Heartbeat' and 'Love's Made A Fool Of You' recorded at Clovis.
- (June) 'Early In The Morning' recorded in New York.
- (June) 'Rave On' reaches number 5 in Britain.
- (July) *Summer Dance Party* tour (mid West states) with Tommy Allsup band (11 dates).
- (August) Buddy marries Maria Elena Santiago in Lubbock.
- (September) 'Reminiscing' recorded at Clovis with saxophonist King Curtis.
- (October) *Biggest Show of Stars for 1958 – Autumn Edition* tour with Frankie Avalon, Bobby Darin, Clyde McPhatter and eight other acts.
- (October) Recordings in New York including 'It Doesn't Matter Anymore' and 'Raining In My Heart'.
- (December) Buddy makes 'apartment tapes' at home in New York City.

1959

- (January) 'It Doesn't Matter Anymore' released.
- (January) *Winter Dance Party* tour begins at Milwaukee. Holly tops the bill.
- (2 February) Performance at Surf Ballroom, Clear Lake, Iowa.
- (3 February) Holly, Ritchie Valens and the Big Bopper killed in the plane crash near Mason City, Iowa.
- (7 February) Funeral of Buddy Holly in Lubbock.

1959

- (February) 'It Doesn't Matter Anymore' reaches number 1 in Britain but only number 13 in the US.
- The first tribute record: 'Three Stars' by Tommy Dee.
- (March) *The Buddy Holly Story* album rush-released in the US, where its highest position is number 11, and Britain, where it reaches number 2 in May.

- (June) Overdub session in New York for 'Peggy Sue Got Married' and 'Crying, Waiting, Hoping'.

1960
- (January) Overdub session in New York for the four remaining new songs on the 'apartment tapes'.
- (March) *The Buddy Holly Story Volume 2* released in US.

1961
- 'Tribute To Buddy Holly', UK hit by Mike Berry, produced by Joe Meek.
- *In Style With The Crickets* released.
- *That'll Be The Day*, an album of Nashville Decca tracks, reaches number 5 in Britain.

1962
- *Bobby Vee Meets The Crickets* album released.
- Norman Petty oversees the first overdub sessions of previously unreleased Buddy Holly tracks.

1963
- (February) *Reminiscing* album released in US and Britain, where it reaches number 2 in April.
- (March) 'Brown Eyed Handsome Man' reaches number 3 in Britain.
- Bobby Vee and the Crickets tour Britain
- (June) 'Bo Diddley' is number 4 in Britain.
- Crickets release the album *Something Old, Something New, Something Blue, Something Else!!*
- Norman Petty produces more overdubbed tracks with the Fireballs including overdubs of the new songs on Holly's 'apartment tapes'.
- (September) 'Wishing' reaches number 10 in Britain.

1964
- (May) *Showcase* album released in US and Britain where it reaches number 3 in June.
- Crickets album *California Sun* released.
- Petty adds overdubs to 'Love's Made A Fool Of You' and 'Wishing'.

1965
- (January) *Holly In The Hills*, an album of overdubbed early recordings, released in the US.

1966
- (April) *The Best Of Buddy Holly* released in US.
- Petty and Fireballs create new versions of 'Maybe Baby' and 'That's My Desire' with overdubs.

1967
- (March) *Buddy Holly's Greatest Hits* released in the US.
- (July) *Buddy Holly's Greatest Hits* reaches number 9 in Britain.

1968
- Final overdub sessions produced by Norman Petty.

1969
- Release of Buddy Holly LP *Giant*, the final album of overdubs of previously unreleased demos.

1971
- 'American Pie' by Don McLean a hit in America and Europe.
- Crickets album *Rockin' 50s Rock 'n Roll* released. Apart from the title track it contains new versions of Holly-era songs.
- Publication of *Buddy Holly* by Dave Laing, in the Rockbooks series.

1972
- Holley family sell their share of Buddy Holly's US publishing rights to MPL, owned by Paul McCartney.

1973
- *Bubblegum, Bop, Ballads And Boogies* by the Crickets released.

1974
- Crickets release two albums of new songs: *Remnants* and *A Long Way From Lubbock*.

1975
- Norman Petty sells his Nor Va Jak catalogue including his share of Holly's publishing rights to MPL.
- Buddy Holly Memorial Society founded in US by Bill Griggs
- Publication of the first edition of John Goldrosen's biography.
- *The Buddy Holly Story*, a five-LP set, the first scholarly collection compiled by Malcolm Jones, is issued in Britain by the World Record Club.
- Filming starts on *Not Fade Away* movie, about the Crickets' tour with black artists. Twentieth Century Fox cancels the film, citing artistic differences with the director.

1976

- Buddy Holly Week proclaimed in Britain, continuing for the next two years.
- Linda Ronstadt's US hit with 'That'll Be The Day'.
- Waylon Jennings records 'Old Friend', his tribute to Buddy.

1977

- Linda Ronstadt's US hit with 'It's So Easy'.
- *Holly Days* tribute album by Denny Laine released.

1978

- Release of the film *American Hot Wax*, including a character wearing a "Buddy Holly Lives" button.
- (May) Release of *The Buddy Holly Story* biopic starring Gary Busey.
- *20 Golden Greats* album is number 1 in Britain.
- First convention of Buddy Holly Memorial Society. The 1979 and 1981 conventions were held in Lubbock.
- Crickets begin five-year period of touring with the Waylon Jennings Show.

1979

- First annual *Holly Hop* at the Surf Ballroom, with DJ Wolfman Jack, Del Shannon, the Drifters and others. These events continue until 1986.
- *The Complete Buddy Holly*, compiled by John Beecher and Malcolm Jones, issued in Britain on six LPs.
- Sonny Curtis writes and records 'The Real Buddy Holly Story'.

1980

- (March) Unveiling of bronze statue of Holly in Lubbock.
- Release of *Holly's House*, an album of songs performed by Buddy's siblings and their children.
- (October) Release in Britain of *Buddy Holly*, a cover version album by the Hollies.

1983

- *For The First Time Anywhere* released in US containing unreleased pre-dubbed versions of ten songs.

1984

- 'I Feel Like Buddy Holly' (composed by Mike Batt) is a British hit for Alvin Stardust.

- (June) The Picks overdub backing vocals on numerous Buddy Holly tracks, released on an album in 1986. They record John Pickering's religiose tribute song 'Buddy Holly Not Fade Away'.
- (August) Death of Norman Petty.

1986

- Buddy Holly is one of the inaugural inductees into the Rock 'n Roll Hall of Fame.
- Release of film *Peggy Sue Got Married*, directed by Francis Ford Coppola.

1987

- *The Real Buddy Holly Story* BBC TV documentary produced by Paul McCartney's MPL company.
- The Crickets record 'T-Shirt', the winning song in the (UK) Buddy Holly Song Contest.

1988

- Auction of Holly memorabilia by Sotheby's in New York.
- Crickets release their first new album for 14 years – variously titled *Three-Piece* and *T-Shirt*.

1989

- Opening of stage musical *Buddy: The Buddy Holly Story* in London, starring Paul Hipp. It ran for over 5,000 performances.
- (February) *True Love Ways* hits compilation reaches number 9 in Britain.

1990

- Opening of Broadway version of *Buddy: The Buddy Holly Story*.
- The Crickets perform 14 Holly-era songs out of 17 in a concert at the London Palladium theatre – a tape of the show is released in the UK in 1992.
- Release of 'Buddy's Waiting On The Flatland Road' by Terry Clarke.

1991

- Sotheby's sell Holly's guitars, etc. in New York rock 'n roll auction.

1992

- Release of *The Buddy Holly Songbook* by Joe Ely.

1993
- (February) *Words Of Love*, a 20-track CD, reaches number 1 in Britain.
- Buddy Holly postage stamp issued in USA.

1995
- Publication of biography by Ellis Amburn.

1996
- *Notfadeaway* tribute album released with cover versions of Holly songs by the Band, the Crickets, the Mavericks, Mary Chapin Carpenter, etc.
- Publication of biographies by Philip Norman and by John Goldrosen and John Beecher.

1997
- Holly is given a Lifetime Achievement Award by the National Academy of Recording Arts & Sciences (NARAS) during the Grammy Awards ceremony.

2004
- *Crickets And Their Buddies* album released with "guest" artists including Eric Clapton ('Someone Someone'), John Prine ('Oh Boy!'), Nanci Griffith ('Heartbeat'), etc.

2008
- Publication of Peggy Sue Gerron's memoirs.
- Release of *Down The Line Rarities* two-CD set in the US by Geffen-Decca records.

2009
- Publication of new books on Holly by John Gribben, Spencer Leigh and Alan Mann.

Endnotes

1 The West Texas Musicscape and Buddy Holly's Musical Idiolect, 1950–1955

1. The reference "Stewart interviews" refers to a long series of question-and-answer interviews conducted by Dick Stewart for the online journal *Lance Monthly* in the years 2002–2006. They can be accessed at musicdish.com and details are given at the end of the References section on page 180.

2. For example, biographers have tried unconvincingly to generate a dramatic character for Buddy based on very limited testimony on such issues as the possibility that he fathered a child that he never acknowledged, that he was riven by religious doubts and that he suffered from debilitating stomach ulcers.

3. According to Philip Norman, Buddy Holly was inspired to ask his parents for a guitar by the sight of Natalie's great-uncle Wayne Maines playing the instrument on the school bus circa 1947 (Norman 1996: 31).

4. Buddy was born Charles Hardin Holley. The change to "Holly" came about when his name was spelt incorrectly on his first recording contract by an official of Decca Records. Buddy decided to adopt this spelling for his stage name.

5. The song was committed to tape by Holly on December 17, 1958, so it must have been written at least 48 days before his death!

6. A "sock hop" was a high-school dance held in a gymnasium or similar room, where participants were required to remove their shoes before entering. The lyrics of 'Ready Teddy', a Little Richard hit also performed and recorded by Buddy Holly, include the lines "All the flat-top cats and dungaree dolls / Are headed to the gym for the sock hop ball".

7. Carr and Munde (1995: 225) explain that in West Texas the term "bootlegger" did not mean someone who manufactured alcohol illegally but a person whose "business was reselling alcohol he had purchased legally in a 'wet' area of the state, or perhaps New Mexico, to customers in 'dry' areas". Many such bootleggers were members of the African-American or Hispanic communities.

8. Stubblefield's continuing role in musical life is evident from the fact that, in the late 1960s, local musicians Joe Ely, Butch Hancock and Jimmie Dale Gilmore would take part in jam sessions at Stubbs's Bar-B-Que establishment on South Broadway in Lubbock.

9. See, for example, John Ingman's review of Truman Godwin's book of interviews with Tinker Carlen in *Now Dig This* 308 (November 2008): 24.

10. Gordon McLendon has been recognized as one of the instigators of the Top 40 pop radio format. He owned several stations in Texas in the 1950s (Rothenbuhler and McCourt 2002: 382).

11. This use of the term "cat music" in 1952 is significant. Two years later Elvis Presley would be billed as "the Hillbilly Cat".

12. A one-stop distribution company served small record stores in a locality by stocking records from every record company, obviating the need for stores to open direct accounts with numerous record labels.

13. John Ingman (1998: 5) says that Buddy & Jack appeared in 1953 on *Around Lubbock*, a talent show on Lubbock's Channel 13 television station hosted by Jack Huddle. Holly was to play lead guitar in 1957 on a Huddle recording, 'Starlight', which Ingman says "features two of Buddy's greatest ever guitar solos".

14. Hester was told by a German fan who had travelled to London in 1958 to see Holly and the Crickets in concert that, before the performance began, Buddy sat at the cinema organ and played and sang the traditional Appalachian folk song 'Black Is The Colour Of My True Love's Hair' which was a staple of female folk revival singers such as Joan Baez and Hester herself (Unterberger 2002: 53).

15. One possible fusion between bluegrass and rock 'n roll in Holly's music was pointed out by Ben Hall who told Alan Munde that, in accompanying the fast bluegrass fiddle playing of Sonny Curtis, "Buddy would start double stripping the guitar [strumming both up and down with the flat pick] . . . and that's where I believe he picked up his lead style he used on his records" (Carr and Munde 1995: 123).

16. Goldrosen and Beecher (1996: 29) include a long quotation from Lubbock radio personality, musician and club owner HiPockets Duncan about a paid Presley gig at the Cotton Club "early in 1955" which was followed the next day by the Pontiac showroom performance. It is possible that this Cotton Club show occurred in the evening of June 3 following the afternoon gig. It might also be the case that Duncan was mixing up two separate visits to Lubbock, although there is no other record of Elvis coming to Lubbock solely to play the Cotton Club apart from the April 29 performance.

2 A Studio Career: Nashville–Clovis–New York, 1956–1959

1. The details of Holly's recording sessions in this chapter are heavily indebted to John Beecher's exemplary "Session Files", included in Goldrosen and Beecher 1996 at pp. 178–188.

2. The Buddy & Bob tracks were unreleased during Holly's lifetime but were overdubbed in the 1960s by Norman Petty who added drums, organ and extra guitars. The overdubbed numbers formed the basis of the LP *Holly In The Hills*, first issued in 1965.

3. Holly's mature vocal style is discussed in detail in Chapter 4 at pp. 92-7.

4. The occasion that Crandall "discovered" Holly was a concert headed by Bill Haley, when it was said that Buddy & Bob backed Haley himself for a few numbers because Haley's group, the Comets, were late in arriving.

5. The Cotton Club at Lubbock was also built from a Quonset hut.

6. Bradley and Cohen were not the only music business veterans to fail to place Holly's music. In New York, the producers and songwriters Hugo and Luigi at RCA Records would later turn down some Holly masters because they were "too country" (Bowen 1997: 49). Bradley, in contrast, found the music not country enough.

7. Alan Mann suggests that Holly may have written 'Reminiscing' himself and gave the copyright to Curtis as "part payment" for the recording session (Mann 2009: 247).

8. Ingman has published a pamphlet on these regional and local labels (Ingman n.d.).

9. Deutch's central role in the process explains why Crickets and Holly records were frequently covered by other singers, since the publisher directly benefited from any

recording of the song, even when these might adversely affect sales of the Crickets or Holly originals. Thus, the first Buddy Holly single 'Words Of Love' was covered by the Diamonds, an established white vocal group with whom Holly had toured. Their version of the song was a (very) minor hit, charting for only one week at number 76. Holly's version did not reach the Top 100.

10. The origin of this name is discussed at some length by the biographers (Amburn 1995: 64–5; Goldrosen and Beecher 1996: 52–3; Norman 1996: 119).

11. Amburn states erroneously that this record was a number 1 hit in *Billboard*.

12. Thiele's autobiography claims that, in gratitude for making 'That'll Be The Day' a hit, Buddy asked him to compose a song for this B-side. According to one source, Thiele wrote the song (which was clearly inspired by 'Blues Stay Away From Me', a Delmore Brothers country song recorded in 1956 for Thiele's label Coral by the Johnny Burnette Trio) "with Buddy in mind" (Goldrosen and Beecher 1996: 66) and probably with royalties for himself in mind. However, this claim is contradicted by the sheet music of the song, which clearly shows the protagonist's lover to be male ("he wrote me only one sad line/Told me he was no longer mine"), which underwent a gender reassignment in Holly's recording. That Thiele is an unreliable witness is shown by various accounts of the provenance of the song 'Sugartime' – a big hit for the McGuire Sisters on Coral. In the autobiography he describes how Sonny Curtis (whom he erroneously calls "the Crickets lead guitarist") pitched the song to him as Thiele was "sitting on the verandah fence at, I think it was, Norman Petty's house" (Thiele with Golden 1995: 56). However, in an interview for Joe Smith's oral history *Off the Record*, Thiele said, "there was some kid on the front porch somewhere. It was like a movie scene. We're all sitting on the porch, and there's this guy sitting on the steps playing guitar and singing 'Sugartime'. I said 'Listen, don't play that for anyone else. When I get back, I'll give it to the McGuire Sisters'" (Smith 1988: 61). In fact, the song was composed not by Curtis but by Charlie Phillips, who would have been the "kid on the front porch". But it transpires that the kid had already recorded the song. Interviewed by Philip Norman, Murray Deutch (who accompanied Thiele on this trip to Clovis) recalled that, during the visit, Norman Petty had given him the demo recording of 'Sugartime' by Phillips, on which Buddy Holly had played lead guitar (Norman 1996: 212).

3 On Stage, 1956–1959

1. While this is a graphic description of the impact made by Buddy at an early stage of his career, Steele's version of the date and place of the performance do not wholly fit with the accepted version of Holly's professional life. In his autobiography, Steele says this encounter took place in the middle of 1955, which is unlikely as the first tours undertaken by Holly, with Sonny James and Hank Thompson, did not take place until the following year. However, the detail of the Gibson guitar is consistent with the 1955 date, as Holly did not buy his first Fender Stratocaster until early in 1956. Steele also says that the day after this concert, he heard 'Blue Suede Shoes' by Carl Perkins on a jukebox, a record that was not released until the end of December 1955. He goes on to say that a few weeks later the film *Blackboard Jungle* was released in Britain. This occurred in October 1955.

2. Although Buddy invariably included cover versions in his shows, it is debatable whether he would perform two songs by the artist who was topping the bill on the same tour.

3. A white shopkeeper in a black section of Washington, DC, in 1939 Feld began to play records in-store to attract customers and soon shifted towards selling them. From 1942 he bought airtime on local radio station WWDC and by the early 1950s he owned three large record stores, a share in a record company, a booking agency and a jukebox distributorship. From the late 1940s, Irvin and his brother Izzy had promoted gospel and R&B shows as Super Enterprise and Super Attractions. In 1956 the Felds promoted the first "fully integrated transcontinental rock 'n roll revue" (Guralnick 2005: 228) in direct competition with Freed. His *Biggest Rock 'n Roll Show of 1956* was headlined by Frankie Lymon and the Teenagers and Bill Haley and the Comets, the only white act among the ten acts on the package show (Gart 1991: 58, 62). By 1958 Irvin Feld and his General Artists Corporation (GAC) had moved into talent management with Clyde McPhatter and Paul Anka (Ennis 1992: 180–1). Feld eventually left the music business to become proprietor of Barnum & Bailey's Circus.

4. O'Connor was to become a minor star of British showbusiness. Many years later he proudly told an interviewer how he had given Buddy some jokes to tell to British audiences, including a racist joke about Pakistanis. "He said it and no-one was offended . . . The audiences loved his accent and jokes I wouldn't get laughs with what would be downright funny when he delivered them" (Leigh 1996).

5. This format contrasted with the 1960 tour by Eddie Cochran and Gene Vincent. This was promoted by Britain's leading rock 'n roll impresario Larry Parnes, who chose various native rock musicians to support the American stars (Collis 2004: 30–2).

6. The reviewer for *Melody Maker* had noted condescendingly at the first show that: "Strangely enough, they unload all their disc hits with feverish speed . . . In Britain the custom is for the best sellers to come as the punch line at the end. By having them at the beginning, the act seems to end on an anti-climax" (quoted in Laing 1971: 35).

7. Holly was also introduced to the very British sounds of skiffle and trad jazz. The skiffle star Lonnie Donegan invited Buddy to attend a benefit concert in London on March 15 to raise funds for the medical treatment of Big Bill Broonzy, the blues singer who had toured Europe several times in the 1950s. Those performing included Donegan, the jazz bands of Chris Barber and Ken Colyer and singer Ottilie Patterson. One of the organizers, Harold Pendleton, recalled that "the place was packed, not a seat left and Buddy Holly comes to the stage saying he really wants to get in to see Donegan. I told him there wasn't any room, but I gave him my seat next to my aged mum. Afterwards I said to her: 'Do you know who that was? Buddy Holly'. 'That's nice dear, who is he?'" (Shapiro 1996: 68).

8. Biographers Ellis Amburn and Philip Norman make a lot of these Greenwich Village experiences, even granting Holly membership of the "beat generation". On the superficial basis that Buddy was inspired by black music, Amburn enrols him as an example of the "white negro" of Norman Mailer's famous 1957 essay (Amburn 1995: 4). Norman claims erroneously that, during the period Holly was resident in New York, "the 'beat' novelist Jack Kerouac and the 'beat' poet Allen Ginsberg nightly declaimed their edgy free-form works to saxophone accompaniment" (1996: 263). In fact, neither Kerouac nor Ginsberg took part in public readings in New York in 1958 with or without "saxophone accompaniment". Kerouac's brief foray into live jazz-poetry reading had occurred at the Village Vanguard in December 1957 (Charters 1973: 297).

9. Some of the correspondence between Petty and Orenstein and Petty and another lawyer, George Schiffer, is included in Philip Norman's book. It seems that Petty obstructed requests for copies of all documentation concerning his contractual relationships with Buddy. He also launched a counterattack by claiming that Buddy had never been a member of the Crickets, a statement rejected by Coral Records (Norman 1996: 304–15, 325–30).

10. Jennings's observation that "he didn't jump around too much" is at variance with the descriptions by band and audience members of the stage act on earlier tours. Perhaps in 1959 Buddy had decided to adopt a different (more mature?) stage persona.

11. Shortly before the tour began, according to Holly's wife Maria Elena, Buddy Holly had considered asking Feld to become his manager (Norman 1996: 292). Carl Bunch stated that "Buddy needed new management and Feld's reputation looked good from where we were standing. But no good manager would put an artist like Buddy in such dangerous and sorry conditions [as those of the final tour]. Buddy was nothing more than a temporary financial windfall for Feld" (Stewart interviews).

4 The Recordings, 1955–1959

1. Although the heroic completist six-LP release of 1979 (*The Complete Buddy Holly*) contained over 100 tracks, with the exception of the 11 tracks recorded in Nashville for Decca, the additional items were not issued in Holly's lifetime and most were never intended to be commercially released. These are discussed in more detail in Chapter 6.

2. Goldrosen does not give a source for this statement by Petty, although Petty is one of those he acknowledges for their help in writing his book.

3. In an interview, Jerry Allison claimed that Norman Petty even recognized that he had made no contribution to the creation of 'That'll Be The Day'. According to Allison, "I remember him getting to see us in the control room and saying, 'OK now, I'm going to put my name on the record, but it won't be on the contract or on taking the money. I'm doing this because I'm popular with the disc-jockeys'" (Goldrosen and Beecher 1996: 62). Petty was claiming that the addition of his name would improve the chances of airplay. And, whether or not Allison's memory of this conversation is correct, Petty took a share of songwriting royalties.

4. Sonny West, co-writer of 'Oh Boy!' and 'Rave On', was less positive about Petty's contribution: "I was all right with giving him publishing rights but he had no reason to take writer's credits. All of his apologists will say that he gave his time and allowed artists to practice in his studio etc. That was not so in my case. I paid him for every session, demo or otherwise . . ." (Stewart interviews).

5. For example, in March 2009, the *Guardian* newspaper published a list of "1,000 songs to hear before you die". The list was divided into seven categories, two of which were "love songs" and "songs about sex".

6. Ellis Amburn describes similar phenomena in 'Oh Boy!' as "falsetto trills and feral growls" (Amburn 1995: 80).

7. *Connie Sings Buddy*. Castle Pie PIESD 262. UK, 2001.

8. Bradby analyses this rhythm and Holly and Allison's variations on it (Bradby 2002: 86–7), while Robert Palmer asserts that "the very concept of the 'Bo Diddley beat' is inadequate; what Bo came up with was a comprehensive theory of rhythmic orchestration" (Palmer 1996: 74–5).

9. This is a method used in structural linguistics to distinguish between the significant and redundant elements in an utterance. If the substitution process changes the overall meaning of the utterance, the original signifying element is significant. The commutation test was introduced to semiotics by Roland Barthes in his 1967 work *Système de la Mode* translated as *The Fashion System* (Barthes 1983).

5 After the Day the Music Died: Memorializing

1. The converse of this perception is the fate of those whose musical voice did "die with them" because they did not record. A case in point is Buddy Bolden – the Buddy who was born in the same year as sound recording itself (1877) but died without leaving a sonic trace; "a cylinder allegedly recorded in the late 1890s has never been located" (Robinson 1988). Bolden was a famous New Orleans trumpeter who was committed to a psychiatric hospital at 30 in 1907. He was said to have originated the style perfected by Louis Armstrong. Jelly Roll Morton wrote and recorded a piece called 'I Thought I Heard Buddy Bolden Say' and the British musician Humphrey Lyttelton attempted to "recreate" the Bolden sound on the 1986 album *Gonna Call My Children Home: The World Of Buddy Bolden*. The plot of *Looking For Buddy*, a 2009 play by the British author Alan Plater, revolved around a search for the "lost" recording by Bolden.

2. Paul Simon's John Lennon tribute song 'The Late Great Johnny Ace' explicitly links Lennon's death to that of the 1950s singer.

3. Some sources claim erroneously that Tommy Dee was a pseudonym of John D. Loudermilk, the country music songwriter and singer (see e.g. Clayson 1992: 139).

4. Philip Norman is wrong to write that the Cochran track was never issued (Norman 1996: 376).

5. However, Barfe incorrectly states that Meek composed 'Tribute To Buddy Holly'.

6. For example, Beecher included three extra Buddy & Bob tracks on the British version of the 1965 release *Holly In The Hills*.

7. Though Amburn has a taste for the more lurid aspects of Holly's life, the reaction against him by Hollyologists seems exaggerated: Alan Mann, for example, dismisses Amburn's book by including it under the heading of "fiction" (Mann 2009: 185). There is sometimes a sanctimonious and proprietorial tendency to protect "Saint Buddy", although that is not unique to Holly enthusiasts in popular culture fandom.

8. Beecher himself contradicts this statement in his 2004 interview with Dick Stewart, where he states that he took over the official fan club which had been in existence for a couple of years.

9. The English singer Billy Fury aroused hatred and jealousy in male audience members whose female partners were captivated by Fury's seductive heterosexual address through his confidential vocal stance and his stage movements: "Billy had seen the Presley films and he was taking it a bit further. He got down on the floor with the mike stand and was rubbing it against his body. The more he did it, the more the girls liked it but the guys in the audience didn't like him at all. One night at Glasgow when he was gyrating they ripped the big brass ashtrays off the stage and threw them at him" (Jim Sullivan quoted in Leigh 1996: 68).

10. After the publication of my 1971 volume on Holly, Georges Collanges of the French fan club sent me a snapshot of himself at the graveside with Buddy's parents.

6 After the Day the Music Died: Presence and Representations

1. The Mexican-American singer Trini Lopez was also offered the job of lead singer. He declined it and went on to make a series of hits with party-style versions of folk revival songs such as 'If I Had A Hammer' (1963) and 'Lemon Tree' (1965).

2. In a few cases, Petty overdubbed the same original in two different versions. This was the case with 'You're The One' and 'Slippin' And Slidin''.

3. The overdub of lead or duetting vocals would later become a frequent event in the world of posthumous popular music. The only occasion when Buddy Holly was subjected to this process was in 1996 when Graham Nash, formerly of the British group the Hollies, harmonized with him on 'Peggy Sue Got Married' for a tribute album. As early as 1981, Holly's former Nashville producer Owen Bradley assembled a duet between the deceased stars Patsy Cline and Jim Reeves on Cline's 1960 hit 'I Fall To Pieces'. According to Bradley, "Mary Reeves, Jim's widow, had already determined that they sang in the same key and approximately the same tempo. It would be much easier now because of the equipment that's available, but we did it the hard way with a razor blade and just a plain old tape machine. We made history all round the world." Bradley's interviewer commented, "They had never sung together in life, but they duetted in death" (Rees 1995: 189).

4. Petty's implicit claim that the Fireballs had inherited Holly's mantle was reinforced by the title of Jimmy Gilmer's album of Holly cover versions which Petty produced in 1964. It was called *Buddy's Buddy*, as if Gilmer had been a friend of Holly. In fact, he had never met Buddy.

5. This doesn't work if listeners do not recognize that the record is a cover version. In 1965 the British Invasion group the Hullabaloos had a small American hit with 'I'm Gonna Love You Too'. When this was negatively compared to Holly's original version by the editors of *Hit Parader*, an angry Hullabaloos fan wrote that "I never heard of Buddy Holly and the Crickets". She was suitably chastised by the letters editor who retorted "it's very unfortunate that you never heard of Buddy Holly. A statement like that means that you don't really care about the music . . ."

6. Canby's jaundiced view of the wooden material is supported by the clunking "irony" of the film's final line, spoken by Busey as Buddy to the audience at the final concert: "Thank you, Clear Lake! C'mon . . . we love you, we'll see you next year."

7. Mansfield and *Buddy* producer Greg Smith later created similar shows about Al Jolson and Jerry Lee Lewis.

8. Spenser, the narrator and hero of *A Catskill Eagle*, refers silently to the agent as "Buddy Holly" throughout a short chapter, finally responding to the agent's farewell statement "Good luck" with: "Sure," I said. "And it's a damned shame about you and the Big Bopper" (Parker 1986: 145). This externalization of Spenser's internal description of the agent is responsible for Ellis Amburn's mistaken claim that Parker's novel casts Holly himself as "an intelligence agent, of all things" (Amburn 1995: 319).

9. The central figure of Denton's novel is a young man conceived on the night of the plane crash in the front seat of a car whose radio was playing 'Heartbeat' at the crucial moment. He becomes convinced that Buddy Holly is his father, and names his motorcycle Peggy Sue and his dog Ready Teddy. At the opening of the story, in 1989, the hero inserts a cassette of the film *The Searchers* into his player only to find the television screen showing a performance by Buddy. During this show, Buddy tells his national audience – the programmes of all stations have been replaced by this broadcast – that he is marooned on Ganymede, a moon of the planet Jupiter

and pleads for help. Interested readers can find the novel free to download under a Creative Commons licence at bradleydenton.net.

10. However, Buddy had retained his respect for Norman Petty's skill as a producer, and some sources say he intended to make Petty a partner in the planned label, which would also have been based at new premises in Lubbock (Norman 1996: 269).

References

Ackerman, P. 1958. "What Has Happened to Popular Music?" *High Fidelity* 8 (June): 34–37, 107–8.

Allen, B. 1988. "Charline Arthur". *Now Dig This* 60 (March): 3–4.

Allison, J. I. 1993. CD booklet notes to *Words Of Love: 20 Classic Songs From Buddy Holly And The Crickets*. PolyGram TV/MCA Records 514 487-2.

Amburn, E. 1995. *Buddy Holly: A Biography*. New York: St Martin's Press.

Barfe, L. 2005. *Where Have All the Good Times Gone? The Rise and Fall of the Record Industry*. London: Atlantic Books.

Barker, G. 1997. "Live Shows: Elvis Presley". *Mojo*, November 1997: 161.

Barthes, R. 1977. *Image–Music–Text*. London: Fontana.

––– 1983. *The Fashion System*. New York: Hill & Wang.

Bayles, M. 1994. *Hole in Our Soul. The Loss of Beauty and Meaning in American Popular Music*. Urbana and Chicago: Chicago University Press.

Beecher, J. 1975. Introduction to *Buddy Holly: His Life and Music* by J. Goldrosen. London: Charisma Books.

Berland, J. 1998. "Locating Listening". In *The Place of Music*, ed. A. Leyshon, D. Matless and G. Revill, 129–50. New York: Guilford Press.

Blackburn, T. 2007. *Poptastic: My Life in Radio*. London: Cassell Illustrated.

Bowen, J., with J. Jerome. 1997. *Rough Mix*. New York: Simon & Schuster.

Brackett, D. 1995. *Interpreting Popular Music*. Cambridge: Cambridge University Press.

Bradby, B. 2002. "Oh, Boy! (Oh, Boy!): Mutual Desirability and Musical Structure in the Buddy Group". *Popular Music* 21(1) (January): 63–91.

Canby, V. 1978. "Screen: 'Buddy Holly Story': Tale of Rock Star". *New York Times*, July 21, 1978.

Carr, J., and A. Munde. 1995. *Prairie Nights to Neon Lights: The Story of Country Music in West Texas*. Lubbock, Texas: Tech University Press.

Chambers, I. 1985. *Urban Rhythms: Pop Music and Popular Culture*. Basingstoke: Macmillan.

Charters, A. 1973. *Kerouac: A Biography*. San Francisco: Straight Arrow.

Clapton, E. 2007. *Clapton: The Autobiography*. London: Century.

Clayson, A. 1992. *Death Discs: Ashes to Smashes. An Account of Fatality in the Popular Song*. London: Gollancz.

Cohn, N. 1969. *Awopbopaloobop Alopbamboom: Pop from the Beginning*. London: Weidenfeld & Nicolson.

Collis, J. 2004. *Gene Vincent and Eddie Cochran: Rock 'n Roll Revolutionaries*. London: Virgin.

Cott, J. 1981. "Buddy Holly". In *The Rolling Stone Illustrated History of Rock & Roll*, ed. J. Miller, 77–82. Revised and updated ed. London: Picador.

Dean, M. 1973 "Wo-uh-ho Peggy Sue: Exploring a Teenage Queen Linguistically". *Popular Music and Society* 2(3): 244–53.

Deffaa, C. 1996. *Blue Rhythms: Six Lives in Rhythm and Blues*. Urbana and Chicago: University of Illinois Press.

Denisoff, R. S. 1974. "Interview with Waylon Jennings". *Popular Music and Society* 3(2): 118-37.

Denselow, R. 2008. "The Lady: Sandy Denny Tribute". *The Guardian*, December 4, 2008: 48.

Denton, B. 1991. *Buddy Holly is Alive and Well on Ganymede*. New York: William Morrow & Co.

Duffett, M. 2001. "Caught in a Trap? Beyond Pop Theory's 'Butch' Construction of Male Elvis Fans". *Popular Music* 20(3): 395–408.

Duke, R. 2008. "Trevor Chance's Legends". *The Stage*, July 17, 2008: 21.

Dylan, B. 2004. *Chronicles Volume One*. London: Simon & Schuster.

Emerson, K. 2005. *Always Magic in the Air: The Bomp and Brilliance of the Brill Building Era*. New York: Viking Penguin.

Ennis, P. H. 1992. *The Seventh Stream: The Emergence of Rocknroll in American Popular Music*. Middletown, NH: Wesleyan University Press.

Fairbairns, M. L. 1956. "Young Singer is Lubbock's 'Answer to Elvis Presley'. Buddy Holly Packs 'Em In". *Lubbock Avalanche-Journal*, October 23, 1956.

Flippo, C. 1978. "The Buddy Holly Story: Friends Say Movie's Not Cricket". *Rolling Stone*, September 21, 1978.

——— 1979. "Buddy Holly". In *The Rolling Stone Record Guide*, ed. D. Marsh and J. Swenson, 173–5. San Francisco: Rolling Stone Press.

Foster, M. 1997. *Seventeen Watts? The First 20 Years of British Rock Guitar. The Musicians and Their Stories*. London: Sanctuary.

Frame, P. 1998. *More Rock Family Trees*. London: Omnibus.

——— 2007. *The Restless Generation. How Rock Music Changed the Face of 1950s Britain*. London: Rogan House.

Friedman, K. 1990. "Buddy Holly's Texas". *Rolling Stone*, April 19, 1990: 103–6.

Garafalo, R. 1997. *Rockin' Out: Popular Music in the USA*. Needham Heights, MA: Allyn & Bacon.

Gart, G. 1991. *First Pressings: The History of Rhythm & Blues*. Vol. 6: *1956*. Milford, NH: Big Nickel Publications.

George, N. 1988. *The Death of Rhythm & Blues*. London: Omnibus.

Gerron, P. S., and G. Cameron. 2008. *Whatever Happened to Peggy Sue? A Memoir by Buddy Holly's Peggy Sue*. Oklahoma City, OK, and Tyler, TX: TogiEntertainment, Inc.

Gillett, C. 1970. "Buddy Knox". *Record Mirror*, June 17, 1970: 11.

——— 1996. *The Sound of the City. The Rise of Rock 'n' Roll*. 3rd ed. London: Souvenir Press.

Gold, M. 1976. *Rock on the Road*. London: Futura.

Goldrosen, J. 1975. *Buddy Holly: His Life and Music*. London: Charisma Books.

——— and J. Beecher. 1996. *Remembering Buddy. The Definitive Biography*. London: Omnibus Press.

Gracyk, T. 2001. *I Wanna Be Me: Rock Music and the Politics of Identity*. Philadelphia: Temple University Press.

Gray, M. 2006. *The Bob Dylan Encyclopedia*. London: Continuum.

Gribben, J. 2009. *Not Fade Away: The Life and Music of Buddy Holly*. Cambridge: Icon Books.

Griffiths, D. 2007. *Elvis Costello*. London: Equinox and Bloomington: Indiana University Press.

Griggs, B. 1997. *Buddy Holly Day by Day*. Lubbock: Rockin' 50s.

Grissim, J. 1970. *Country Music: White Man's Blues*. New York: Paperback Library.

Groia, P. 1983. *They All Sang on the Corner. A Second Look at New York City's Rhythm and Blues Vocal Groups*. Port Jefferson, NY: Phillie Dee Enterprises.

Gross, M. 1963. "Album Sales Keep 'Em Alive". *Variety*, February 6, 1963.

Gunning, J. 1998. "Oh Boy! Holly's trademark glasses in city's hands. Civic Lubbock donates $80,000 item to exhibit". *Lubbock Avalanche-Journal*, May 29, 1998.

Guralnick, P. 1971. *Feel Like Goin' Home: Portraits in Blues and Rock 'n Roll*. Boston: Outerbridge & Dienstfrey.

——— 1994. *Last Train to Memphis: The Rise of Elvis Presley*. London: Little, Brown.

——— and E. Jorgenson. 1999. *Elvis Day by Day*. New York: Ballantine Books.

——— 2005. *Dream Boogie: The Triumph of Sam Cooke*. London: Little, Brown.

Hardy, P. 1973. "Bobby Vee: Not Just the Sound of Muzak". *Radio One Story of Pop* Part 6: 148–49

——— 2001. *The Faber Companion to 20th Century Popular Music*. London: Faber.

Hicks, M. 1999. *Sixties Rock: Garage, Psychedelic, and other Satisfactions*. Urbana and Chicago: University of Illinois Press.

Ingman, J. 1998. CD booklet notes to *West Texas Bop*. Ace Records CDCHD 699.

——— 2008. "Memories will follow me forever". *Now Dig This* 300 (March): 14–17.

——— n.d. *AOK: Record Labels of West Texas and New Mexico*. Chesterfield.

Jackson, B. 1996 "Buddy Holly's 'Not Fade Away' ". *Mix*, July 1996: 202, 212–6.

Jackson. J. A. 1991. *Big Beat Heat: Alan Freed and the Early Years of Rock 'n Roll*. New York: Schirmer.

Jensen, J. 1998. *The Nashville Sound: Authenticity, Commercialization and Country Music*. Nashville: Vanderbilt University Press.

Kerns, W. 1998. "That'll Be the Day: For a true collector, Buddy Holly left a vast legacy in albums and memorabilia". *Lubbock Avalanche-Journal*, September 4, 1998.

—— 1999. "A sour note for Holly festival: Dispute leads to name change". *Lubbock Avalanche-Journal*, June 9, 1999.

Kloosterman, R. C., and C. Quispel. 1990. 'Not Just the Same Old Show on My Radio: An Analysis of the Role of Radio in the Diffusion of Black Music among Whites in the South of the United States of America, 1920–1960". *Popular Music* 9(2): 151–64.

Laing, D. 1969. *The Sound of Our Time*. London: Sheed & Ward; Chicago: Quadrangle.

——— 1971. *Buddy Holly*. London: Studio Vista; New York: Macmillan.

Latour, B. 1987. *Science in Action: How to Follow Scientists and Engineers through Society*. Cambridge, MA: Harvard University Press.

Lawson, M. 2008. "Hot under the collar". *Guardian Weekend*, November 15, 2008.

Leadbitter, M. 1973–4. "Serving the South: The Stan Lewis Legend". *Blues Unlimited* 105 (December–January): 5–7.

Lehmer, L. 1997. *The Day the Music Died*. New York: Schirmer.

Leigh, S. 1996. *Halfway to Paradise: Britpop, 1955–1962*. Folkestone: Finbarr International.

——— 2003. *Puttin' on the Style: The Lonnie Donegan Story*. Folkestone: Finbarr International.

——— 2009. *Everyday: Getting Closer to Buddy Holly*. London: SAF.

Lewis, M., with M. Silver. 1982. *Great Balls of Fire! The True Story of Jerry Lee Lewis*. London: Virgin Books.

Lewisohn, M. 1988. *The Complete Beatles Recording Sessions. The Official Story of the Abbey Road Years*. London: Hamlyn/EMI.

Lubbock Avalanche-Journal. 1958. " 'Rockabilly' holding own among music followers. Lubbock youths share in spotlight". August 17, 1958.

Lydon, M. 1968. *Rock Folk: Portraits from the Rock 'n Roll Pantheon*. New York: Dell.

McCarthy, E. 2002. *Morbid Curiosity: Celebrity Tombstones across America*. Monagco.

Malone, B. C. 2002a. *Country Music USA*. 2nd rev. ed. Austin: University of Texas Press.

——— 2002b. *Don't Get About Your Raisin': Country Music and the Southern Working Class*. Urbana: University of Illinois Press.

Mann, A. 2002. *Elvis and Buddy: Linked Lives*. York: Music Mentor.

——— 2009. *The A–Z of Buddy Holly and the Crickets*. 3rd ed. York: Music Mentor.

Marcus, G. 1969. "Records". *Rolling Stone* 35 (June 28): 36.

——— 1977. *Mystery Train: Images of America in Rock 'n Roll*. London: Omnibus.

——— 1991. *Dead Elvis: A Chronicle of a Cultural Obsession*. New York: Doubleday.

Mazzarella, S. R., and T. M. Matyjewicz. 2002. "'The Day the Music Died' – Again: Newspaper Coverage of the Deaths of Popular Musicians". In *Pop Music and the Press*, ed. S. Jones. Philadelphia: Temple University Press.

Meinig, D. W. 1969. *Imperial Texas*. Austin: University of Texas Press.

Mellers, W. 1984. *A Darker Shade of Pale. A Backdrop to Bob Dylan*. London: Faber & Faber.

Millard, A. 1995. *America on Record. A History of Recorded Sound*. Cambridge: Cambridge University Press.

Minhinnett, R., and B. Young. 1995. *The Story of the Fender Stratocaster: Curves, Contours and Body Horns*. San Francisco: Miller Freeman Books.

Moag, R., and A. Campbell. 2004. "The History of Early Bluegrass Music in Texas". *The Journal of Texas Music History* 4(2) (Fall): 22–48.

Monaghan, T. 2009. "Rock Around The Clock: The Record, the Film, and the Last Historic Dance Revolt". *Popular Music History* 3(2): 123–48.

Morton, D. 2000. *Off the Record: The Technology and Culture of Sound Recording in America*. New Brunswick, NJ, and London: Rutgers University Press.

Norman, P. 1996. *Buddy: The Biography*. London: Macmillan.

——— 2000. *Sir Elton: The Definitive Biography of Elton John*. London: Sidgwick & Jackson.

O'Keeffe, G. 1976 (1917). *Georgia O'Keeffe*. London: Black Dog & Leventhal.

O'Neal, S. 1996. *Elvis Inc. The Fall and Rise of the Presley Empire*. Rocklin, CA: Prima Publishing.

Oliver, P. 1969. *The Story of the Blues*. London: Barrie & Rockliff.

Palmer, R. 1996. *Dancing in the Street: A Rock and Roll History*. London: BBC Books.

Parker, R. B. 1986. *A Catskill Eagle*. London: Penguin.

Pecknold, D. 2007. *The Selling Sound: The Rise of the Country Music Industry*. Durham, NC, and London: Duke University Press.

Peer, E., and R. Peer II. 1972. *Buddy Holly: A Biography in Words, Photographs and Music*. New York: Peer International Corp.

Porterfield, N. 1992. *Jimmie Rodgers: The Life and Times of America's Blue Yodeler*. Urbana: University of Illinois Press.

Rees, J. 1995. "I Fall to Pieces". In *Lives of the Great Songs*, ed. T. de Lisle, 184–9. London: Penguin.

Regev, M. 2006. "Introduction to Special Issue on Canonisation". *Popular Music* 25(1) (January): 1–2.

Repsch, J. 1989. *The Legendary Joe Meek*. London: Woodford House.

Rich, F. 1990. "In a Rock Star's Story, the Music is the Thing". *New York Times*, November 5, 1990.

Riley, T. 2004. *Fever: How Rock 'n Roll Transformed Gender in America*. New York: St Martin's Press.

Robinson, J. B. 1988. "Bolden, Buddy". In *The New Grove Dictionary of Jazz*, ed. B. Kernfeld, 133. London: Macmillan.

Romanowski, P., and H. George-Warren (ed.). 1995. *The Rolling Stone Encyclopedia of Rock & Roll: Completely Revised and updated*. New York: Simon & Schuster.

Rosenberg, N. V. 2005. *Bluegrass: A History*. 2nd ed. Urbana and Chicago: University of Illinois Press.

Rothenbuhler, E., and T. McCourt. 2002. "Radio Redefines Itself, 1947–1962". In *The Radio Reader: Essays in the Cultural History of Radio*, ed. M. Hilmes and J. Loviglio, 367–88. New York and London: Routledge.

Roxon, L. 1978. *Lillian Roxon's Rock Encyclopedia*. Updated and revised by Ed Naha. New York: Grossett & Dunlap.

Ryan, J., and R. Peterson. 2001. "The Guitar as Artefact and Icon: Identity Formation in the Babyboom Generation". In *Guitar Cultures*, ed. A. Bennett and K. Dawe, 89–116. Oxford: Berg.

Salem, J. M. 1999. *The Late Great Johnny Ace and the Transition from R&B to Rock 'n' Roll*. Urbana and Chicago: University of Illinois Press.

Sandford. C. 1996. *Bowie: Loving the Alien*. London: Little, Brown.

Sandison, D. 1978. *Oxtoby's Rockers*. Oxford: Phaidon Press.

Sanjek, R. 1988. *American Popular Music and its Business*. Vol. III: *1900–1984*. New York: Oxford University Press.

Schafer, R. M. 1977. *The Tuning of the World*. New York: Knopf.

——— 1986. *The Thinking Ear*. Toronto: Arcana Editions.

Schwarz, B. 1982. "The Social Context of Commemoration: A Study in Collective Memory". *Social Forces* 61(2) (December): 374-402.

Scientific American. 1877a. "A Wonderful Invention". *Scientific American*, November 17, 1877: 304.

——— 1877b. "The Talking Phonograph". *Scientific American*, December 22, 1877: 385.

Shapiro, H. 1996. *Alexis Korner: The Biography*. London: Bloomsbury.

Shelton R. 1966. *The Country Music Story*. Secausus, NJ: Castle Books.

Smith, J. 1988. *Off the Record: An Oral History of Popular Music*. Ed. M. Fink. New York: Warner Books.

Specht, J. 2003. "I Forgot to Remember to Forget: Elvis Presley in Texas – 1955". *Journal of Texas Music History* 3(1): 1–7.

Stambler, I., and G. Landon. 1971. *Golden Guitars: The Story of Country Music*. New York: Four Winds Press.

——— 2000. *Country Music: The Encyclopedia*. New York: St Martin's Griffin.

Steele, T. 2006. *Bermondsey Boy: Memories of a Forgotten World*. London: Michael Joseph.

Sterne, J. 2003. *The Audible Past: Cultural Origins of Sound Reproduction*. Durham, NC, and London: Duke University Press.

Tagg, P. 1981. *Fernando the Flute*. Gothenburg.

Tapp, R. 2009. "The Margaret Lewis Story. Part 1". *Juke Blues* 67: 16–18.

Thiele, B., with B. Golden. 1995. *What a Wonderful World: A Lifetime of Recordings*. New York and Oxford: Oxford University Press.

Thomas, M. 1999. "Family disputes royalty payments". *Lubbock Avalanche-Journal*, March 17, 1999.

Unterberger, R. 2002. *Turn! Turn! Turn! The 60s Folk-Rock Revolution*. San Francisco: Backbeat Books.

Von Appen, R., and A. Doehring. 2006. "Nevermind the Beatles, Here's Exile 61 and Nico. 'The Top 100 Records of All Time': A Canon of Pop and Rock Albums According to Sociological and Aesthetic Criteria". *Popular Music* 25(1) January: 21–39.

Waksman, S. 1999. *Instruments of Desire: The Electric Guitar and the Shaping of Musical Experience*. Cambridge, MA: Harvard University Press.

Wall, D. 2003. "Policing Elvis: Legal Action and the Shaping of Post-mortem Celebrity Culture as Contested Space". *Entertainment Law* 2(3) (Autumn): 35–69.

Walser, R. 1998. "The Rock and Roll Era". In *The Cambridge History of American Music*, ed. D. Nicholls, 345–87. Cambridge and New York: Cambridge University Press.

Ward, B. 1998. *Just My Soul Responding: Rhythm and Blues, Black Consciousness and Race Relations*. London: UEL Press.

White, C. 1985. *The Life and Times of Little Richard, the Quasar of Rock*. London: Pan.

Williams, R., and M. Orrom. 1954. *Preface to Film*. London: Film Art.

Williams, R. 2003. *Phil Spector: Out of His Head*. Rev. ed. London: Omnibus Press.

Wyman, B., with R. Coleman. 1990. *Stone Alone. The Story of a Rock 'n Roll Band*. London: Viking.

Wyn Jones, C. 2008. *The Rock Canon: Canonical Values in the Reception of Rock Albums*. Aldershot and Burlington: Ashgate.

Zak, A. J. III. 2001. *The Poetics of Rock: Cutting Tracks, Making Records*. Berkeley: University of California Press.

Dick Stewart interviews

The following interviews can be found at http://musicdish.com/mag/index.php3?id= with the addition of a four-figure number:

- Beecher, John   9427, 9428
- Bigham, David   8272
- Bunch, Carl   9704, 9705
- Carlen, Tinker   interview at http://lancerecords.com/news2.htm
- Curtis Sonny   8948
- Gerron, Peggy Sue   9577
- Griggs, Bill   8749, 9078
- Pickering, John and Vicky   8595, 8596, 8597
- Tollett, Gary and Ramona   8104
- West, Sonny   8408

Index

Unless otherwise stated, songs and albums are as recorded by Buddy Holly or by Holly with the Crickets